Mitt, Set Our People Free!

Mitt, Set Our People Free!

♦

A 7th Generation Mormon's Plea for Truth

Michael D. Moody

iUniverse, Inc.

New York Bloomington Shanghai

Mitt, Set Our People Free!
A 7th Generation Mormon's Plea for Truth

iUniverse books may be ordered through booksellers or by contacting:

iUniverse
1663 Liberty Drive
Bloomington, IN 47403
www.iuniverse.com
1-800-Authors (1-800-288-4677)

Because of the dynamic nature of the Internet, any Web addresses
or links contained in this book may have changed
since publication and may no longer be valid.

The views expressed in this work are solely those of the author and do not necessarily
reflect the views of the publisher, and the publisher hereby disclaims any responsibility
for them.

ISBN: 978-0-595-51178-5 (pbk)
ISBN: 978-0-595-61789-0 (ebk)

Printed in the United States of America

In loving memory of my maternal grandparents:
Oscar Virgil "Peck" Kelly, 1901–1980 and Inez Ivy "Ike" Thompson Kelly,
1904–2000.

Contents

Acknowledgments

I'm grateful for the enormous help given me in creating this memoir. My wife was always there to encourage and critique my effort throughout, and our dear friend, Tammy Smith, provided technical support when I needed it. I benefited from several people who gave their precious time to read the manuscript and made my mission of passion more readable and understandable as it developed. Pastor Ray Christenson, Carolyn Talbot, and Al Sciarrino offered their special knowledge and skills to direct me toward my best effort.

As the project progressed, The Utah Lighthouse Ministry staff was always there to answer questions and provide written material, confirmation or clarification on Mormon history and doctrine. Ministry co-founder Sandra Tanner reviewed my manuscript and gave me insight and guidance concerning historical Mormon temple ordinances and the recent changes.

I'm especially indebted to author William D. Schroder (*Cousins of Color* and *Soldier's Heart*) who read the manuscript and critically evaluated the grammar and syntax line by line. Friends since the beginning of our days in the Army over forty years ago, Bill's efforts were invaluable to my understanding of the writing craft.

Finally, I was motivated by several members of my extended Mormon family who are unable or unwilling even to consider the possibility that LDS Church dogma isn't true.

1

An Open Letter to My Cougar Club Brother

Mitt, we graduated from Brigham Young University thirty seven years ago, and time passes ever faster. I confirmed that watching Florence Henderson doing a Polident commercial. In 1970–71, I remember the Cougar Club buzzed that you planned to run for President someday, and it became a fait accompli by 2006. Early and aggressively, you began your long-planned push for the U.S. Presidency. After making all the right business moves and a few snazzy dance steps to the political right, you were suddenly a top tier contender for the Republican nomination with significant insider support and a freshly reinvented persona. The ultimate goal for which you so long strived suddenly was within the realm of possibility. Not my preference, however. I want you to use your talents and Mormon pedigree ancestry to ignite the intellect of the LDS Church's pioneer family descendants who remain trapped in a perpetual state of denial about their real history and the validity of Church doctrines.

I'm not surprised time speeds up over the decades. Grandpa Kelly told me that time passes faster as we get older, and my life would be over before I knew it. He had only a sixth grade education and spent his adult life in a small Utah pioneer village named Oasis. Like him, the village is dead and gone, but he was right. The years slipped away quickly as I darted in and out of the fast lane and tried to control my road rage. Strangely, the sense of accelerating time felt right—and Moroni, son of the *Book of Mormon* warrior Mormon, assured us near the end of that book that we can trust our feelings and emotions. According to the LDS Church, our first spiritual impulse is the correct and most important one, providing us clarity of vision only distorted by unnecessary concerns about devilish details and complexities.

Non-BYU astrophysicists believe the faster we go, the slower time passes and the slower we age. Einstein, Hawking and others claim there is no past or future—but what do they know? They're not prophets like Joseph Smith, Brigham Young or Gordon Hinckley. Notwithstanding their cosmic insight, those scientists are mere gentiles, never ordained to the restored ancient Priesthoods or even baptized by one. How could gentiles, never schooled in our teachings, know more about the universe than Joseph Smith and generations of Mormon Living Prophets? I never heard of the theory of relativity from Church leaders and the concept sounds warped to me. Go figure.

I doubt Einstein or Hawking studied Joseph Smith's revelations or Father Abraham's description of the universe in the Mormon scripture, *The Pearl of Great Price*. Then again, maybe these astrophysicists are on to something. Certainly, the past is dead and the future blind. And compelling twentieth century scientific evidence indicates time is a man-made creation. Confusing, it makes a person wonder how to feel about the nineteenth century universe eternalized by the Prophet, Joseph Smith. Could it be that the Mormon Church correctly instructs members to trust the Living Prophets' revelations and not clutter or confuse their minds with "the mysteries?"

Knowing when and what to think is often a mystery to many, but one thing is clear to me. After we left BYU, you and I diverged onto different paths through what Einstein called "the ever present now." Today, we disagree fundamentally on earthly and eternal concepts ranging from time and space to politics and the purpose of life. With that in mind, I call your attention to our correspondence of 1999. I congratulated you on your appointment to lead the Salt Lake Olympic Committee and you were flabbergasted I remembered the theme of your 1971 Valedictorian presentation. I listened attentively as you told fellow graduates not to accept "pabulum" in life.

Eventually, I became smart enough to stop eating that gooey kids stuff, but I assure you not everyone agrees with your observation, "What a mind," for remembering your speech. Nineteenth century writer, George Eliot, wrote, "A patronizing disposition always has a meaner side," but I think she would have given you the benefit of the doubt and agreed that your comment about my intelligence was sincere. The flattery worked, too. Having spent much of my life with a fanciful opinion of myself unjustified by reality, I'm more susceptible to adulation than most. False pride was a natural pitfall for me, as it is for many Mormon men. From Childhood, we were told we were born into the LDS Church in the "latter days" because we were special spirits in primordial life.

At eighteen, my Patriarchal Blessing rattled through my brain like a coronation and a call to arms. Patriarch J. Harold Brinley laid his hands on my head in 1963 and told me I was a valiant, true son in the preexistence with important earthly responsibilities. He said when I raised my voice in defense of the truth the Lord would magnify and enhance me in the eyes of my fellow men. Of course, I hoped the girls would be impressed, too. The instructions in my blessing, which I believed came directly from Jesus, motivated me to seek a career in government and politics. Considering my imagined eternal standing, I think it understandable that non-Mormon friends and associates were subjected for years to my delusions of self-importance and grandeur.

During the 1982 gubernatorial campaign, former Nevada Governor, Mike O'Callaghan, warned me that a local political hustler was telling everyone within earshot I was crazy. Hey, maybe it was a form of insanity. My foreordained destiny had called me, and the words of my blessing swelled in my chest. I did my duty to the Mormon Gods and ran for Governor to expand our kingdom and help you lead the world into the Millennium. Actually, that isn't true. By then, I had begun my long journey out of the cult. One step in my political and spiritual recovery was to annoy Nevada's corrupt political system, including numerous Mormon politicians. I attacked the incumbent Governor, questioned his morality and took negative campaigning to a therefore unheard of level. Nor divinely inspired, but I had fun breaking the 11th Commandment to never speak ill of a fellow Republican, even if the criticism is true.

Mitt, in that 1999 letter, you responded to my critical comments about the Mormon Church by stating its rules and fees are indeed demanding and assured me the Church had been very good to you and your family. You were sorry my experience had been so unpleasant and invited me to visit your Olympic digs, saying you would be happy to see me. Despite our differing views, I'm sure you would have treated me graciously and respectfully. Later, I complimented you for putting a tight lid on the bribery scandal that developed while Salt Lake City officials aggressively pursued the Olympic bid. You erased their budget deficit and generally did a magnificent job in difficult circumstances. Your leadership saved the Salt Lake City Olympics and turned a festering international embarrassment into a sterling success. You bailed out LDS leaders and Utah pioneer families still chafing under the yoke of an historical persecution complex, made more irritating and frustrating by cultural delusions of grandeur.

In 1999, I planned to visit you in Salt Lake City, but events intervened. Instead, I spent 2001 and 2002 trapped in a very public train wreck. I discovered a trusted colleague was a thief, called in the FBI, and watched my career at Moody Investment Consultants flash before my eyes. Using faked documents and doctored faxes, he embezzled millions from my wealthiest clients' accounts and gambled it away at his favorite Las Vegas pleasure palaces. He went to prison, and I closed my shattered business and staggered home to my wife and infant son. At the time, I doubted Plato's observation: "Nothing in human affairs is worthy of any great anxiety."

But your success as a venture capitalist has already been told, and my wild ride on America's biggest bull market is a tale for another time. Your Mormon God put you on a path to the Massachusetts Governorship—and possibly the White House—and my God sent me home to be the primary care giver to my children. Not to brag, but I'm doing a better job than Michael Keaton in Mr. Mom. Once they transitioned from pampers to preschool, I found time to give your 1999 letter a serious response.

2

The Only True School

I have vivid memories of our year together in the BYU Cougar Club, and recall your graduation admonition not to settle for Gerber's mush. You had returned from your mission a year earlier, and I returned from five adventurous years off campus. Once again attending what we half jokingly called the Only True School, it was an important time for me. The Church wanted no Greek fraternities on campus to compete with its myth fraternity, so we joined the Cougar Club. I hadn't performed my rite of passage—a Mormon mission—but was accepted into the elite club and met you.

As a new Cougar Club member, I resolved to swim in formation with the Returned Missionaries and prepare for whatever the Mormon Gods directed. Heady days for young men who held the restored holy Priesthood and were fore-ordained before birth to help usher in the Millennium and the Second Coming of Jesus Christ. Joseph Smith, the "Greatest Prophet since Moses," we believed, had restored the only true church to earth. Following excruciation delays dating to the nineteenth century, the LDS Church was destined to redeem the world and rule from the promised land of America. The end days were near, and we were assured the Mormon Gods were tanned, rested and ready for 2000. Those Gods had high expectations for young men like you and me. You haven't let them down.

I remember traveling to Salt Lake City for the 1970, BYU/Utah football game. As always, the Cougar Club brothers sat together in a privileged section of the stadium. During a time out, the Utah student section suddenly stood and shouted, "BYU-BYU, where the girls are girls, and the boys are, too." Placid compared to raunchier taunts, but at that moment, I paused and looked around. I sat sandwiched with a group of mild-manner returned missionaries, most too sweet to swear. I was no longer an aide to a General, and no longer monitoring communication lines to the Paris peace talks. The military and my experiences in the

Vietnam War were behind me. Now, I wore the uniform of a student again back at my beloved BYU, where I always wanted to be since my Utah childhood.

The Cougar Club got special privileges at sporting events because of their powerful fund-raising capacity, and how much money a member got in pledges to the University was a competition. During our fall fundraiser, I quickly got a couple donations totaling $1,000 and took the early lead. When commitments were announce to everyone, we made eye contact, and you flashed me a look like a cornered wolf. Then, you pounced on the fundraising project and won the annual "smile and dial" contest—along with my attention and respect. There are Alpha males, and then there's Mitt Romney.

As President of Cougar Club in 1970–71, you had decided you should be President of the United States, having asked the brethren; "If not you, then who?" Everyone, including me, agreed. So, I decided serving as Nevada Governor or Senator before being appointed to your cabinet to start the millennium sounded like a reasonable plan. After all, we were two of the greatest "organized intelligences" to ever come to earth from the preexistence. This was why I was startled in 2006 to read your words quoted in *The American Spectator,* "I have to admit I did not think I was going into politics." In November, 2007, you made similar comments at town hall meetings in Marshalltown, Iowa and Las Vegas. Did you change your mind as your business career developed, and then decided to follow your earlier plan to be President after all?

Everyone in the Cougar Club had most of the answers back then—except me. During the intervening years, I had developed serious questions and concerns that you and our brethren did not share. Notwithstanding, I chugged the Mormon Kool Aid, prayed earnestly, and committed to help our generation of Mormon men save the world. A major Mormon prophecy about a White Horse and America remained unfulfilled. Like previous generations of Mormons, we were reared to believe the US Constitution needed saving, and the LDS Church would do it. We knew our reward, because of primordial valiance, was a chance to play major roles in the ensuing end day events. Jesus and "God the Father" had told the prophets, and our patriarchs had told us personally. We were a special generation.

That the US Constitution is in eminent danger and will "hang by a thread as fine as silk fiber" in the latter days before the LDS Church rides to its rescue is a continually restated claim beginning with Joseph Smith and persisting through every subsequent Mormon generation. The Church Priesthood holders will swoop in like knights to save the Constitution then set it aside to reestablish the theocratic Kingdom created by Joseph Smith and nearly perfected by Brigham

Young. The stated plan is to pave the way for the political Kingdom of God and Joseph Smith's version of the Millennial Kingdom on Earth. This belief was made public by Utah Senator Orrin Hatch during his run for President, when he said that, despite one of the most prosperous times in American history, the Church might need to step in to fill the breech should America collapse. Your own father, Mitt, also expressed the Mormon White Horse Prophecy in a similar comment decades earlier.

Ultimately, I concluded life is too valuable to prostrate before disproved prophets. I prefer a Democratic Republic government over the social and economic systems created by Joseph Smith, Brigham Young and Fundamentalist LDS leaders like Warren Jeffs. However, it wasn't always that way. While you served your Mormon mission in France, where you said people constantly made you defensive about the Vietnam War, I went to Southeast Asia in 1968, missionary lessons in hand, bosom burning, and eager to redeem gentiles. I envisioned serving my Mormon mission in Vietnam, where I could preach the restored Gospel to save people at the same time I held up dominoes to protect the Western World from Communists. Dedicated to country and certain of my duty to the Mormon Gods, I toted Mormon literature and searched for a chance to redeem some souls.

The best laid plans of mice and Mormons. The first chink in my Mormon armor came courtesy of an Air Force officer over a game of chess. Smirking and sucking his pipe, this hot prospective convert entered my room one evening. Reacting to my claim that no man could have written the *Book of Mormon*, he proceeded to read King James sounding scriptures he created for my benefit. This man made me laugh in spite of my pompous self. His material sounded as authentic as Joseph Smith's and equally as repetitive and drab. Verily, I say unto you, I chuckled and finally begged for mercy. And it came to pass that my friend made his point well, and I directed my frustration toward the chessboard.

Years later, I realized not serving a Mormon mission had been a blessing, and meeting men like the Air Force officer helped me to become a thinking human being. However, in 1968, I focused my efforts to spread the Mormon truth to the nations of the earth, cornered fellow officers and dreamed of when I could return to the only true school, where other chosen spirits from the preexistence were educated. Assured we had been held back in Heaven and blessed with the opportunity to be born in the very last days of wars and rumors of wars before all hell broke loose. Surely, I would return triumphant to BYU and find my first wife, waiting to marry for "time and all eternity" and "keep sweet" for her future God.

Mitt, I met you in the fall of 1970, only a month after leaving Vietnam. I had returned to BYU to salvage credits lost in 1965, and to give my Church and cultural heritage another chance. A seventh generation Mormon chosen and called before birth, I remained hooked on one of the greatest American fables ever formulated. Determined to play an important role in the culmination of events leading to the Millenniam, I faced my first temptation at Granny's Kitchen in downtown Provo. I couldn't resist going there to sneak a peak at the international news and indulge my Army coffee habit.

One day, relaxing between classes at Granny's, I read the *Salt Lake Tribune* and drank my java black, when a Cougar Club brother sat beside me at the counter. We carried on a strained conversation, while his eyes darted between my sinful "hot drink" and my defensive blue eyes. Today, I would tell him coffee is an antioxidant, even suggest a glass of red wine for both good health and self-righteous constipation. However, at the time, I only felt embarrassment, guilt and fear. The Church begins the guilt training early, and I suspect Mormon guilt makes Catholic guilt feel like fun. Catholic Priests listen and turn penitents into bead counters, but Mormon Bishops dispense condescending lectures and threats. If the guilt becomes too intense, Catholics can ease the pain by self medicating with alcohol, but Mormons have only punch, cookies, and prescription drugs.

Mitt, I tried hard to be a good BYU student like you, but I was single and far more sinful. Besides dealing with Granny's temptations, I wrestled with a campus full of beautiful young women who looked like they just stepped out of heaven. These well-programmed girls would ask where I went on my mission, then looked startled when I deadpanned, Vietnam. Petting with a female student had already gotten me in trouble with the BYU Standards Committee again. I had been banished three weeks before 1965 final exams, and now the current standards boss, a retired light Colonel, had just heel-locked me and waived my dusty old water-balloon-throwing, pant-raiding, fist-fighting file in my face. I didn't need him to hear I was downtown at Granny's breaking the Word of Wisdom by drinking coffee with the local Jack Mormons. It was harsh and insulting for a man of twenty-five just home from war to be browbeaten and threatened like a teenager. It reminded me of the Hemingway World War One novel in which the protagonist returned from Europe, where he had watched his lover die in his arms, only to be informed he couldn't be trusted with the family car.

Many contemporary Mormons would be shocked to learn their beloved Prophet, Joseph Smith, didn't live the Word of Wisdom and wouldn't be granted a Mormon Temple Recommend today. Although Church records systematically have been altered in failed attempts to hide this from historians and researchers, the Prophet smoked cigars and drank whisky, beer and wine. This dandy loved to lead parades through Nauvoo wearing his Napoleon-style hat and basking in prophetic adulation. Yes, Mitt, Lieutenant General Joseph Smith rode "Charlie" through town in his flashy military uniform with a big stogie in his mouth. His Mormon militia, four thousand strong and second only to the US Army in size, proudly marched behind him before an adoring crowd of the newest chosen people.

When the greatest prophet since Moses arrived at his mansion, his lap-dog loyal bartender, young Orrin Porter Rockwell, opened the bar for business or pleasure. Rockwell, later known in Utah as the Son of Thunder, served as one of the Church's Avenging Angels who intimidated or murdered at the Prophet's request. He was undoubtedly one of the scoundrels of whom Brigham Young spoke when he "dared the world to produce as mean devils as we can; we can beat them at anything. We have the greatest and smoothest liars in the world, the cunningest and most adroit thieves, and any shade of character you can mention." Orrin Porter Rockwell was on trial for murder when he died, yet still a hero in Lehi, Utah where he has been memorialized with a statute.

Joseph Smith's lifestyle and Porter Rockwell's behavior were of no consequence when I met you in the fall of 1970. I didn't know about the revealing and burgeoning New Mormon History. I only worried that another semester's credits might be pilfered. Given permission to contact my former professors and retrieve any grades I could, my kindly Chemistry Professor, near retirement, had just checked his old class records and agreed to credit me four hours with a B grade. Remembering me, he wondered why I never showed up for the final exam when I had an A. He shook his head and pierced his lips when I shared the sophomoric adventures that left me humiliated, my young life in shambles, and resulted in my 1966 draft notice.

Nobody likes to hear excuses, but to quote Flip Wilson, "The Devil made me do it." Our big brother Lucifer, the "Son of the Morning," was messing with my mind. Revelations warns us "the Great dragon was cast out, that old serpent, called the devil and Satan, which deceiveth the whole world." Old Beelzebub, the original bad boy, has been leading men and women like me astray since he lost the war in heaven. He was responsible for my naughtiness back then, and thanks to contemporary Mormon social attitudes, there's even more to blame him for in today's evil world. There would have been real trouble in River City if I had been spied racking them up at the Provo pool hall with a cigarette dangling from my mouth like Brando or Dean.

By the way, Mitt, my God appreciates a good joke. Kind and understanding, he sometimes gives a courtesy laugh to bad ones. We were reared to believe Mormon Gods are resurrected men with bodies of flesh and blood, so why shouldn't those guys have a funny bone, too? You have a sense of humor, so I hope you'll bear with my attempts at merriment and pray my arguments are as well developed as my sarcasm. To paraphrase Will Rogers, there's no trick to being a humorist, when you have the Mormon Church working for you, and the more I learn about Mormonism the harder it works for me. It took a long time to bring any form of humor to the Mormon farce, but then I finally understood how silly and easily satirized it is.

Numerous Christian groups want to love Mormons to their view of heaven, while scholars, scientists and researchers prefer reason and logic to usher Mormons forward in the universe. I think we all need a few good laughs along the way. Too many members still don't realize it, but Mormons need good humor served up like sugar to help the medicine go down. I predict it will be increasingly difficult for Mormons to simply turn away from bitter tablespoons of truthful medicine. One heaping spoonful of unpalatable truth for the LDS Church is that the "Millennium" has arrived, and there's still no Mormon Jesus with a train of adoring wives following behind. Mitt, perhaps equally disheartening for true believers is that not one of the thirty cities mentioned in the *Book of Mormon* can be found for us to hold a Cougar Club reunion some summer.

To paint an accurate picture of the Mormon Church, past and present, it's helpful to use the brush of humor, including sarcasm and ridicule. The finished portrait depicts an organization stretched on a canvas of lies, sketched and re-sketched so many times over the past generations, that it appears to discerning eyes humorously discombobulated. Certainly, fresh humor is desperately needed to augment the Mormon classics. The joke about excommunicated Mormons getting Sundays off and a ten percent pay raise has become shopworn. It's also inaccurate because the Church has always financially drained members far beyond the ten percent tithing requirement, while systematically sucking up their time and energy. And the decades-old joke about being quiet when you walk by the Mormons in Heaven—because they think they're the only ones there—is equally exhausted.

Sarcasm may be a weak form of humor, but not as distasteful as unsanitary potty humor, which still makes my kids giggle. I won't resort to that. Whatever style, it won't elicit laughs from the self-proclaimed chosen people in the latter days. Unable to accept or appreciate how ludicrous their beliefs are, devout LDS members have zero tolerance for any humor about their history and doctrines. Mormon leaders and members have mocked and laughed at other churches for generations, but remain too thin-skinned to laugh with those who laugh at them. If they dared pay attention to outside views, Mormon members might develop their sense of humor and lose testimony in their only true Church, though unlikely because perpetual lies have diverted their eyes and fooled their hearts. Still, reality can be more interesting and fun than fiction, Mitt, and I remain optimistic you and the Mormons someday will agree with me. With some original Mormon shtick, a man like you could help many members swallow the truth and at least snicker about the silliness.

There was more seriousness than humor at BYU in 1970–71. Already married to your high school sweetheart, and in the marriage you planned for years, you had found the woman you call your soul mate. Your relationship was an envious one. You got married three months after returning from France, only waiting that long to honor your family's request, but many weren't so fortunate. The Church had instructed returned missionaries to find their first companion for time and all eternity and marry her within six months. Several guys, long overdue for matrimony, were naturally frustrated, cranky and stressed out. One despondent brother speculated his wife had been killed, a crossfire casualty between our big brothers, Jesus and Lucifer, during their War in Heaven.

A proverbial kid in the candy store after two years in Vietnam, I was looking for my eternal harem Queen, too. I needed a first wife on earth who could later coordinate date nights around baby sitting chores and menstrual cycles in heaven. I constantly scanned the campus crowd of potential partners in search of one that would be a supremely skillful executive secretary in the Celestial Kingdom. Mormon men are destined to marry innumerable wives in heaven, but having the concubine over for dinner on a Saturday night, as Brigham Young liked to do on earth, is only acceptable so long as a God doesn't let several ladies party too late or spend the night. Considering a marital ménage a trios is apparently disgusting and absolutely out of the question for Mormon Gods.

Competition for earthly and eternal companionship was stiff, so when word circulated I was in trouble with Standards, some guys attack to further their cause. Nevertheless, I couldn't let pompous returned missionaries, who used a missionary deferment to avoid the draft, claim all wasn't fair in love and war. After all, while I suited up to help create havoc and cultural destruction across Southeast Asia, you and fellow missionaries soldiered in the Mormon war on Christianity. Now, we were all back at BYU with a burning in our bosom and a yearning to find our eternal harem queen. Mitt, thankful and somewhat relieved,

I learned you told club members to leave me alone and let me work out my problems with school officials. And I did. Since it was an open secret our imported basketball star, Kresimir Cosic, was slam-dunking wide-eyed coeds across campus, maybe the Standards office decided to give me some slack for having Russian hands and Roman fingers. Whatever happened, I finally was treated like a decorated war veteran and allowed to complete my long-disrupted undergraduate work.

After graduation, you went to Harvard for a degree in Business/Law and graduated in the top tier. I stayed at BYU and pursued a Masters in Public Administration. I didn't find a wife on my second trip through BYU, but was granted a scholarship to intern with former BYU professor Mark Cannon on Chief Justice Warren Burger's staff at the U.S. Supreme Court. There for the spring semester of 1973, I experienced the historic time of Roe v Wade when the Court was under siege by anti-abortionists. While you finished at Harvard and entered the business world to amass your fortune as a venture capitalist, I was hired as a Republican congressional aide and returned to Las Vegas to prepare to help you change the world. I entered the underworld of local politics and found myself unexpectedly at war on the front lines of Watergate. Not surprisingly, in retrospect, I was again at loggerheads with Mormon Church leaders.

3

It's Vegas, Baby

It's easy to agree with those who think my hometown was more fun in the days when casinos were financed by mob families, run by wise guys, and the Mormon Sheriff escorted unwanted visitors to the edge of town with a warning not to come back. Many old time Las Vegans are nostalgic for the small town with racketeers in turtle necks and Duke of Earl pompadours—and clean cut Mormon front men sporting crew cuts. The era before button-down Wall Street types counted each bean and comps became as scarce as a straight flush. Then again, maybe the melancholy crowd is mostly composed of old cranks. My big city wife grew up in a suburb of Cleveland and says Las Vegas is getting just large enough to interest her. It's definitely not the place where I spent my teenage years or returned to a few decades ago.

Like you when you left BYU for Harvard in 1971, Mitt, I was a Mormon fair-haired boy in 1973. I left Washington DC and returned to Las Vegas with write-ups in both local newspapers. Mobsters were still King in this company town, but some Mormon Jacks powerfully fronted for their interests. LDS Church members permeated the school district and local governments, as they still do today. Congressman David Towell's wife, Sherry, once told me, "Someday people will say they remember you when you were just a Congressman's aide." Though vertically challenged and already balding, she thought I had the right stuff for a bright political future in Nevada.

As an eager congressional aide, I quickly learned my hometown was a shadowy world where some bribes masquerade as campaign contributions and others are just plain bribes. Now, a big-time city on the surface, Las Vegas remains a corrupted political place where "juice" dictates public policy, from the penthouse to the courthouse, and most politicians, many of them Mormons, are bigger whores than the Strip's street walkers. The worst bent nosed thugs have been driven off the Las Vegas Strip, and their successors garnered financial credibility on Wall Street, but the political corruption was woven into the community fabric generations ago and continues unabated. Gaming Inc. has always been as secretive as Mormon Inc. and still holds its cards close to the vest, even after the companies became publicly traded. Now, some corporations are going private again, where they will face less scrutiny from regulators.

My foray into local government was when hired by the court system in 1976 to build a misdemeanant diversion program for first and youthful offenders. The program operated under a federal grant and was controlled locally by Mormon politicians. Still naïve, and inspired by my Supreme Court experience and social beliefs, I began a political street fight with county commissioners and the City Manager to get the Lower Court Counseling Program permanently funded. Chief Municipal Judge "Moon" Mullen was unhappy because I had taken my crusade into the media and flashed his pistol at me menacingly in chambers one day, saying he didn't think I had the personality for politics. One County Commissioner and the assistant City Manager, both Mormons, did their best to throttle me. I won the political battle to save the alternative sentencing program for the court system then resigned and began my career in business. Mitt, I'm proud to say the program still serves youthful and minor misdemeanants under the capable management of my former assistant.

Overcoming angry opposition and getting permanent funding for the court program was rewarding, but, at the end of the day, Judge Mullen was right about me not having the personality for Las Vegas politics. It was acceptable and profitable to be a corrupted political hypocrite, but pushing for change and not playing the game was inexcusable to the good-old-boy network. Young, adventuresome and then a lot more self-righteous, I decided to change the system by seeking election to public office. Choosing to no linger drink the Mormon Kool Aid, I ran for public office twice, first for City Commissioner and then Governor. With a great deal of idealism and little money, I taunted the corrupted good-old-boys, including their Mormon co-conspirators, and got politically smothered in an avalanche of casino chips. I had fun doing what I felt was right at the time and walked away with no shame.

Mitt, I ran away with the political circus a few years, believing it my religious destiny, and forwarded you news clippings to show my progress. Never performed under the political big top again, but still find it fun to watch the greatest show on earth. Nationally and locally, it never stops entertaining. In 2006, the Los Angeles Times did a three-part expose on Nevada's tainted judicial system, the mob's former big mouthpiece is our mayor, and we have our first Mormon Governor whose bungling kept a cadre of defense attorneys, late night comedians and scrambling reporters busy for months. To paraphrase the late Molly Ivins, politics is the greatest entertainment in America—and it's free! Well, almost free. You still have to pay for the popcorn.

These days, between Presidential elections, I am entertained watching the local political circus. Nevada politics rarely stops amusing. Following the media's disclosers of major corruption by elected officials in the 1970s, a new generation of Mormon political hacks have grabbed the cash and in a nasty new twist, lavished in the lap dance of luxury. For generations, Mormon politicians pretended to protect the public good, while stuffing their pockets, shirts and faces with freebees. Las Vegas was built on luck, and some of the most successful people are those lucky enough to own a few Mormon clowns in the local political circus. It's natural for the LDS Church to want a piece of the Vegas action, too. Brigham Young once said, "We can pick out Elders of Israel right here who can beat the world at gambling, who can handle the cards, cut and shuffle them with the smartest rogues on the face of God's foot-stool."

The Mormon Church distains Las Vegas values, Mitt, but your religious leaders gladly accept tens of millions of dollars that annually flows to Salt Lake City from money earned and tithed in that despotic place. For decades, bag men departed Las Vegas with laundered and skimmed cash to Chicago and other destinations, while every week the Mormons got their cut of the sin city largesse routed to Salt Lake City. Local Mormons insisted a Temple be built in Las Vegas as a return on their investment, so Church leaders relented and built a big white one on the Salt Lake City side of town overlooking the evil. Mormons bought many of the homes around it to be closer to their Mormon Jesus. Now, gambling executives sucker living people in their Strip Temples, and local Mormons save dead ones in their Sunrise Mountain Temple.

The Mormon and gambling industries have more in common than their symbiotic financial relationship in Las Vegas. Both function in their respective states as corporate oligopolies. Surrounded by their Temples, Salt Lake City Church leaders anoint politicians who covenant to do the Church's political bidding. In Las Vegas, the gambling apostles invite political candidates into their gaudy temples for blessings and money. A core group of pioneer Mormon families, who became powerful and wealthy players in the LDS financial kingdom, think they're preordained by the Gods to collect billions annually in tax-free money and rule over religious rubes. On the flip side, a new generation of rich and powerful Las Vegas corporate suits, who inherited the house odds, believes they're geniuses for annually plucking billions from pigeons.

Whether the Gods or the odds, few can beat the house in Salt Lake City or Las Vegas. Mormon, Inc. and Gaming Inc. are content to keep and customers uneducated and invest money in more temple construction around the world. Salt Lake City based Mormon leaders don't care whether their people are educated as long as they loyally serve the Church and regularly pay their tithing and other "offerings" to support Mormonism's expansive building programs. Gaming leaders aren't concerned whether Nevada citizens are educated so long as they provide a workforce in construction and basic service industry jobs to build and support more gambling temples. Las Vegas is one of the richest cities on the planet, but gaming taxes remain the lowest in the nation and intimidated politicians let education spending languish at levels to compete with Mississippi and a few other States for the nation's bottom slot.

Mormons and mobsters enjoyed a decade's long affair in Las Vegas, a place where strip joints proprietors naturally guarded their hen houses more closely than the old Mormon polygamists did their pagan harems. Each espoused strong family values and, whether Mormon or Cosa Nostra, believed their families came first and demanded social loyalty. Both hated whistleblowers. Family renegades of either group who spoke up or wanted out were considered snitches and traitors to be punished for disloyalty. Granted, punishment methods have evolved from Bowie knives and cement boots to more subtle and humane means of control.

Other control methods have improved in Las Vegas and the Salt Lake City in recent years. No longer considered the Mississippi of the West, Las Vegas governments and businesses are nicer to black people than they were decades ago. Meanwhile, some Negroes reportedly now live in Salt Lake City. Vegas no longer segregates Negroes on the "west side" or forces them to sneak in casino back doors, like Sammie Davis Jr. had to do when a member of the Rat Pack. Salt Lake City allows black people to hold the Mormon Priesthoods and finally treats them like human beings. While undoubtedly wiser to avoid both enticements, Negroes today can walk in the front door of Las Vegas gaming temples to gamble, and they can enter LDS temples to compete for a high seat in Mormon heaven.

The Grand Canyon of moral decay, Las Vegas is a modern day Sodom reviled by America's religious right and self-righteous Mormons. However, I'm pleased we met as preteens and grew up together. Now married, but not for time and all eternity, I love the place because, despite the comparisons—some admittedly stretched—there are big differences between Salt Lake City and Las Vegas. The LDS Church in Salt Lake sells work, subservience and sacrifice, but the Las Vegas gaming industry merely deals play, fun and more fun. Sin City is a land of freedom where good and evil coexists, even flourishes, while Salt Lake City's Mormon leaders try to mandate good behavior and punish evil—or the enforcer's version of it.

In spite of continuing political corruption, Las Vegas is a city where personal freedoms are appreciated and people have the right to sin if they choose. We cultural Mormons were taught as children that Lucifer is our big brother—the second born after Jesus—who presented God the Father with an earthly plan to force humanity into righteousness and mandatory salvation. In response, Jesus countered with his plan of "free agency," which our Heavenly Father accepted for his spirit children over Lucifer's plan. We primordial intelligences purportedly cheered our approval when informed we would be allowed to come to earth, knowing Jesus would die for our sins and redeem us. So, tell me, Mitt, why are LDS leaders so determined to obstruct free agency and restrict the freedom to think, choose and have fun?

4

All in the Family

Our ancestors, true believers, traveled west in the nineteenth century and arrived in the Salt Lake valley. Already traditional Christians, they were susceptible to Joseph Smith's stories of gold bibles, ancient civilizations and a marvelous Gospel restoration directly from heaven. Well-intentioned people got swept away by a charlatan with a big ego and brazen lines. For the most part, your ancestors and mine converted, joined the Saints in eastern settlements and, with a song in their hearts, put their shoulders to the wheel on the journey to Salt Lake City. When I think of the physical indignities and psychological assaults our families endured, it makes me want to drop to my knees and beg again for Mormonism's alternate version of reality to be real. Then, I remember Huckleberry Finn, as real as any *Book of Mormon* character and considerably more interesting, said we can't pray a lie.

Mitt, neither you nor I can pray the Mormon Church true or wish it into reality. Not for you, me, or my pioneer forefathers, many of whom lie in graveyards along the old railroad line that cuts through the Utah valley, where as a child I was indoctrinated. They rested there on Memorial Day 2006, while their great-grandchildren listened to patriotic speeches praising President Bush and the Iraq War. They wait for the Mormon Morning of the First Resurrection, when Jesus will call priesthood holders to rise from their graves first, and these worthy men will call their wives to rise up beside them. Our forefathers died believing they will enter the Mormon Celestial Kingdom of heaven and dwell with their families, Father in Heaven and the Mormon Jesus forever. Sadly, they will wait forever because Mormonism originated in Joseph Smith's imagination, and he couldn't simply create his own reality and make it universal.

Our ancestors didn't have the education, knowledge or information necessary to evaluate intellectually and unemotionally the earnest testimonies of missionaries with exciting tales of a new prophet and his golden gospel's freshly minted Christ. Most converts were lured to Salt Lake City without being informed by the missionaries of polygamy and other non-Christian doctrines. Others were too young to have a choice. Mitt, our family histories are replete with poignant generational stories of our forefathers' heroism and heartache as they dealt with the harsh frontier environment, federal authorities and Indians. They listened to their prophets, built new communities, led expeditions, hauled freight and helped build the transcontinental railroad. Their deprivations and deaths from disease and hardship helped lay the foundation for our comfortable lives.

My great-great-grandfather Moody migrated to Salt Lake City in 1853 after freeing his slaves and leaving much of his wealth behind in Texas, as required by law. William Crestfield Moody didn't fit the poor, working class profile of most early converts to the Church. His grandfather had been a Virginia doctor and his father, John Wyatt Moody, rode with Sam Houston as a Major in the Texas army. John Wyatt became the first Auditor of Public Accounts in the new Republic of Texas, a position he held until his death of "congestive fever" in 1839. The large Moody farm once sat near Buffalo Bayou, in the middle of the present Houston business district.

William Crestfield Moody arrived in Zion with a herd of cattle, fire in his belly and claimed he spoke in tongues. Moody's tongue talking—and his cattle and wealth—impressed Brigham Young, masterful at manipulating new converts with talent and money. Young also spoke in tongues and had impressed Joseph Smith by doing so at a prayer meeting in the Prophet's home on the first day they met in 1832. Moody was dispatched on missions to Texas and then England before Young sent him to southern Utah's "Dixie" to grow cotton and help build the St. George Temple. Over the years, Moody settled several places in the Utah/ Nevada territory, including Eagle Valley and Ersine, Nevada. He eventually moved his family to Deseret, Utah in the early 1880s so his numerous children could marry somebody other than their brothers or sisters. Later, when polygamists went on the run to avoid arrest, he left his family behind and migrated to Arizona.

Many of my ancestors, including the Bess, Kelly and Hunt families, had already reached Zion when Moody arrived. His second of five wives came into the Salt Lake valley as a child with a company led by Apostle Heber C. Kimball. Lola Eliza Bess traveled west with her siblings and widowed mother against their family's wishes. She buried one of her sisters along the Mormon Trail, ate roots to survive and, like most pioneer children, received meager schooling. This courageous woman reared eleven children of her own and helped raise five more when one of her sister wives died young. She endured primitive frontier conditions in several new settlements as Moody dragged her from place to place before leaving her behind in Deseret.

My Kelly ancestors joined the Latter Day Saints and traveled to Salt Lake City after Joseph Smith's death. A great-great-grandfather, Virgil Kelly Sr., became an influential law enforcement figure in central and southern Utah. He was deputy US Marshal for the Utah Territory and in charge of Indian affairs for the southern region. Later, Kelly was elected Sheriff of Millard County for several terms and entertained his wide-eyed descendants for generations with the telling and retelling of his adventures with horse thieves and Indians. My favorite Virgil Kelly story is recorded in a family history written by my great uncle, Hilton Kelly. According to Uncle Hilt, a band of Piute Indians had come to the house looking for the man they called "Masamaquapits." They were angry about a regional water shortage, and Virgil was unable to reason with them. When the Indians started beating Virgil, his mother-in-law, Amanda Barron, charged from the house pulling the pins from her long dark hair, screaming like a banshee. She carried on until the Indians mounted and rode away. The punch line was Indians believed it bad luck to hang out with crazy people.

My great-great-great-great-grandfather, Jefferson Hunt, converted to Mormonism in 1835. Not wanting to be left out when wife, Celia, accepted baptism, he reportedly dropped the plow and headed for a dunking, too. In 1838, after joining the Saints in Far West, Missouri, he fought in a bloody brawl called the Battle at Crooked River, in which both Mormon and Missouri militiamen were killed. That confrontation inspired Joseph Smith's Mohammad Speech in the town square. The Mormon prophet said that, if he were not let alone, he "would be a second Mohammad to this generation, and make it one gore of blood from the Rocky Mountains to the Atlantic Ocean." He further warned he "would tread down his enemies, and walk over their dead bodies." Mormons, boldly claiming divine right to the land in Jackson County, Missouri and believing the Millennium and Second Coming were imminent, hurried to prepare their New Jerusalem.

Many were impressed by the Prophet's threats, but not Boggs, the Missouri Governor. Three months earlier—on the Fourth of July—influential early Church leader Sydney Rigdon had delivered a fiery speech in which he used the term "war of extermination" to threaten non-Mormons. In response, and amidst reports of Mormon looting, Governor Boggs said Mormons had made war upon the people of his state and issued "extermination orders" to drive the Mormons out. That led to the Haun's Mill Massacre at a small Mormon settlement near

Far West, which set the stage for even more violence and provided the foundation for Mormons to lay claim to persecution for years to come. Even today, Haun's Mill is used to justify past Mormon violence, although the Church fails to mention the Mormon militia attacked the Missouri militia a few nights earlier.

In 1838, a secret society of men known as Danites was formed in Far West. Also known as the Sons of Dan, after the warrior tribe of Israel, these men stole from the gentiles, burned the homes of innocent people and murdered apostates and enemies of the Church. Jefferson Hunt, a major figure in the Mormon Wars was a known participant in the Battle at Crooked River and a member of the elite group of Church enforcers organized to defend the Prophet and Mormon interests, violently if necessary. In 1844, Jefferson Hunt escorted Joseph Smith to the Carthage, Illinois jail and was "within hearing distance of the shots" that killed the Prophet. Hunt, a Major in the Nauvoo Legion, and other loyalists loaded the bodies of Joseph and Hyrum Smith on a wagon and returned them to the Nauvoo Mansion House.

I was recently startled to realize one of my family's pioneer heroes was almost certainly a member of the Danites, but blemishes are more interesting—and human—than any Church attempts to whitewash Mormon history under a sparkling coat of disinformation. Leaders in the clandestine Danite organization were invaluable to Brigham Young after he moved the Mormon Kingdom to Utah, and Jefferson Hunt and Brigham Young had forged a lifelong friendship. As Mormon preparations to move west began in 1845, Brigham Young sent Jefferson Hunt and Porter Rockwell to explore sections of Mexico and the west coast. Known as the Hunt-Rockwell expedition, it returned with recommendations for Mormon settlement in Southern California and Oregon. Young later ignored those recommendations in favor of the Great Salt Lake Valley.

With the Mormon move west from Nauvoo in full motion, Jefferson Hunt played his first major role in American pioneer history in 1846, when he was appointed the highest-ranking Mormon in the Mormon Battalion. Hunt was a "conspicuously effective" captain in Company A of the five hundred man group called by the US to fight in the Mexican/American War, and he briefly led the battalion when the federally appointed commander died. The Mormon Battalion traveled more than 2,000 miles from Council Bluffs, Iowa to San Diego, the longest infantry march in history. Mitt, according to your great-great-grandfather, Parley P. Pratt, the Mormon Battalion helped take and maintain California. Mormon Battalion members were some of the first men to discover gold and set off the second gold rush. The first gold rush came when the Mormons hastily headed west with a copy of Joseph Smith's new gold-plated Bible in hand.

Following his Mormon Battalion service, Jefferson Hunt arrived in the Salt Lake valley in the fall of 1847. Wagon trains of Latter Day Saints had begun arriving with Brigham Young in July, and Hunt was appalled to find them living in squalor. In response, he began freighting supplies from California and soon guided wagon trains carrying gold rushers. On one occasion, the fortune seekers became frustrated with the slow pace of the one hundred wagon caravan Hunt led. When a young man rode in with a John C. Fremont map he claimed showed a shortcut to the coast, nearly all the wagons left Hunt's group and immediately encountered difficult terrain. Within days, most of the defecting wagons returned to the main group, and all arrived safely in California with Hunt. However, twenty wagons continued west on their own and ultimately became known as the Death Valley 49ers. With limited provisions and no food for their animals, they slaughtered several oxen and burned wood from their wagons to make jerky at Burned Wagons Camp. As they hiked out, a woman turned, waved and said, "Goodbye Death Valley." Rescued by Mexican Caballeros, the wayward pioneers lived to recount their adventures—and the name Death Valley was born.

During the 1850s, Jefferson Hunt founded cities in California and Utah, including Provo and Parowan. The citizens of Parowan elected him to serve as Iron County's representative to the Utah Legislature. In 1851, while in Salt Lake City for the first legislative session of the new territory of Utah, Hunt and Brigham Young held a conference. Brigham Young finally saw the wisdom of a wagon route to the coast and a way station to support it. "Hunt had long believed a Mormon settlement in southern California was wise" and his choice was soon-to-be-named San Bernardino. The California outpost was to serve as hub in a string of Mormon settlements for an immigration route stretching from Salt Lake City to the Pacific. The Prophet and Apostles were determined to get the English converts, particularly the young immigrant girls to Salt Lake City faster by sailing them to the west coast and bringing them overland. The motto was, "I don't care how you bring 'um, just bring 'um young."

Hunt was told to prepare quickly and pilot the mass departure. One hundred and fifty wagons carrying three hundred and fifty people left Utah for southern California in 1851 with Jefferson Hunt and your great-great-grandfather, Apostle Parley P. Pratt, piloting parts of the wagon train. The pioneers suffered blizzards, mud holes, the withering desert and Indian attacks. Mitt, Piute Indians raided the train led by Apostle Pratt between Las Vegas and "Resting Springs," endangering lives and killing livestock. Once camped in California, Jefferson Hunt, Parley Pratt and two other Apostles traveled to northern California on the steamer Goliath, where they raised $25,000 from Saints and minors Hunt knew from his Battalion years. The money was used to purchase the land for San Bernardino and its fort.

Jefferson Hunt was an elected representative in the California Legislature and served for five years as an assemblyman from Los Angeles County. He became know as the "Father of San Bernardino County" after introducing legislation to create it. He was a Lieutenant General in the California militia when word came from Brigham Young that he was needed back in Salt Lake City. Newly elected President James Buchanan had declared Utah in a state of rebellion in 1857, and, as the confrontation escalated, Young ordered Hunt and the California colonist to return to Utah. Buchanan opposed polygamy and felt Young's theocratic dominance of the Utah territory defied American principles. Before surrendering the title of Governor in 1858, Young ordered Hunt and others to circle the wagons and threatened to burn the city as a federal army marched toward the Great Salt Lake valley.

Jefferson Hunt founded Huntsville, Utah in 1860 and served in as a Utah territorial legislator from Weber County in the early 1860s before moving on to Oxford, Idaho where he died. There's a monument dedicated to him on the Old Spanish Trail near Enterprise, Utah.

Mitt, few can match your pedigree in the Mormon Church. Joseph Smith appointed your great-great-grandfather Parley P. Pratt and his younger brother Orson as two of the first Twelve Apostles. Parley Pratt read the book of Mormon soon after its publication and according to his autobiography—written posthumously by his son—esteemed it, "more than all the riches of the world." The Mormon Church only a few months old, the elder Pratt traveled to Palmyra looking for Joseph Smith, met his brother Hiram and was baptized by Oliver Cowdrey in September, 1830.

Now one of the first members of Joseph Smith's new Church, Parley P. Pratt left Palmyra to inform his mentor Sydney Rigdon of the exciting news, along with the other followers of Alexander Campbell, known as the Campbellites. Pratt convinced the scholarly Rigdon that Joseph Smith was a Prophet, and together they cajoled hundreds of Campbellites to convert to Mormonism. Before his tragic death, your famous forefather single handedly brought thousands of converts into the Church, including his brother Orson. Like Orson, Parley P. Pratt was a bright, articulate man and the Pratt Apostles became two of the most able defenders of the early Mormon Church. Mitt, leadership skills and intellectual talent run like sap through your family tree.

In 1835, Joseph Smith selected Parley P. Pratt to the group of twelve men who supposedly mirrored Christ's Apostles, making him part of the "traveling high council," responsible for taking the Restored Gospel to "all nations, kindred, tongues and people." Despite his shortened life, Parley's fiery writings defended Mormon Doctrine for much of the nineteenth century. Now more humorous than inspiring to read many of his pontifical orations and proclamations, in his day, he was a master at explaining away contradictions to keep members convinced and potential converts listening. Arguably, Parley P. Pratt deserves the title of Father of Mormon Apologists.

Both Jefferson Hunt and Parley P. Pratt were in the Battle at Crooked River, which led to the Missouri militia's mad-dog revenge at Haun's Mill. When Apostle David W. Patton, a Danite Captain, ordered his men to "rake them down," Apostle Pratt took a sniper's aim and killed a Missourian. Another Missouri militiaman, Samuel Tarwater, was wounded and badly mutilated, but lived to press murder charges against Pratt, who was imprisoned in 1839. It is not known how, but like many early Church leaders, Pratt subsequently escaped from prison and resumed his position in the quorum of Twelve Apostles.

For reasons unclear to me, Jefferson Hunt took a second wife in Nauvoo and extended the polygamist lifestyle no further. Parley P. Pratt, whom Joseph Smith called the Archer of Paradise, had twelve wives and had he lived would have claimed more. A fluffy peacock who loved the ladies, Pratt married several young women over a four year period whose average age was twenty-four—the youngest seventeen, when he was forty. Jefferson and Parley differed on more than just the plural marriage doctrine. While Jefferson earned money leading gold rushers to California, Parley set up toll roads to collect fees as they passed through Zion.

It was a sad day for the Saints when beloved Parley P. Pratt's girl-crazy ways proved his undoing. A fanatical supporter of polygamy, he was sent home to meet his maker in 1857 at the hand of the outraged spouse of his twelfth wife, Eleanor McLean. Parley P. Pratt showed the Mormon leadership's contempt for civil marriage and authority when Brigham Young sealed him to the woman while she was still legally married to Hector McLean. Then, Pratt helped her hatch a plan to snatch the couple's three children from New Orleans and take them to Utah. Hector, known as a mean drunk, was furious and apparently didn't want to share joint custody with Eleanor. Taking the kids fishing on weekends presented logistical problems with his children stashed in 1850s Salt Lake City. When attempted court action against Pratt failed, McLean tracked him down in Arkansas and killed him in a murderous rage. Not "shot in the back" as Mormon propaganda alleges, Pratt was stabbed with a knife as the two men fought from their horses, then shot and gruesomely left to bleed to death. A terrible way to die and adds a strange twist to the "shot by a jealous husband" scenario.

Parley P. Pratt achieved Mormon martyrdom and his death, which flamed the Saint's long-seething anger over the death of Joseph Smith, became a precursor to the most evil, disgusting event in pioneer history—the Mountain Meadows Massacre. When Pratt was killed, Brigham Young said nothing had bothered him so much since the death of Joseph and Hyrum Smith at Carthage jail. It's understandable because Parley's irresistible charm had lifted him to hero status, and his brilliance—along with brother Orson—had breathed live into the Church from its earliest days. Young and others wanted revenge, and within a few months, they extracted it with murder in the once serine meadows. A wagon train of innocent Southerners, mostly from Arkansas where Pratt was killed, was attacked in Southern Utah by Mormons who historically tried to blame it on Indians. Mormon leadership has lied about this event for 150 years and, before *September Dawn* in 2007, successfully blocked attempts to make it a movie.

The butcher at Mountain Meadows took place after the victims were lured from their position under a flag of truce—hungry, battered and terrified. The bodies and personal items were scattered across the valley, and their valuables later reappeared in the possession of Southern Utah Mormons. Mitt, none of these sorrowful souls were spared, except for the smallest children, themselves inconsolable after watching their families killed in cold blood. Much is written about this event, but none more thoroughly researched than Sally Denton's 2003 book, *American Massacre.* A former Boulder City, Nevada resident and also a descendant of Mormon pioneers, Sally presents the slaughter and surrounding events in vivid detail.

Only a few years after Joseph Smith ordained Parley and Orson Pratt Apostles, Orson's long career as a powerful and influential Mormon leader suffered a temporary disruption. While Orson Pratt was away on a mission, Joseph Smith made sexual advances on his wife, Sarah. Orson reacted angrily when he returned and in the aftermath, was excommunicated from the Church in 1842. One can only wonder at the negotiations that convinced Orson Pratt to ignore his wife's dishonor, and abandon his own self respect and return to Mormonism as a reinstated Apostle in 1843. Whatever was said, he put away his anger and skepticism about Joseph Smith's calling as a prophet. Orson Pratt was reappointed to the Twelve Apostles, although he lost his seniority and subsequently, the chance to serve as Prophet.

Orson Pratt clearly decided it better to be an Apostle with several sweet wives than an apostate with just one angry one. Sarah remained livid about the greatest prophet since Moses trying to jump her while her Apostle husband was away recruiting for their Kingdom of Heaven on Earth. At first, Orson didn't accepted polygamy, but before long, moved by the spirit, he boldly announced "the great Messiah, who was the founder of the Christian religion, was a polygamist." Apostle Orson Pratt had shared the absolute power of Joseph Smith and then lost it. Uncomfortable out of power, he repented, pledged allegiance to the new polygamist club and once more became a powerful man. Then, he assembled his own "train," which grew to seven wives and forty five children.

In the summer of 1847, reinvigorated Orson Pratt beat Brigham Young and the main party of Saints into the Salt Lake valley by three days, but Sarah Pratt chose a different direction for her life. After her husband's reinstatement, she left both him and the Church. Sarah Pratt later said polygamy was the "direst curse," which demoralizes "good men" and made "bad men worse." In an 1886 interview, Sarah Pratt said Joseph Smith's attempted seduction system included telling her "God does not care if we have a good time, if only people do not know it." Joseph Smith, a product of the writings and philosophies of his day, was influenced by numerous men, including Ralph Waldo Emerson. Emerson taught that we please God by responding to our desires and pleasing ourselves. Joseph Smith and Emerson were in harmony on what later became the cry of the 1960s sexual revolution: "If it feels good, do it!"

A power struggle developed between Apostle Orson Pratt and Brigham Young that persisted into the 1870s. When Apostle Pratt would disagree with Young on doctrine of policy issues, Young, the boss, would simply say your great-great-great-uncle Orson was preaching false doctrine again. The struggle between the man who would be King and the man who was may have been inevitable. Pratt was described as a rational thinker; Brigham Young viewed as more intuitive. Both Brigham Young's and Orson Pratt's approaches to theocracy were rooted in nineteenth century frontier life and its base of knowledge. Though influenced by rational Aristotelian metaphysics and Newton, Orson Pratt mostly viewed the universe through the monocle of Hermetic philosophers of the Renaissance and the occult world of Hermeticism. Hermes was the grandson of one of the earliest and most primitive Greek Gods, and over the centuries, varying forms of Hermeticism influenced human belief systems, including the Masonic movement and Mormonism.

One of Orson's uninspired works, *Key to the Universe*, published in 1879, was saturated with nineteenth century mathematical theories covered by a Newtonian veneer. Like Joseph Smith and Brigham Young, Orson Pratt was trapped by his provincial Gods, and the concepts he believed self-evident have proved illusions.

On one occasion, French writer Jules Remy traveled to Salt Lake and criticized Orson's philosophy as "old hat." In his book, *A Journey to Great-Salt-Lake City*, Remy wrote it was "the old materialism of Epicurus." He added that Orson's work was "hardly anything more than an echo of many a philosophical school in Boston and Philadelphia." Now, well over one hundred years since Remy wrote those words, and even Orson Pratt's philosophical echo has faded.

The surname you carry, Mitt, is also imbedded in early Mormon history records. Your great-great-grandfather Miles Romney converted in England and arrived in Nauvoo in 1841, where he joined Jefferson Hunt and others working on the Temple. Like Brigham Young, Miles Romney was a master carpenter who eventually supervised the construction of the St. George, Utah Tabernacle. Both assigned to the construction project by Brigham Young, certainly William Crestfield Moody and Miles Romney also knew each other. Unlike Moody who had five wives, Miles Romney was apparently not a polygamist, although there are conflicting records about his marital status. Romney died an unusual death in 1877 when he accidentally fell from an upper floor window of the St. George Endowment House.

Miles Romney's son, Miles Park Romney, and another of your great grandfathers, Helaman Pratt, became earnest polygamists. These men moved to the Mormon Mexican colonies, where they became leaders and practiced plural marriage after it was officially banned by the Church in 1890. Just five years after your father was born to Gaskell Romney and Anna A. Pratt in 1907, the Mexican Revolution forced the Mormon colonists to return to America. Typical of the Mormon's preoccupation with narcissism and melodrama, their 1912 migration back to the US, which included young George Romney, was called The Exodus.

Mitt, our Mormon ancestral roots run deep into America's pioneer soil. These men and women bravely colonized in the American west, and believed themselves major players in end day events. Since Joseph Smith said Jesus would come before the end of the nineteenth Century, every subsequent Mormon generation has believed it would happen in their lifetime, including our own. I remember Grandpa Moody told me we lived in the last days and would live to see Christ's return. He had heard that pronouncement all his life, too. Now, our ancestor's views appear more pathetic than prophetic, at least for those who dare to question. I suspect the Pratt brothers would look askance at the Church's decades-long intimidation of members who dare engage in open discussion of historical and doctrinal inconsistencies.

The LDS end days rubbish continues as every Mormon generation views its time as the last days when even "the very elect" are in danger of being misled before Joseph Smith returns with Jesus. Contemporary devout Mormons view these as the last days and smugly believe themselves the elect of God who will see Jesus in their lifetime. Sadly, like their forefathers, they remain deceived and sublimate their free agency to a blissful but false eternal promise. Were Jefferson Hunt alive today, I believe he would advise us to avoid the Death Valley of Mormonism and return the wagons to the Old Spanish Trail of traditional Christian values. Mormon pioneer descendants should remember the words of the woman who said, "Goodbye, Death Valley" and tell their barren belief system goodbye.

Our Mormon generation has the information to discern the truth, but without independent inquiry, members mentally capitulate to Church leaders and ventriloquize their pronouncements on history and doctrine. Church public relations professionals flood Mormon homes with endless mind/molding malarkey, and not surprisingly, our clannish people hold strong convictions based on feelings, not facts. Church members are constantly comforted, told to be faithful and not clutter their minds with troubling details or contradictions. In reality, Mormons desperately need less blind faith and credulity to escape this behemoth of certitude. Pioneer descendants must open their spiritual eyes and bestow real honor on their ancestors by rescuing another generation of children from this wagon train lost in Death Valley. Mitt, help free our people stranded and unable to escape, and redirect new converts just beginning their descent into this Valley of Death.

5

Rents in the Family Fabric

Mitt, this memoir was motivated by influences beyond reminiscing about our years in Provo, Utah, torturing Salt Lake City/Las Vegas analogies or delving into our family histories. It's seated in frustration, driven by a powerful personal passion and galvanized by a desire to fight Mormonism's most bitter contemporary fruit; the division of family and friends because of a discredited religious belief system. My youngest aunt, like a big sister to me, discarded two books I gave her, one by a Mormon scholar and the other a Mormon Scientist, because she didn't want them in her home. She wrote to tell me I must never bring up religion around her family again. She said she knows what I believe, and I should respect her beliefs. That day, I realized my aunt doesn't know what I believe because I'd never expressed myself beyond a passing comment, and her unwillingness to review "anti-Mormon literature" limits her knowledge of Church history and doctrines so much that she doesn't know what she believes. Thus challenged, I began researching Church's history and doctrines and really thinking about what I believe.

How disheartening and morally repugnant for Mormon leaders' to firmly admonish members not to concern themselves with the Church's secretive historical past or to interact with anyone who challenges them on Mormon doctrine, It has created an attitude that enlists Mormons, including members of my family, into a pious form of anti-intellectualism. In 1993, Apostle Boyd Packer, sometimes referred to by apostates as Darth Packer, said the three greatest dangers facing the Church are feminists, homosexuals and intellectuals. In truth, the real threat to Mormonism was stated clearly by Wallace B. Smith, President Emeritus of the Reformed LDS Church, now known as the Church of Christ. He said, "One thing is clear, the genie is out of the bottle and cannot be put back. Facts uncovered and questions raised by the New Mormon Historians will not go away."

In the 1960's, Hugh B. Brown, then a member of the Mormon First Presidency, said, "I admire men and women who develop the questioning spirits, who are unafraid of new ideas as stepping stones to progress." Boyd Packer contradicted that comment in 1976, when he told former BYU professor and Mormon historian D. Michael Quinn, "I have a hard time with historians … because they idolize the truth." Packer went on to say the truth is destructive, not uplifting. On another occasion, Packer announced that "Some things that are true are not very useful." His astonishing comments epitomize the serial dishonesty and willful undermining of truth by generations of Mormon leaders and revisionists. By all appearances, truths discovered and reported in recent decades only strengthened Church leaders' resolve to perpetuate their deception on current and future generations.

Mormons desperately need someone with credibility to convince them that while the Church emphasizes education, it condemns those who research and write about unaltered Mormon history. The Church Educational System (CES) has become increasingly parochial, anti-intellectual, anti-science, and intolerant of those who question Church policies. And how many church members know the American Association of University Professors (AAUP) censored BYU in 1998 because its "climate for academic freedom was distressingly poor."

The Church taught us at BYU the "Glory of God is Intelligence." I read those words on the campus library wall every time I entered, yet students were not to engage their brains fully without permission from administrators who took their management orders from the Prophet or Apostles. Despite pictures of long-haired, bearded Mormon Prophets hanging in hallways, no long hair or beards were allowed and most student leaders reviled rock and roll. Church leaders were certain we looked better clean-shaven and hair cropped short off our ears. Some contemporary dancing was allowed when I returned from Vietnam, but mostly our minds and bodies were encouraged to waltz or square dance as our elders had done before us. As I learned firsthand, no one defied the leaders of that Church-run university without penalty.

In the 1980s, Apostle Packer's nephew, BYU instructor Lynn Packer, was fired and, as he put it, "beaten to a pulp" when he revealed that First Council of Seventy member Paul H. Dunn had spent his Church career telling false stories about his military service and other personal events to embellish his image as an heroic figure. I attended BYU Devotional services to hear Dunn, a student favorite, tell his invented World War II stories and fabricated experiences as a professional baseball player. Meanwhile, Lynn Packer, a real Mormon hero, suffered because University policy prohibiting criticism of Church leaders even if it's true.

It's no wonder that in 1988, author D. Michael Quinn compared the academic environment at BYU to an Auschwitz of the mind.

D. Michael Quinn, a former BYU professor and openly gay, was ex-communicated in the 1993 Mormon Purge that included some of the bravest and brightest men and women in the Church. He said that being excommunicated from the Church was like a form of death and compared it to attending his own funeral. However, Sandra Tanner of the Utah Lighthouse Ministry recently confirmed Quinn still believes in Joseph Smith's calling as a prophet. Hopefully, this heroic man didn't spend so much time at BYU that he'll never again be able to think clearly. Who needs inductive or deductive reasoning when one has the Prophet's magic? Quinn, like so many others, may believe the *Book of Mormon* city of Bountiful will suddenly burst from the bushes like Brigadoon. Until it does, Church leaders and BYU professors should wear tall pointy hats adorned with seer stones, planets and divining rods.

Too many Mormons stubbornly cling to ignorance and denial because the Church offers easy answers, emotional comfort, financial security and a sense of superiority. They willingly adorn the dunce cap and obediently follow the flock herded by Church leaders. Then, even though the academic environment at BYU is distressingly poor, they send their children there to be coached on life's meaning and purpose by the guys in the pointy hats. However, a glimmer of hope emanates from Happy Valley these days. The *New York Times* reported hundreds of students at predominantly Republican BYU demonstrated in protest of the university's invitation to Vice President Dick Cheney to give the 2007 commencement address. One student even dared to say Cheney is a morally dubious man. Hopefully, he got his diploma and left Provo before the Standards Committee summoned him.

Mitt, the Mormon mosaic is a jigsaw puzzle with so many pieces missing or miss-sized that LDS families have little chance to assemble it and view a reality based picture. Determined Mormon apologists and revisionists perpetuate the falsehoods, and members are instructed how magically to assemble the puzzle. Men and women of integrity tell the truth, but others grasp at words or phrases from antiquity, attach Mormon meaning, and are rewarded by Church leaders for diverting the conversation or confusing the discussion. In a 2002 article posted on the internet, Mark Cannon quoted studies that showed a much higher percent of Mormon Scientists believe in disproved theories than non-Mormon scientists. Some Mormon men have degrees technically designating them scientists, but disciplined scholarship is overwhelmed by religious motivation to per-petuate the deception.

Mitt, use your loud voice to tell our people what church leaders call anti-Mormon literature is, in most cases, better described as pro-truth. It's where integrity is found—and it's our pioneer families' gateway to personal and intellectual free-dom. Demand Church leaders stop intimidating members with their "don't read the anti-Mormon literature" scare-a-thon. Will you stop Mormons posting fake research on official church websites to fool our people into believing in magic and mystery? Will you keep Church apologists from frantically filling holes in history and doctrine with tape, soft plaster and paint? How many more revisionists and fake Mormon scientists will mislead our people before leaders finally admit it's make believe? How long will missionaries be allowed to prey on the vulnerable and uninformed to engulf people in Mormon deception?

The Mormon Church is an imposter and rogue organization that claims a quest for knowledge while systematically showing a day-to-day aversion to it. Like other of history's greatest scallywags, Joseph Smith effectively hid behind worthy causes and good things, and like the most dangerous historical imposters, the contemporary Mormon Church is secretive about its past behavior and clev-erly camouflages future plans. The Church only pretends to share concepts with Christianity and, according to non-member scholar Jan Shipps, is "an idiosyn-cratic form of Christianity." More than that, it's non-Christian by definition.

Like a rattler under a rock, the Mormon Church hides behind the Biblical Christ and selective self-serving twentieth century social programs. It's disgusting to watch this disingenuous organization slinking along behind its "pray in the streets" support for high morals and strong family values. Not to forget the mul-tiple youth programs so proudly displayed—which exist primarily for the pur-pose of indoctrination and ongoing control of young, impressionable minds. Mormonism is a series of non-glorious non sequiturs cobbled together into an impressive but phony organization that mangles Christianity and insults the intelligence of thinking human beings.

The LDS Church commandeers Bible quotes to complement the Book of Mormon and other Mormon scriptures to argue it's a Christian Church. "By their fruits ye shall know them" (Matthew 7.20) is one scripture the Mormons love to recite as proof their faith is superior. As a young member of the clan, I heard it repeatedly. Mitt, in its brief history, the LDS Church has produced really awful fruits. Still, Mormons quote the scripture and proudly point to themselves as fulfillment of its meaning. Devout Mormons are somehow oblivious to the fact that bitter treats from Mormonism include aggressive attacks on traditional Christian denominations, institutionalized racism, pagan polygamy, *Old Testament* priesthood paternalism, blood atonement, lying for the Lord, murders and castrations.

Other unpalatable fruits from the Mormon Gospel orchard are the systematic repression of scientific and historical discoveries, hateful homophobic activism and turning family members against each other. All of it is sustained by a pattern of intimidation and deception to keep faithful members, potential converts and the gentile populations from knowing the Church's true history, doctrines and goals. Whether still bearing these face-puckering fruits, or disavowing them, Mormon leaders cultivate the orchard and incredulously proclaim to members and prospects that Mormons are also the people whom the Bible calls "the salt of the earth."

Mitt, Mormonism isn't a Christian fruit orchard, and its people aren't the salt of the earth. The LDS Church is a heretical organization based on the teachings of a huckster with a pair of stones. Joseph Smith had a pair of magic stones, and I discovered in 1964 that First Presidency member N. Eldon Tanner believed in magic, too. After I confessed to my Bishop I was unchaste, he sent me to Salt Lake City to meet with Tanner. All teenage fornicators—at least those who admitted it, were required to interview with a General Authority before given clearance to serve a mission. So, I sat in Tanner's elegant office and met my first member of the First Presidency. An overwhelmed nineteen year old, I didn't have the stones or maturity to follow my first instinct and challenge Tanner to prove it when he sternly instructed me to tell him the truth or he would read my mind. I spilled my guts. Surreal now, because I know Tanner could no more read my thoughts than I could peek into his.

I returned to Tanner's office a year later to tell him what happened with the BYU Standards Committee and beg him to intervene. I believed this great man would help me when he heard the truth and corroborated it after reading my mind to confirm. However, President Tanner left me at the mercy of the Standards Committee. By his action, or inaction, he called me a liar. One of us lied, and his name was N. Eldon Tanner. He possessed the business acumen to help lift the Church from its mid-twentieth century financial crisis, but his mind reading ability was severely limited—definitely not one of his God-given talents—at least not one he had developed. Given the Mormon Church leader's history of believing in magic and the occult, today I would challenge President Tanner to lay his hands on my head to feel my phrenology bumps or read my palm. After losing a semester's credit hours those many years ago, I was drafted and, in what I would years later see as a positive twist of fortune, became Captain Moody instead of a returned missionary.

Today, I've focused my efforts to stop an organization obsessed with marketing a humungous American-based lie to the world. Joseph Smith—and N. Eldon Tanner—intuitively knew or quickly learned what Hitler stated in *Mein Kampf.* Human beings will more easily fall victim to a big lie than a small one. Like Hitler's Third Reich, Mormons historically have had a low opinion of people of color, and current Mormon leaders show little compassion for the plight of homosexuals. Just two of Mormonism's bitter fruits, Mitt, and you're chewing hard on the second one.

As a result of the condescending and contemptuous treatment I received from a handful of Mormon family members and long-time LDS friends in recent years, I reflected on my experiences in the Mormon Church, and then directed my energies toward the repressive institution determined to continue deceiving humanity. For three decades, I had walked away and focused on my career and, for the most part, maintained a live and let live attitude about Mormonism. However, in 2005, I sat alone on a Cancun hotel balcony and decided to join the fight against the ongoing LDS deception of our people and the world. Coffee in hand, as my family slept in, I began to write what I believe.

Edward R. Morrow hosted a radio program during the 1950s entitled, "This I Believe." The series aired on 196 radio stations, and millions gathered to hear compelling essays written by famous and average Americans. Morrow said the program sought "to point to the common meeting ground of beliefs, which is the essence of brotherhood and the floor of our civilization." Revived on National Public Radio in recent years, the program allows average Americans to state what they believe in five minute essays. I'm finally on my long-delayed Mormon mission, but not to solicit gentiles to join the Great American Cult. Mitt, my objective is to encourage you to lead our deceived pioneer families off the Mormon compound. Meanwhile, know what I believe.

I believe an ethical belief system should be based on humility and tolerance not arrogance and exclusivity. Otherwise, religion becomes an excuse for self-righteousness, condescension and judgmentalism. I believe we should give knowledge and opinions equal opportunity for honest examination. Even more important to consider other's opinions when religious or political figures actively discourage the discourse. A closed mind really is a terrible waste.

I believe in Christ's words as recalled by John: "Love one another, as I have loved you, so you must love one another." Mitt, Mormons don't love their fellowmen—as my best friend once said—they love their fellow Mormons. The LDS Church is a closed society, so Mormons give gentiles the bum's rush, and then, if prospects don't join, they refit the fake smile and shake the dust off their shoes.

I believe God is a more tolerant and loving being than the one worshipped by religious fundamentalists found in Father Abraham's world religions and the Mormon Church. I subscribe to Edmund Burke's comment, "It is the day of no judgment that I fear," but I retain faith that Atheists are wrong to claim, "We come and we go." I expect enlightenment, healing, forgiveness, and, yes, some rude awakenings on the Day of Judgment. Whatever the nature of the hereafter, I believe something is fundamentally wrong with religionists who dwell on wedge issues to stir hatred and intolerance toward their fellowman on earth.

I believe Jesus lived and died for our sins in a veritable culture of real people, who lived in real cities. I believe He blesses those who struggle against selfishness, intolerance and arrogance to learn selflessness, tolerance and humility. Victor Hugo said, "The ones who live are the ones who struggle; the ones whose soul and heart are filled with high purpose. Yes, these are the living ones." I believe you are one of those people, Mitt, so I challenge you to struggle free from birth and historical circumstances and accept a higher purpose in life.

I believe in a greater God than those created by Joseph Smith, and I support more important causes than those endorsed by contemporary Mormon leaders. I believe it's important to seek fulfillment in our day-to-day gift of life, and wrong to expend energy and resources saving the dead—while praying for an inevitable dark future to quickly befall mankind so Joseph Smith and his Mormon Jesus can save us.

I believe the two of the most important Commandments are "Judge not that yet you be not judged" and, acknowledging my constant need for forgiveness, "Let him who is without sin, cast the first stone." I believe in the Sermon on the Mount and all Christ's other teachings during His short ministry, including the *Parable of the Talents.* Mitt, you and I were practically weaned on the concept: "Where much is given, much is expected." We were given much and taught to believe in Gods who grant us little or no grace if we don't meet expectations. It was ingrained in my psyche and drove me throughout my life. Now, I have faith in the grace of God and know I'll need a lot if it.

Mitt, I believe the *Parable of the Talents* fueled the fire of your life achievements, too. You're on a "Faith without works is dead" treadmill, constantly striving for a version of uniquely Mormon perfection. Don't you see that rather than full of God's grace, Mormonism is almost grace-free? Free yourself and our well-meaning people from endlessly striving for a contrived form of perfection dictated by graceless leaders. You became who you said you would be and achieved almost everything expected by family, friends and the Mormon Church. Now, I believe you can step outside yourself, look around and rise above this Mormon Myth machine.

For Mormons, there are so many dos and don'ts that the grace of Christ—his gift to believers—is secondary to the litany of rules and expectations. Richard Abanes observed in *Becoming Gods* that, "for many Mormons, the idea of having to work their way back to God is a crushing burden that produces doubt, fear, guilt and no end of anxiety." Yet, according to *Ephesians*, we gain access to God's presence, "not by works, lest any man boast." One of the scriptures the boastful Joseph Smith undoubtedly would have corrected had he lived to finish his planned retranslation of the Bible. He would have changed it to read, "Only by works, so proud men can boast."

Mitt, Abanes, a non-Mormon Christian, was correct to observe that you and I were reared to believe returning to the presence of God is a reward to be earned, rather than a gift to be graciously received. Mormon doctrine states everyone will be resurrected, but the highest level of the Celestial Kingdom, where God the Father and Jesus dwell, is closed to all except the "exalted." Only the very elect, who were valiant before birth and practically perfect on earth will rejoin the Mormon Gods for eternity. From childhood, Mormons are expected to attain salvation by starting chores before daybreak and singing for their supper. Mitt, you're center stage and still singing for your supper.

I believe the concept of working for salvation is merely an effective management tool for Church leaders who benefit when members busy themselves in the beehive. I believe good works should be by-products of faith, not to earn stars by our names in Heaven. By my early thirties, I realized I couldn't use my talents to perpetuate one of the history's enormous lies, no matter how financially lucrative or ego thrilling. I also knew I couldn't save myself, no matter how hard I tried. Only Christ or someone like him can do that.

I believe governments should be secular, tolerant and pluralistic, creating an environment where cultures thrive in peace and individuals have free agency to act without guilt or fear. Spiritual beliefs should never be polarized by zealots with theocratic agendas, and science should never be vilified in the name of God, or Gods. I believe it evil to teach children to disrespect secular governments and scientific advancements or feel superior toward other races, cultures and beliefs. I believe individuals have a moral responsibility to stay informed and question authority so humanity is free of political and religious tyranny. I believe religious fanaticism is a form of insanity, which inhibits free agency to make critical judgments.

Mitt, I believe in anthropology, archeology, biology, chemistry, genetics, mathematics, paleontology, linguistics, physics and evolution. My God created this universe as sciences reveal it, not as Joseph Smith, Brigham Young or the Pratt brothers described it. I believe God wants his creations to gain as much learning and insight into scientific disciplines and scholarly research as He gave each of us the ability to understand and enjoy. I believe, as a result of reinvigorated thinking, that Mormons are mentally trapped in an intellectual and spiritual compound.

6

Out of the Wilderness

My new mission to the Mormons is serious, so I only have one choice. Mitt, I'm calling you out! No, I'm not suggesting we have a dust-up, duke it out or wrestle around in the dirt like a couple of dorks—as the Prophet Joseph Smith frequently did. Fisticuffs are not my proposition. We're a little long in the tooth for that stuff, anyway. Sir, I challenge you to treat yourself to a Starbucks White Chocolate Mocha Venti and step forward as a modern day Moses to the Mormon people. Instead of living out a falsely founded political mission to save the world for your Mormon Jesus, accept this challenge to organize and lead a team of experts on Mormonism to free our people. Take the baton of the bravest and brightest heroes excommunicated in recent years for daring to tell the truth and carry on the marathon to end this mass confusion.

Mitt, this mission of passion is to convince you, Mormonism's titular leader and someone akin to a Thirteenth Apostle, to be the leader of a spiritual mutiny. Maybe, more appropriately called a plain old mental jailbreak. A new leadership role requires much of you, including the refutation of deceptive statements made by Michael Otterson, the Church's Director of Media Relations. He visited Washington in late 2006 to "put some of the myths to rest—polygamy being the most enduring." Continuing his national campaign to influence the media, Otterson was in Las Vegas in the fall of 2007 to spread disinformation and tell the media always to call the Church first if it has any questions. This Mormon convert claims the Church is neutral on politics and much untrue folklore surrounds Mormon Church beliefs. "The Church," according to Otterson, "is about preaching the gospel of Jesus Christ. Anything else is a distraction."

Brother Otterson told Time magazine he has a "no dumb questions" policy and urges journalists to call his cell phone, day or night. Mitt, please give this spinmeister a wake-up call at 2 a.m. and tell him there are no dumb questions—only dummied down or deceptive answers to deceive minimally informed or intimidated press members. Then, ask him how the Mormon Church can preach the Christian Gospel of Jesus Christ when it doesn't believe in the Jesus Christ of Christendom and has attacked Biblical Christianity for 177 years. Before Otterson nods off or hangs up, request he explain how polygamy can be a myth when, even though not officially practiced today, it remains central to Mormon theological beliefs about eternity and the purpose of life.

Speak up to characters like Otterson, Mitt, and begin the exodus of our people out of Joseph Smith's wilderness of polytheism, polygamy, coveted levels of Heaven, Masonic-based temple rituals, and a simplistic Newtonian/Copernican universe. Lead our pioneer families from this multi-generational religious wilderness, back to the Biblical teachings of Jesus Christ and into the twenty-first century. Only you, a highly respected man of pedigree Mormon ancestry, can save our people from another generation of deception. Even with billions to pay smart lawyers, loyal apologists and clever revisionists, LDS leaders cannot indefinitely censure and alter historical facts to protect their empire. Mitt, mercifully end it now.

Eighteenth century German poet, Johann Goethe, said, "None is so hopelessly enslaved as those who believe they are free." The travesty for Mormons is that they are mentally enslaved to a dictatorial organization, yet believe they have the truth and it has set them free. Even as the federal government erodes our personal liberties, our people allow the Mormon Church government to dictate restrictions to their right to question, speak, write and think. How much longer will LDS leaders control members and punish Mormon scholars and scientists who understand and speak up? This modern day Trial of Galileo mentality must stop and will end only when someone of your stature raises his voice to demand it. As Paul Harvey would say, it's time for members to hear the rest of the story on Mormonism.

Leading a rebellion will sorely test you. Gullibility and denial are old roommates that quickly draw curtains to block enlightenment and knowledge. Even a man of your talent and prestige will struggle to help our people grow up spiritually and rise above the animalistic, primitive dictatorial belief system that caused much persecution, pain and death. May the spirit of truth wash over you and help you see all the unnecessary suffering our ancestors endured and the lives cut short because of egotistical men lusting for power and women.

Mitt, the Mormon Church is true or not. There's no middle ground and nowhere to hide from reality. Logic defines it as the Law of Non-contradiction. We learned in grade school that if any part of a statement is false, then, by definition, the entire statement is false. The LDS Church's claims are preposterous, but members chose to hide behind denial, the first line of defense against painful realities and advancing truths. Regardless, truth must prevail and millions of Mormon members will have to face a rude awakening. The Church is not divine. It's a financial and social trap, and someone like you must intervene.

Mitt, to break ranks with Mormon leaders and stand tall with the apostates will be a major transition because a gargantuan gap exists between what you apparently still believe and what actually happened since the 1820's—between myth and reality. Nineteenth century philosopher Arthur Schopenhauer proposed that truth passes through three stages. First, ridiculed, second, violently opposed, and then accepted as self-evident. A big lie follows a reverse process. First, vulnerable people embrace it as self-evident, second it's questioned and evaluated, and finally it's discredited and cast into the intellectual trash dump. Founded on lies, Mormonism is visionless, and the *Book of Proverbs* states that where there is no vision, the people will perish. Mitt, don't let our people perish.

Think of this request as more of a coffee challenge then a Pepsi challenge. Although both use caffeine and can keep Mormon members out of their temples and highly coveted Celestial Kingdom, researchers continue to discover benefits to humans in coffee. In addition to antioxidants, coffee makes us more focused and better disposed to logical arguments. So drink a pot of fresh brew while you finish reading this. According to research, coffee enhances one's ability to evaluate the merits of arguments. Combine the coffee with your fine mind and you could read this book in thirty minutes, while on the tread mill, and not resist the urge to shout—"yes!"

Understandably, it will be more difficult for you to escape Mormonism than it was for me. Two of your ancestors were members of the first Twelve Apostles and you may feel you owe it to your famous forefathers to continue the crusade. Also, I've never had a near death experience as you did on your French mission, not even during two tours of duty in Vietnam. Being declared dead by the French Police and seeing a fellow missionary die in your head-on collision with a drunk driver is a harrowing experience that has affected your life in ways I can only imagine. You must feel the Lord spared you to fulfill your earthly Mormon destiny, and you have an obligation to your famous ancestors to perpetuate the faith.

An alternate perspective is that since your Apostle ancestors played major roles in creating and sustaining this confusion, your true calling might be that of master myth-buster. It's entirely possible the Creator spared you to lead our people out of intellectual and spiritual darkness. Research highlights the disturbing reality that once a myth has been implanted in peoples' minds, it's difficult to dislodge the idea, and even repetition of evidence dispelling the myth often only reinforces it and drives it deeper into the subconscious. It brings to mind the old saying, "Once a Mormon, always a Mormon." Still, while many remain smugly devout and determined to stay that way, a large percentage of Church members know it isn't true. Some acknowledge they are cultural Mormons and remain active even though they know the *Book of Mormon* is historical fiction. Others simply lack the courage to break free, rationalizing that it's preferable to keep quiet and go along. Some men and women continue to attend Church regularly and others become Jack Mormons, who drift away but send their children to Church.

Rationalizing the Mormon Church a good organization with youth programs and a strong emphasis on the family isn't good enough for my family, and I propose it isn't good enough for devout or conflicted Mormons. A decision to remain Mormon, neither hot nor cold, is damaging to personal growth and a form of intellectual and spiritual cowardice. Mitt, some hide in the mushy middle to protect their businesses, family ties or political careers and need you're help to find the strength to walk into the sunlight. Those deceived need powerful leadership and inspiration to climb the compound barricades, get over the psychological barbed wire and down the emotional wall. Better yet, lead them all out a Mitt Romney exit door. Show them how to leave with dignity.

Helping Mormons escape is a higher calling than any other you could pursue because the Church is not merely a social club. It's an insidious organization triumphantly declaring itself the only true church and the eternal order of the universe. Mormon leadership, adept at stirring emotions to divert attention and control the subject matter, will continue their course if good men do nothing. The editorial staffs of Church publications and speech writers for Church presentations and videos will forever serve members emotionalism to manipulate them. Bringing this to a halt will be the challenge of your life. Mormonism is emotional, spiritual and financial tyranny, and Thomas Payne said, "Tyranny, like Hell, is not easily conquered."

Mitt, refuse to accept Mormonism as good enough for you and your family. Have another cup of coffee and listen to what I'm sharing with you. I ask you not to dress in ash clothe and preach from the top of Mt. Timpanogos overlooking BYU—not in this microchip age. You don't have to proclaim Jesus and his Dad appeared in a grove—or gave you prophetic directions in King James's English. Just be unthinkably brave, accept the truth and make life altering changes. Honestly review the history and science and make your own emotional escape so you can free current members and future generations. Tell the millions of Mormons who admire you the facts of life. Mormonism is not the blue print for eternal civilization, and the *Book of Mormon* is not a record of an ancient earthly one.

Two decades ago Apostle Boyd Packer said, "There is a war going on, and we are engaged in it." Packer was referring to the Mormon version of evil in America and the world, but that's not the real war. A war rages for Mormons' minds and souls, and Captain Moody is on a mission to recruit a general to the battle. Those who escaped the Church's clutches need leadership to battle Lieutenant General Joseph Smith's modern day band of non-Christian brethren. Use your skills to organize a Mormon revolution that will redirect misguided devout Mormons marching weighted down by backpacks filled with deception. Mitt, as the most powerful political force of our Mormon generation, lead the charge on their closed compound doors so men and women like me can step forward to help take down its barbed fences, wire by wire. I have old Vietnam combat boots somewhere—and leather gloves, too.

Join the war, speak truth to power, and replace General Joseph Smith as a real modern day prophet. Sir, there is no other Mormon prophet but you! The Church is wrong and the longer wrong, the more certain it's right. Tell LDS leaders and members that Mormon Church doctrine is neither the eternal law of the universe, nor is it above American law. Assure them BYU isn't the "Lord's university," and the GOP isn't "Gods Own Party." Free our pioneer families and all Church members from this religious organization, which past and present has been secretive, dictatorial, and dishonest about the critical issues of Heaven and Earth. Fortunately, for now, all Church leaders can do is whine and pontificate about media and citizen freedoms, while politically and financially supporting those who whittle away at liberty.

A broader war exists beyond the Mormon enclave. We wage a cultural battle to keep our Republic, maintain our liberties and defend ourselves from Mormonism and pop culture fundamentalist groups. Mormon leaders and political leaders know that labeling individuals or groups evil bonds followers and makes them feel superior and somehow threatened. The technique legitimizes their existence and justifies collecting and spending money to wage war against phantom enemies. Mitt, freeing our people is far nobler than running for President as political ambassador for the Mormon Church.

In Army Officer Candidates School, candidates were "washed out" for quibbling on any topic. A classmate at Ft Gordon, Georgia was sent back to the enlisted ranks for quibbling with an officer over some issue I've forgotten. Because I liked the candidate and felt the infraction minor, I defended him and questioned the fairness of the officers' harsh treatment. Today, I appreciate what happened and why the policy existed. Reflecting on that experience forty years ago makes it even more disturbing to watch LDS leaders callously wash out the Church's bravest members for telling the truth and reward those who defend deceitfulness.

Mormons have preached so many damning distortions and quibbling positions for so long that it will take courage to champion heroic Mormon scientists and researchers systematically patronized, trivialized and marginalized for telling the truth. The Mormon's standard historical practice has been to demonize the Catholics and Protestants, but in recent decades Church leaders have turned their ferociousness against fellow Mormons who dared follow their conscience and publicly reveal the obvious. Figuratively speaking, if these truth warriors don't kneel to kiss the Priesthood ring or swear their allegiance with a hand on the Book of Mormon, brave hearts are quickly disfellowshipped if they recant, or if they stand firm, excommunicated from the only religion they know. When this humorless, self-righteous Church stops smiling and no longer extends a strong hand-shake, it peddles fear, stern judgment and rejection.

Mitt, when you take your stand for truth and some members listen, purging will intensify as Church leaders desperately try to choke off dissenters. Persistent General Authorities don't want truths planted in their membership garden for fear they will root, grow and flower. Like other entities, Mormonism has a corporate life, and its goal is not just to survive, but thrive. Determined to spread Joseph Smith's religious weed garden around the world, Mormon leaders painstakingly water new color plants to obscure old trash plants, and they guard their growing garden with well-paid apologists and public relations masters of horticultural heresy. I am reminded of Dorothy Parker's witticism that you can lead a whore to culture, but you can't make her think. Encourage our people to think so they can begin to free themselves from Mormonism's cultural weed garden

Content to live in the religious right's black and white world, Mormons—with their unique distortions—happily join those who want to judge for everyone. Mitt, use your skills as a corporate turn-around expert to pluck Church members out of this drab world and into a multi-colored montage of Christian love and tolerance. Modern researchers seeking the historical Jesus find no evidence to support the Joseph Smith/Brigham Young version of the figure Christians call Christ. The real Jesus would run modern day Mormon Pharisees from Mormon temples, along with their Republican money changers. Actually, there's no Christian reason for Mormon temples to exist at all.

Apostle and President George A. Smith once remarked that "If a faith will not bear to be investigated; if its preachers and professors are afraid to have it examined, their foundation must be very weak." He spoke at a time in the Nineteenth century when Mormons accepted scrutiny, but described precisely what the Mormon Church has become. Today, those inside and outside the Church who investigate Mormonism are punished or ridiculed by Church leaders, while members are treated as children grateful to eat what is harvested from the weed garden and served in the Church cafeteria. Now, your presence is requested at the table with those who know this reconstituted pabulum isn't fit for consumption, but regurgitation! As old Clara put it, "Where's the beef?"

Use your prodigious standing to lead our pioneer families from the stifling box in which they were born. Spiritually and intellectually starving, they need meat and potatoes. It's painful to watch indoctrinated family and friends compartmentalize factual data for fear that if considered, it will compromise their structured belief system and threaten their exaltation. Robotic behavior robs them of the right to proper knowledge in this life. Sad to see they mistakenly use their antiquated belief system to hide from reality and look down on others who won't join or rejoin them in the Mormon cafeteria.

Fortunately for twentieth century Church leaders, naïve members followed their nineteenth century ancestors and ate the mush. Faithful Mormons accepted the contradictions, doctrinal changes and emotional propaganda served from Salt Lake City by pretend Prophets and Apostles. Members' demography and shared experiences acted as mental glue to bind them together and clog their brains. In their calculated push for homogeneity, Church leaders isolated members who rarely made deep friendships with people of dissimilar world views. Mitt, it's difficult to examine one's beliefs if everyone in the social group is a trained parrot shouting out canned answers in Priesthood or Relief Society meetings. Urban myths, old wives tales and hardened lies die hard, so I'm calling you to a daunting, almost impossible task. Shame a shameless leadership, and simultaneously coax spiritually frightened people out their emotional comfort zone.

The LDS Church, like the Bush administration, is in an aggressive empire-builder and works tirelessly to impose its version of community standards and eternal standards on citizens of the world. Creativity crushing LDS Prophets and Apostles are determined never to let truth interfere with their organizational goals as they dispatch an unapologetic army of zealots to belittle Christian faiths and raid their flocks. Mormonism has distinguished itself as a determined, powerful institution, and Church leaders continue repressive self-serving techniques to preserve power over members. However hard it is to change them, Mitt, like me, once you accept the truth, it's even harder to idly watch bright, often highly educated men and women deny the obvious and fearfully cling to mythology and magical beliefs as if their eternal lives depended upon them.

It will take a man like you to intervene because, just as sailors were once happy to stay in their comfort zone for fear they would fall off a flat earth, Mormons are content to ride in the theological fog on a tall ship I named Farrago. Stiff backed and teeth to the wind, they sail in circles and pretend to lead a great religious regatta. They don't understand or care that their behavior creates an intellectual vacuum for themselves and their families. I don't want my descendants floating for generations over frothy seas on a fantasy ship. Mitt, once you accept the truth about Mormonism, it's unfathomable you could contently watch your family sail endlessly on this farcical ship of fools.

Being a high seas navigator for the Mormon people will take great courage, but if given permission to think, millions would be ready to reconsider their spiritual direction and escape the maelstrom. Encourage them by providing the personal, business and political cover they need. Setting our people free from what never happened and leading them back to a belief system based on the New Testament teachings of Jesus will challenge and refine your character. You'll be ridiculed, patronized, ostracized, shunned, called a traitor to your people and face the ultimate control weapon—the Church Disciplinary Council. Church leaders glower when someone tells members its okay to dismiss lingering distrust of books not Church approved. Dare to back talk and tell the truth about Church history and doctrines, and those pious boys will force you off the boat quickly. Be assured the intellectual and spiritual rewards for walking their plank are worth it.

Seriously Mitt, there's no reason to fear excommunication. It isn't as difficult as in nineteenth century Salt Lake City, where people were stripped of property and visited by the "whistle and whittle" boys with Bowie knives. If they didn't repent or run for their lives, King Brigham sent Avenging Angels to intimidate or murder them. Now, throats are no longer slit so blood can gush onto the ground to atone for sins. You need only catch a plane for Bean Town or stay in Salt Lake City and take the fight directly to them. Attack the deception with the same methodical approach you applied to your Presidential campaign, and you can lead those determined to free our people. If not, you are destined to continue stretching and ripping truth to please Republican political advisors, self-righteous evangelicals and lost Mormon leaders.

After I was excommunicated in 1977, people questioned why such harsh action was taken toward me, when Las Vegas was full of Jack Mormons unbothered by Mormon leaders. The answer was simple. Well known in the community, I ruffled the political feathers of powerful Mormons who attempted to intimidate and control me. Unsuccessful, to punish me, they tarnished my reputation. When threatened during a Bishop's Interview in 1974, I told Las Vegas Bishop Boyad Tanner, soon promoted to Stake President, I would not be intimidated or bullied by Mormon religious or political leaders anymore. I stood my ground with Bishop Tanner, and that conversation laid the foundation for excommunication. Dating from high school, that was my fourth time subjected to Mormon threats, and enough was enough. So, at age twenty-nine, I decided to build a career on my own terms instead of limping through life on the comfortable "Mormon crutch," a guarantee of temporal success for men like me.

Mitt, throw away your Mormon crutch and dare to get excommunicated for speaking truth to self-righteous, power-crazed Mormon leaders. When you're attacked, attend the witch hunt—also known as a Disciplinary Council. I threw away the summoning paperwork hand-delivered by two Elders one day in 1977. Regretfully, I didn't attend my Mormon inquisition to confront my accusers, not righteous men prepared to punish a sinner but politicians out to get another politician. It would have been priceless to watch several local Mormon hacks remove their political hats and don Priesthood hats in a parody suitable for a Moliere play. Experience is the greatest teacher, and I regret missing that adventure.

Mitt, don't repent at your trial and promise to be faithful, allowing Church leaders only to disfellowship you. Through excommunication, you will provide a unique example to Mormon members, Americans and the world. After which, tell Church members their Church was founded on magical/pagan traditions prevalent in nineteenth century New England, and Mormonism is just another of the quirky cult movements that sprouted around charismatic leaders during the Second Great Awakening. Explain that, from the beginning, Mormon Prophets read unorthodox interpretations into Christian scripture to support deviant doctrines unsupported by biblical scholarship in Joseph Smith's era or today. Your bravery will be received warmly by real American Christians waiting to embrace you and welcome Mormons back into the fold.

How wonderful, Mitt, to have Mormons not stomping around the world in pride's oversized, empty shoes, showing no humility when telling others what to believe and how to live. Your courage could end the aggressive preaching of falsehoods and start a healing, unifying process for Mormons who historically alternated between being victims and creating them. Once you're committed and free, you can tell Church leaders one hundred and seventy-eight years of disparaging Christian Churches and stealing their members disqualified the Mormon Church to play the poor, misunderstood organization, while at the same time hiding its history and changing its doctrines. Truth is everywhere and Mormon attitudes and behavior grow ever more tiresome and hypocritical.

Mitt, a proven master of monopoly and politics, you now aspire to the title of master of the universe. Not a pretend galaxy far, far away, or one universally guided from the Mormon planet, Kolob, but an earthly one centered in America that politically will benefit Mormonism's universal cause. The problem is that Mormons are masters of repression, not masters of the universe, and you positioned yourself as the political champion of a religious organization that repeatedly defied our secular laws. Refined by centuries of blood and tears, western culture established the rule of law and America's founders incorporated them in our system of government. While historical Mormon leaders benefited from the US Constitution and Bill of Rights, they schemed to overthrow the American Republic in favor of a theocracy. Restriction on free speech and free thought is one of the most dangerous subversions and LDS Church leaders notoriously subverted members' freedom of thought and speech for generations. Their predilection for dishonesty in the name of faith continues today.

Mitt, beware of the dark side and read the words of Isaiah: "The people who walk in darkness will see a great light. For those who live in a land of deep darkness, a light will shine."(Isaiah 9.2). I once read that the eternal stars come out when it's dark enough. Our people have lived in spiritual darkness for generations, and now its dark enough. Rather than continue your quest to champion the destructive policies of neoconservative zealots and enforce the dogmas of religious zealots, lift your enlightenment sword and lead the good fight against the Prince of Darkness and his disciples who deceive our people. Shine as only you can shine and become a noble warrior to thirteen million deceived Mormon worshippers of false doctrine.

Don't be discouraged when Church leaders rescind your Temple Recommend and confiscate your sacred underwear. Remember the old proverb: Fool's praise is censure. Fight the Mormon leaders, crash through their shields, and then warpspeed Mormons to universal enlightenment and spiritual freedom. Demand that Mormon General Authorities open the Church vault in Salt Lake City—also known as the black hole—so scholars and historians can report to members and the press on documents still hidden in the archives. Stop Mormon Prophets and Apostles from ruling with fear, guilt and false promises. Almost two centuries of arrogant piety, religious imperialism and non-Biblical babble is enough.

Free Mormons to worship the true Jesus, Mitt, not the one leading a train of wives through eternity. Take Joseph Smith from his pedestal and dropkick him into his proper place in history—a charlatan and writer of religious fiction. Humanity doesn't need the world cluttered with absurd Mormon claims about our universe's structure and the meaning of life. It was disgraceful to create a new Christ to confuse mankind and then dispatch an aggressive army of naïve teenagers in white shirts and black ties to preach it. To believe in what C.S. Lewis called *Mere Christianity* is difficult enough without adding horns and a tail.

7

The Hero's Big Test

Over the years, several Church members told me, "Don't judge the church by the people in it." Our generation of young Mormons also had the "Life is a test" challenge imbedded in its collective brain. I accept life is a test and strive, sometimes without much success, to be less judgmental toward tightly programmed Mormon people born into the Church. However, the Church teaches that members are to exercise free agency and make correct decisions with no memory of primordial life and only selective perceptions about our existing one. Can Mormons pass the test and make vital life decisions with limited knowledge of real Church history or the realities of modern science? Mitt, the real Mormon test is first to think and then escape from spiritual and intellectual prison on earth. Help members study for the test, accept the truth and correctly answer questions. Testify to your Mormon peers and admirers that they must not blindly live the lie until they die—also known in Church vernacular as "endure to the end."

Hope springs eternal, and I ask myself who can tear the Teflon off this growing child of lies and expose the Church for the cult it is. If you don't accept the challenge and tutor the Mormon masses, who will? Ten years ago, award-winning cartoonist Steve Benson told me nothing can stop the Church. He's a hero for escaping, standing for truth, and becoming an outspoken critic of Mormonism. He realized Mormon Prophet Ezra Taft Benson wasn't leading the LDS Church if he could no longer recognize his own grandson. Benson not only passed the hero's test, he held his own when mocked and patronized by President Hinckley on 60 Minutes. Benson told Mike Wallace, "The cultural mindset of the Church is when the prophet has spoken the debate is over." He added that when the prophet has stated his position, its incumbent on the members to pray, pay and obey. Stand with Steve Benson, Mitt, because many who should join him and impact the discussion can't pass the test.

In 2005, Kim Clark resigned from Harvard Business School to be President of BYU-Idaho, and he will never muster the courage to challenge Church leaders.

Bubbling with pride and a little defensive, Clark performed like a puppet when a Prophet like Moses pulled his strings. He gushed, "You have to appreciate what this is like; we behold him to be a prophet. Imagine yourself getting a call from Moses." Gee whiz. The Gods told their Mormon Prophet what they wanted done, and Hinckley told Clark. Kim Clark knew no one puts Gordon Hinckley on hold and ponders test choices. After all, Hinckley relays orders directly from Jesus himself. Especially hard for Clark to say no when he's under consideration for promotion to the Twelve Apostles. This man, a Harvard graduate and professor, can't pass the test. No hero here. Meanwhile, Clark's new educational mission is to make a repressive Mormon institution the "Harvard of the West," which will be interesting to watch.

Heroism 101 is unknown to Senator Harry Reid. Desperate to build a political career in Southern Nevada, young Reid joined the Democratic Party and converted to the influential Mormon Church. A Mormon Brethren and quick study of the gambler's Golden Rule, local media ordained him one of the Gold Dust Twins. Operators who play the house and have the gold sprinkled on him with a dusting of casino chips. Some men make money, as you did, then enter politics. The other Gold Dust Twin, former Nevada Senator Richard Bryan, made his money after retiring with distinction from public life. Ostensibly in public service, Harry Reid became one of the richest men in the Senate during his life as a career politician. In reality, the poor boy from Searchlight has used political influence to enrich himself, his family and friends during forty years of self service.

The first time I met Harry Reid, he was Nevada's Lieutenant Governor. I introduced myself at a political function in 1973 amid speculation he was considering a run for Republican David Towell's congressional seat. When Harry said he had no plans to run against my boss, I said Democrats would find someone to replace him. Expressing the arrogance that trademarked his dealings with people, he said, "No one can replace me." He was correct about that. Harry definitely has staying power. Opponents beat him in the 1975 Mayor's race and came within 500 votes of bringing him home in his 1998 Senate reelection run, but he keeps turning up like a bad penny—or several million dollars.

Like many who acquire a taste for the trappings of power, Harry Reid steadily moved down the slippery slope into a pool of political and religious confusion. It has been said Reid is a man who defies description, and in recognition of his prodigious political leaping ability, one writer designated him a "kangaroo rat." A man who defies description could be called a political chameleon, and Senator Reid jumps all over the place like a kangaroo rat on key political issues then lands and, like a chameleon, changes color to blend in. Hopefully, he will blend into oblivion soon.

Reid's jumping and blending theatrics occasionally land him in the right place. Although very late, he now accepts the dangers of global warming, and when Mormon leaders pressed their determined stand for the dark side of what *Las Vegas Review Journal* columnist Jane Ann Morrison called the "perfect wedge issue" of gay marriage, he balked and stood for freedom. Reid stopped lining his pockets with sweetheart deals and greasing financial and political skids for his kids long enough to vote against the Federal Gay Marriage Amendment. In the process, he incurred the wrath of a former Mormon Stake President named James Howard. Enraged by Reid's vote, Howard wrote, "You chose your party's agenda over Nevadans', over your prophets' wishes and defied God in the process."

Stake President Howard didn't expect to see his rant in the Las Vegas newspaper because he added, "Having sold out your Church, your State and possibly your soul for political power, I will have a hard time supporting you or voting for you in the future, should you attempt to hold your seat. Your soul is vacant, and you have lost your moral compass." Short term, Senator Reid will pray there are more gay voters or sympathizers in Nevada than Mormon voters. Long run, for opposing Mormon political leadership and standing by Ann Coulter's "Faggots," Senator Reid may compete with me for one of the last slots in Mormonism's lowly Telestial Kingdom of Heaven. In his recent memoir, Senator Charles Schumer wrote that Reid "is soft-spoken and polite and is a deeply religious Mormon," but "he will also kneecap you if you cross him." Though some Mormon brethren crossed him, with his 2010 reelection bid looming, I doubt Reid will kneecap the Nevada LDS leadership or call the big bosses in Salt Lake City false prophets.

Speaking of damaged kneecaps, Reid never became the mobsters' man in old Las Vegas. In FBI wiretaps during a major corruption case thirty years ago, wise guys referred to him as "clean face," and later a bomb planted in his car failed to explode. More recently, as part of his political jumping and "verbal wanderings," Senate Majority Leader Reid called President Bush a liar and condemned his foreign policy fiasco in Iraq—which by itself qualifies him for near hero status. Reid even called for a federal task force to investigate the demeaning of women, domestic violence and child abuse in Fundamental LDS polygamous communities after Warren Jeffs was arrested. In October, 2007, he told four thousand people on the BYU campus that conservative political leaders like former Church President Ezra Taft Benson had ill-served the Mormon people. Still, he won't have the courage to challenge the LDS Church on the veracity of its theological doctrines. There's no Mormon hero-in-waiting behind Reid's pious, dour demeanor.

If Harry Reid missed his chance to pass heroism 101, Professor Richard Lyman Bushman isn't aware it's part of the curriculum. In his biased cultural biography, *Joseph Smith: Rough Stone Rolling,* Bushman admits he and his wife love Brother Joseph as much as they worship the biblical Jesus that Joseph Smith corrupted. Bushman, a career university professor with stints at BYU and Columbia, ignored the importance of integrity in presenting his material. In the process, he disrespected his peers in the higher education community. Bushman cooked up a pot of impressive rhetoric that settles like Gerber's peas on intellectual taste buds. He wasted his prestige and failed to have a potential heroic impact on Church members.

However, Bushman did admit Joseph Smith was a man driven by the occult. Observers point out he had no choice to maintain any credibility with his academic associates. That admission and examples of Joseph Smiths magic practices apparently dissuaded the LDS Church from its planned strong endorsement of Bushman's book. Published near the bicentennial of Joseph Smith's birth in 2005, Mormon leaders backed away. Truth is dangerous to members who might start thinking and begin asking impertinent questions in Sunday school class. Who needs doubters interrupting the Church's structured lesson plans with rude questions, when everyone is feeling special and secure on a nice Sunday morning?

The hero definition doesn't fit Clark, Reid or Bushman. They can't pass the test. Short of a great awakening, they're relegated to the role of gophers in the game of life. Gophers have a good ground game, but they can't pass. No champions of the truth in that group, but, Mitt, you can pass, so step forward, plant your feet and loft a Hail Mary into the end zone. Better yet, step away from your current playing field and discover the higher path. Be a real hero and modern day prophet to our people. If not a new Moses, then become like the Pharisee, Saul of Tarsus, who became Paul after his religious epiphany on the road to Damascus.

8

The Great American Cult

When confronted with the term cult, Mormons doth protest too much. Programmed to flash anger at the mere mention the "C" word, Church members adamantly reject efforts to free them. Cults share basic characteristics, but create their own culture or subculture, and Mormonism follows the classic pattern. Christian-based cults demand a loyalty and devotion to their founders that eclipse Jesus and his Gospel. LDS Church leaders are accomplished cultist who made con man Joseph Smith an eternal icon unfairly persecuted for restoring the true Church. The serial dishonesty persists into the twenty-first century and, as a result of the deception, members believe themselves warriors in a religious war for the soul of humanity and not remnants of an imperialistic nineteenth century theocratic cult.

Mitt, devout Mormons quickly become defensive and challenge real Christians, scientific critics or ex-members who point out that you and I were born and reared in a cult. A mere mention of anything perceived as anti-Mormon draws patronage from uninformed family, friends or LDS acquaintances. If I persist or use the word cult, eyes glaze over, they pull a Pavlov, and the salivation begins. Consequently, I was cautious around the uncle who told me never to bring up religion again, and then he brought it up at a family function in 2006. When he informed me his grandson, on a mission to Romania, was having difficulty finding converts to baptize, I resisted the urge to say that most newly freed eastern Europeans probably weren't interested in joining an American cult.

When asked recently what branch of Christianity the Mormon Church is most like, a CBS expert answered that the LDS Church is most similar to the Moonies. Ouch! Those who correctly see the Mormons as non-Christian view the LDS Church more like Scientology without the celebrities. *Slate* Editor Jacob Weisberg has characterized Mormonism as "Scientology plus 125 years." Both cults are relatively new, with the Mormon cult surviving since the Second Great Awakening and Scientology a product of the new age movement. Tom Cruise is now the celebrity face of Scientology, and you, Mitt, are the telegenic national face of Mormonism. No doubt exhilarating to be the Mormon political star and pursue the political goals you set as a young man. You are Mormonism's prized pugilist in the political circus center ring, diligently and dutifully fighting to lead our nineteenth century cult into the White House and assume the world's most powerful position. However, typical of faithful cult members, neither Cruise nor you realize you belong to one.

Mitt, you're in a cult and it won't be some politically tough Curse of Cain guy like Barrack Obama who drops a straight right between your sagging gloves. Prepare for a barrage of hard body shots from the fists of truth. The early Mormon practice of lying for the Lord, co-mission and omission, sits like a shadow over Church character. Dutiful members refuse to listen to any speech not approved by Church leadership and ignore literature conveniently poisoned as anti-Mormon. Equally disheartening, Church leaders continue to lie to faithful members about historical and doctrinal issues. Uninformed missionaries lie to potential converts and give false comfort to people the world over. From my childhood to early adulthood, I understood the great comfort found in a complex myth. This Great American Cult has confused my family for generations and fooled me half my life.

Programmed to feel persecuted since the first generation, Mormons perpetuate their persecution complex ad nauseam and believe divinely inspired General Authorities should never be scrutinized. No membership criticism of thin-skinned leaders is allowed without consequences. Apostle Dallen Oakes emphasized, "It does not matter whether the criticism is true." The expectation of blind loyalty has strong historical LDS precedent. Both the Nauvoo Legion and Danites were committed to defending Joseph Smith, whether he was right or wrong. As in times past, Mormons today follow the Prophet's every command, defend the Church fervently, or risk salvation and exaltation in the Celestial Kingdom.

A fundamental cult characteristic is to filter member information so their thoughts, emotions and behavior are controlled. LDS leaders' successful mind control programs leave victims unaware they are brainwashed cult members. Your father knew the term brainwashing. He said he had been brainwashed by military generals about Vietnam and his Presidential bid unraveled in six months. Possibly, you know the truth about Mormonism but don't dare admit it for fear people will think you're brainwashed and reject your continued political aspiration. Mitt, to remain cult-bound and defensive about it for fear of doing otherwise is the wrong thing for the wrong reasons.

As I try not to judge you, and remind myself I always liked you, I can't help wondering what you're thinking. Has a fine mind and superior education lead you to the conclusions I reached, yet you continue your alpha male charge down the life-long road of plan A? I respect you too much to believe it. Maybe, you have some knowledge about the New Mormon History but remain conflicted and choose to mentally compartmentalize information. Most likely, you still believe Church teachings and feel destined to pursue your dreams, believing it your foreordained purpose in life. Did you make up your mind long ago and chose not to revisit the possibility we were reared in a cultural trap of intergenerational deception? Enough of this, I'll leave the mind-mining work to professionals like Dr Phil.

Whatever you think, God knows our childhood programming was intense and total. A few years ago, when two friends from my Utah childhood went on a Caribbean cruise to see ruins of the *Book of Mormon* cities, I told them there were no Mormon ruins to see. They didn't believe me then, but admitted it upon their return. When I tried to pursue the conversation, I was politely told they wouldn't talk to me further if I persisted. Their cruise was planned out of Salt Lake City, and the Church sent along a "wonderful speaker" to answer questions. Apparently, the Church representative explained everything. A veterinarian specializing in horses, the husband should have recognized horse manure when he smelled it. Sadly, his eyes are glazed with cultural cataracts, and his nose clogged with magical incense. Far more crucial than what we know or don't know in life is what we don't want to know. My friends did not want to know, and now a childhood friendship is lost. They plan to endure to the end, and will not let me lead them astray—end of discussion.

My friends and I were reared in a central Utah valley where a few thousand people live in small villages founded in pioneer days. As children, we respected President Eisenhower, but loved our silver-haired Mormon Prophet, David O. McKay, a figure more important than any President. The first clean shaven, modern looking Mormon President, McKay helped usher our subculture into the twentieth century—a half century late. I still respect this educator turned Mormon prophet who coined the phrase, "every member a missionary," and once scolded the nation for not paying for outstanding teachers. Mitt, you agreed with McKay, and said teaching should be recognized as the profession it is, because it is not making widgets.

I listened when President McKay emphasized the importance of education to our generation. Lamentably, Mormons leaders believe in education to a point, and then draw a divisive line to prevent the faithful from learning what the

Church doesn't want them to know. Perhaps, I have a better education than President McKay would have wished. Then again, maybe McKay would agree that the mind, like pliers, is a worthless tool if permanently closed or laid aside in favor of blind faith. Of Church leaders and members who always elevated faith over all else, the poetic McKay once remarked, "Perfect people would be awfully tiresome to live with; their stained-glass view of things would seem a constant sermon without intermission, a continuous snub of superiority to our self-respect." Amen, my childhood hero—rest in peace.

One of antiquity's great thinkers, English philosopher John Stewart Mill, said any attempt to resist another opinion is a "peculiar evil." If the information is right, we're robbed of the opportunity to exchange error for truth. If wrong, we're deprived of a deeper understanding of truth's collision with error. Sadly, Mormons reinforce existing beliefs by only accepting new information that will substantiate their preconceived ideas. The concept of confirmation bias—grasping at nuggets of new information to reinforce previously held positions—is so pervasive that people suffer from the malady without realizing it. It robs good judgment, whether buying a bad stock or defending a false religion. Mitt, instead of ignoring new ideas or shrugging off dissenting views, I want my family and Mormon friends progressing intellectually and spiritually freed from their cult's mesmerizing leaders.

Rather than seek enlightenment, most Mormons are proud to be a peculiar people—even relish their uniqueness. They have limited perspective about their preposterous belief system and naturally become defense, self-righteous and exhibit false pride when challenged. Having displayed that behavior myself in the past, I know the pattern well. Now, decades after climbing the barbed wired wall, I still wonder why I was born into this cult. I have concluded that being born Mormon was either happenstance in a random universe or the toughest test of my life. I believe the latter. With faith that life has meaning and purpose, I ran the Mormon maze, escaped over the wall and now challenge you to do the same. Off the compound for decades, albeit still carrying heavy baggage, I outgrew or quieted most simmering anger toward the Church and its leaders. Anger finally subsided; I don't take it so seriously and as much as possible, turned my sense of humor on myself and our ritualistic religious gibberish.

There is also solace in knowing I can educate my children and keep them free of this cult. As they mature, I will explain how first generation Mormons were driven from several early frontier settlements because of self-righteous behavior and implied superiority that repeatedly raised fear and hatred in non-Mormons.

My son and daughter will understand that much violence leveled at their Mormon forefathers was solicited or self-induced. They will learn Joseph Smith and his followers destabilized and tried to take control of every state into which they swarmed. Mormons and their Gods' showed little tolerance and respect for either Christian gentiles or the US Constitution standing in the path of their kingdom on earth.

Ironically, escaping Mormonism is my response to our childhood mantra that still rings in my ears—where much is given; much is expected. Now, more is expected of me than saying good luck and see you at the judgment. Families continue to fracture, and too many members must sit quietly in the back rows on Sunday to avoid losing their loved ones, friends and careers. Harsh rules set by uninspired, often mean-spirited cult leaders—and enforced by member behavior—make fees for leaving Mormonism financially and socially severe. Mitt, do what you can to end the heartbreak caused by those Mormon leaders and members exhibiting cult behavioral characteristics. Endure the emotional disenfranchisement for climbing the compound fence. Only then can you learn to enjoy as much spiritual and intellectual freedom as is possible for tightly programmed people like us. Understand complete freedom is impossible, but do the right thing, anyway.

Throughout decades of Mormon Church attendance, I listened to members "bear their testimony" at the monthly Testimony Meetings, stating how grateful they were to belong to the only true church. They added, "I know Joseph Smith is a prophet of God." As an usher passed the microphone, emotionally overwrought members waxed weepy, revealed their knowledge deficiencies, and then smiled proudly as their six-year-olds took the microphone to declare they too knew the Church was true. Another generation of brainwashed little warriors was preparing to march in the Mormon's culture war on traditional Christianity and intellectual freedom. Nothing is so firmly believed as that about which least is known.

The idea has intrigued and humored me, but I can't legally or financially afford to have all my Mormon friends kidnapped and deprogrammed. I can share with them, and you, some important things I know. I know the Church is too harsh, unforgiving and un-Christian with members. In 2006, I talked about religion with a former Mormon county commissioner in the midst of his corruption trials. He had been excommunicated but still believed in the Mormon Church with "all his heart." When I told him some facts about the Church, he told me to say something good about my Church and not be critical of his.

Although the young man converted to Mormonism, and his Church was my Church before he was born, he expressed a defense stratagem I've heard many times in one form or another. A cousin threw out similar comments the day she told me that my family was unwelcome in her home if I again mentioned anything negative about Mormonism. This cousin, a Jack Mormon who didn't practice what she was suddenly ready to defend, forgot what most Mormons conveniently forget. The Mormon Church builds its flock by raiding the congregations of Christian churches. Since 1830, Mormons have been disrespectful and judgmental toward Christian denominations yet bristle if not shown the respect they feel they deserve.

Some time later, when the former commissioner and I connected again, I told him he was welcome at my Lutheran Church and offered to introduce him to the Pastor. Like many imperfect people, he was persona non grata in the self-proclaimed only true Christian Church just when he needed Christian love, understanding and forgiveness. Although not portrayed as the most trustworthy man in Las Vegas (He later joined two other former Mormon county commissioners in prison) he seemed genuinely moved. Just then, defensiveness and self-righteousness melted away, and a man not usually at a loss for words didn't know what to say.

Mitt, who will propel our people out of this nineteenth century cult and into the twenty-first if I can't compel you to action? Though I can't be ordered like a common criminal to appear at a Church tribunal again, I could never free them. I was marginalized long ago. Only someone like you can provide the leadership, soften the blow and escort members into a new Great Awakening. Tell pioneer family descendants it's okay to stop compartmentalizing conflicting information, or avoiding it altogether, and free them from the spiritual and intellectual death grip of their egocentric subculture.

I could die trying to change the Church and not accomplish it. Actually, a guy once told me I was lucky someone hadn't yet killed me. Maybe, my gene pool attracts conflict. Jefferson Hunt fought in the Battle at Crooked River and his Grandson, my great-great-grandfather, George Jefferson Hunt, was killed in an 1880s Virgin City, Utah street fight. His brother died three weeks later from injuries inflicted in the same brawl, fought with Mormon brethren over admission to a Church dance. The Hunt boys, emulating the Prophet Joseph Smith, were street fighters who liked strong drink. The death of her father set a series of negative events in motion for great-grandmother, Lydia Isabelle "Belle" Hunt Kelly, which eventually left her stranded in old Mexico. Infected with small pox, Belle was quarantined in a shack on a mountain outside Juarez. Almost all her family had died and their belongings buried or burned. In the spring of 1891, her face still scared by pox and her long red hair gone, fifteen-year-old Belle traveled back to Virgin City, accompanied by Mary, her ten year old sister. With little money, they traveled by train and hitched rides with sympathetic freighters to complete the trip.

Short of dying in a brawl or shot by some modern day Avenging Angel, I'm still a liar long ago excommunicated and dismissible as a defiant fornicator. They would try, but the Prophets and seers in Salt Lake City can't ignore, dismiss or smear you. Church leaders employ defense strategies—hang tough, divert attention and shoot the messenger. Those most in need of the messenger's words are most inclined to gun him down, and Church leaders would come after you like old west gunslingers. Most Church members as well will be initially angry with you, Mitt. Experts at segregating information to protect themselves from mental and emotional conflicts, the General Authorities and devout members won't tolerate anyone warring on their beloved Church and its eternal mission. However, battling this continuing multigenerational Mormon war on reality mustn't be avoided.

Adding to a long line of Mormon leaders' war comments, Prophet Gordon Hinckley reiterated that a war rages Mormons must win. In June, 2007, in *Ensign Magazine* for Church members, Hinckley wrote, "We must be united. An army that is disorganized will not be victorious. It is imperative that we close ranks, that we march together as one." Hinckley's Mormon war is waged across the world for the minds of men and women, the front lines manned by missionaries emotionally prepared to fight over the issues of truth and error. Thirteen million Mormons know the truth about who gets those special seats in heaven, while six and a half billion gentiles are in error. Granted, Mormons give better heavenly odds than the Jehovah's Witnesses one hundred and forty-four thousand limit.

Enlisted in the same war, but with a different army, I belong to the growing ranks of soldiers who want truth accepted and Mormon lies rejected. However, despite a plethora of enlightening information, Church leaders serve Gerbergoodies and members eat it up. Mitt, tell our people that books written and carefully researched by heroic Mormon historians and scientists should be studied not avoided or dismissed as unauthorized reading material. Help free misguided Mormons who mimic the book burning mentality found in historical dark periods. Sir, there is a war on, and you are in it—on one side or the other.

As a general in the army of truth, you could tell our people to wake up and pay attention. You have my permission to slap Church leaders and members if necessary. Smack the faithful upside the head with Grant Palmer's book, *An*

Insiders View of Mormon Origins, or Simon Southerton's, *Losing a Lost Tribe*—preferably with the paperback versions. I would suggest whacking them with a copy of Jerald and Sandra Tanner's book, *Mormonism, Shadow or Reality,* but the book is so big it could brain damage the most stubborn Mormon mules. Besides, it's not available in paperback. Mitt, I only joke about slapping sense into our pioneer families' heads. There's been too much violence in Mormon history. Even without violence, thousands of Mormon apostates would enjoy watching Church leaders frog-marched from their Salt Lake City headquarters and held accountable for perpetuating this deception into the twenty-first century.

The Mormon train of logic and common sense was derailed long ago by its leaders' mysticism and emotion, leaving members struggling to cling to discordant, contradictory beliefs for fear they will lose faith in the future. Dale Carnegie said, "Faith is one of the forces by which men live, and the total absence of it means collapse." Pastor Ray Christenson once told me, "Mormons turn away, and there's nothing there." Christenson counseled numerous ex-Mormons during his long ministry, and I knew immediately what he meant. Mere Christianity seems incomplete when compared to Mormonism's humanized religious philosophy, with its personalized answers for almost everything. It's devastating for a person's self-esteem once to believe himself part of God's chosen people, the very elect from primordial life, and then admit he clung to a cult, either afraid to let go or unable to completely break free.

Once one accepts reality—that Mormonism is false—there seems nowhere to turn. We were taught from childhood that the Christian churches are abominable before God. Referring to Jesus, Joseph Smith said all their creeds were an abomination in His sight. Mitt, use your celebrity status and credibility to stop this blasphemy and guide our people back to reality. The LDS Church must accept that its sacrosanct doctrines are simply silly when unemotionally and objectionably scrutinized. Though frustrating, I finally find some humor watching friends and relatives behave like ostriches, hiding their eyes from the elephant standing in the middle of their exclusive Mormon stairway to celestial thrones and crowns.

A cupful of confirmation bias, a few more dutiful Church chores stirred in, a dose of denial sprinkled on top—and presto, our people feel they're ascending the celestial stairs. Mitt, the Church's emotional grip stifles. Relieve the immense pressure on our pioneer families who strive to meet Church expectations in this closed society. Besides "every member a missionary," male members are expected to perform like potential Stake Presidents and women like candidates for Relief Society President. Admittedly, a social class structure exists in the Church hierarchy of layman workers. However, it's difficult to say no when the Prophet wants a new General Authority or the ward Bishop wants to fill a Sunday school teaching job.

Not surprisingly, law enforcement once called Salt Lake City the "bunko capital of America." It's also a happy-pill-heaven for pharmaceutical companies delighted to help depressed Mormon men and women meet their responsibilities. Who misses out on a great investment opportunity if they hear their Bishop or Stake President is in the deal? Who turns down another volunteer job when it's a calling directly from Jesus? Lifelong training to trust authority figures resulted in good people being swindled because they were easy marks. Through it all, they sweat out an endless regiment of Church work for a cause that's not real.

Mormon subculture instills women and men with anxiety and anger, which many manage with prescription drugs instead of confronting the authority figure making the demand. Comic, Steven Wright, joked "Depression is merely anger without enthusiasm." Church obligations tire and depress too many Mormon people. They don't have enough energy to be enthusiastic and feel guilty if they complain or become angry. Mormons who would never down a Bud Light or smoke a joint will pop legal pills as needed. For the most trusting and dutiful members, happy pills are almost mandatory to meet the Church's endless expectations.

Notwithstanding the negatives and miseries of Mormonism, the Church provides a comforting support group for members. Mormons behave normally when they stay with their dominant social group. Hanging with the tribe and running with the pack served our human ancestors' needs since time immemorial. However, while all organized religions give their members a support system and a sense of community, Mormon leaders practice a level of control that has been perfected to cult status. It's wrong for tribal leaders to keep people isolated, ignorant, lead them in false directions and drive them like pack animals.

Mitt, powerful forces emanating from a sophisticated cult drive you to seek political leadership. You feel "called" to the Presidency of the United States and are motivated by expectations emanating from everyone ranging from the Mormon Jesus to your lifelong peers and ancestors. That powerful belief makes it acceptable to change your position on the social issues like a pool hustler setting up his next shot. Who dares refuse the calling to be President, Vice President or a Cabinet member when refusing a direct order from Jesus to a teach Priesthood meeting can make a Mormon man feel nervous or depressed? Sir, just say no to the drug of Mormonism and its false sense of euphoria. Accept a more important position. Help our people break their addiction and become emotionally drug-free.

Former Supreme Court Justice, Louis Brandeis, said, "Sunlight is the best disinfectant." When you're ready to step from the waiting room to greatness, there's a growing number of historically and scientifically trained Totos eager to help you pull back the "Zion Curtain" to reveal the wizard's darkest secrets. Not foreordained to be President in a Mormon-made primordial existence, you have a nobler calling to free our people from the Great American Cult. Break the cultural knot that binds our people and shine light through the darkness that blinds them. Since you wrapped yourself in the Ronald Reagan mantle, I paraphrase his Berlin wall comment and beseech you: Mr. Romney, tear down this Zion Curtain, and set our people free!

This higher calling will require you and a team of biblical scholars to correct the Mormon blasphemous perversions of Christ's life and purpose. Joseph Smith claimed he needed to restore the only true church because, over the centuries, the Christian Gospel was distorted and its authority lost. According to the Prophet Joseph, Christ established a detailed, highly structured organization during his ministry. Then, the "whore who sits on many waters" (Revelations 17-1), which Mormons believe is the Catholic Church, distorted and perverted the eternal plan, requiring a latter-day restoration. The whore's naughty daughters—the Protestant Churches—sought to correct the errors, but didn't get it right because they lacked authority from Heaven and the restoring authority of the holy ancient Priesthood.

Mitt, tell Mormon pioneer families that the "Meridian of Time" Jesus never installed a massive new religious bureaucracy to replace the old Jewish system, so this supposed new structure was never distorted or lost over the centuries. In Biblical scriptures, Jesus chastised the Pharisees and other sects for burdening the people with too many rules and rigid customs. It's an historical stretch to conclude Jesus even wanted to found a church, yet Mormons purport he established a complex flow chart filled with titles and positions. How arrogant for Joseph Smith, early Church leaders and present day Mormon authorities to distort and attack nineteen hundred years of Christian history and attempt to create a new Christian reality.

As America moved from Joseph Smith's era of magic and mysticism to an age of science, research and reason, Mormon views remained frozen in time. Religious faith in a higher power is only contrary to reason when steeped in the absurd. When viewed through the un-glazed eyes of reason, real faith can develop and be sustained. Clear eyes and open minds see that traditional Christian scriptures—and even the *Book of Mormon*—contain no references to the Mormon terms and doctrines—Heavenly Mother, pre-mortal intelligences, eternal progression, first estate or second estate.

Mitt, Brigham Young and our early cult leaders skipped Bible class when they preached the blasphemous doctrine that God, Jesus and Adam were all polygamists. These uneducated seers ditched geography class then announced that, instead of south of Baghdad, the Garden of Eden was in Jackson County, Missouri where the Mormon's New Jerusalem will be built. King Brigham Young led Mormons further astray when he spent twenty-five years teaching that Adam is God, our Heavenly Father, in addition to being Michael the Arc Angel, the Ancient of Days. According to Brigham Young's proclamations dispersed in the *Journal of Discourses*, our multi-talented, multi-faced Father in Heaven starred in all the big roles. I know all that can't be possible. God may be Adam and some other leading men, but everybody knows John Travolta was Michael the Arc Angel.

Mormon heresy continues unabated. Although Jesus and Peter warned to beware of false prophets, President Hinckley and Apostle Dallen Oakes admit that Mormons believe in a different Jesus, not the Christ found in original Biblical Gospels who actually lived in Biblical times. In 1995, Oakes told members that Mormons believe in a different God, or Gods, than Christians. Then, in 2002, Hinckley said the Church doesn't believe in the same Jesus worshipped throughout Christendom. At the Church's 2007 fall conference, Hinckley stated God and Jesus are two separate physical beings. Mitt, when you say you believe in Jesus Christ as your Savior, which one do you mean? Have you spent your life believing in a different God and Jesus, too?

President Hinckley also announced at the October, 2007 conference, "A great miracle is taking place right before our eyes." He proudly proclaimed, "This work will continue to grow and prosper and move across the earth." Mitt, while Mormon sheep remain credulous, deceived, and devoid of free agency, the wolf relishes his role as the father of lies. The master of confusion has created a new Jesus in Mormondom and found a willing audience of gullible people. Satan smiles and peaks through his sheep face to admire his perfect handiwork. Pleased, the old shyster retreats behind his disguise, trying not to laugh too loudly. He is gratified to see that attempts to free our proud people from his quagmire of lies are cleverly twisted into the belief that it is he—the Devil—who is trying to lead them astray.

Mormon members, herded like sheep, insist vital Bible concepts were lost or badly mangled in translation, while the *Book of Mormon* remains the most correct book on earth. According to Joseph Smith, the Bible was so poorly translated he was instructed by Jesus to correct it. Although the original *Book of Mormon* was filled with horrendous misspellings, grammatical mistakes, double negatives and syntactical errors reflecting his social class, Smith began his literary attack on the Bible. Ironically, soon after he began to retranslate it, the Mormon Prophet was welcomed to his eternal rewards. Apparently, having his Bible re-written by a nineteenth century swindler with an over-stimulated libido was more than even a benevolent Christian God could take.

The Bible is a compilation of heavily edited works by numerous authors, and scholars admit to contradictions and inconsistencies in the *New Testament*. Some lost their belief in Christ's mission as a result of their research. Early Greek manuscripts, which didn't contain punctuation or capital letters, were translated by amateur often confused scribes, who, from time to time, simply added their own meanings. Biblical researchers, acknowledging these and other problems, continue to rectify the errors and clarify contemporary translations. Meanwhile, millions of conservative Christians believe the Bible word for word, and Mormons barely believed it at all.

A few years ago, Americans were entertained when Southern Baptists held their annual conference in Salt Lake City and sent missionaries to proselytize local residents. Mormons were not amused. The LDS Church joins with the Baptists in America's contemporary cultural wars, but rejects Baptist missionaries trying to convert their members. In the country's founding period, Baptists championed the first amendment as their protection from majority churches. Today, they join forces with Mormons and others seeking political power to impose a strict version of legislated morality on our secular society.

Independent scholars know the scribes' mistakes and additions to the Bible don't support Joseph Smith's unorthodox assertions about its original structure, and whatever its problems, the Bible is not an unambiguous lie like the *Book of Mormon* and Mormon religious philosophy. Ongoing Bible research and scholarship offer little to legitimize the Mormon theology from Joseph Smith and Brigham Young to current leaders—not records found on papyri, parchment, the printing press or computerization. Contradictions between the Bible and Mormon theology don't matter to Mormon leaders and apologists systematically defending the cult's unorthodox twist on Christianity. Even though the possibility is summarily dismissed beyond LDS educational circles, the Mormon mantra remains that early recorded proof of their quirky doctrines were mistranslated, lost or deleted from the Bible.

Mitt, that didn't happen to the Bible, but independent scholars know Mormons have revised, reinterpreted and simply subtracted information from their previous organizational material. Revealed religion is dangerous because anyone can justify anything by sudden revelation or slowly mutated scriptures. Still, nothing is new about revisionist history. It happens in all cultures, particularly the repressed authoritarian societies. Today, the Bush Administration works quietly to rewrite some of our Twentieth Century American history. Notwithstanding, it's particularly despicable behavior from a religious organization that claims to be divine and bristles when called a cult.

In 2004, I asked Pastor Ray Christenson to re-baptized me because I wanted membership in an organization that believes in Jesus and God as described in the New Testament and other recently found documents. Rebaptism wasn't necessary for membership in Community Lutheran Church. This open-armed Christian church grants membership to all people, even those baptized Mormon. The Catholic Church stopped accepting Mormon baptisms in 2000 and, of course, the Mormons don't accept the baptisms of any Christian churches. Now a traditional Christian, I still remain partly trapped in the Mormon subculture, including vestiges of the Utah "Mormon twang" when I speak. And like all ex-Mormons, I continue to sort truths from blasphemies and rebuild myself emotionally—as will you, when you join us.

9

Mormon Living Prophets

Today's Mormon members are programmed, like our forefathers, to only concern themselves with what the Living Prophet and Apostles proclaim. The "indeed demanding" Church rules and fees mentioned in your 1999 letter come in various forms, and the most insulting is the requirement that members never question Church authority. Ordinances previously revered as eternal are changed, hidden or simply deleted, making Mormonism magically become whatever the latest group of geriatric windbags proclaims. This never seems to matter to devout members. Gullible early Latter Day Saints were more enthralled with the process of revelation than the long term value of the product, and current members willingly follow their Living Prophets without questioning why their Gods seem so fickle and confused.

It seems an Orwellian twist, a form of Newspeak, that Mormon doctrines and ordinances are hidden, twisted or labeled heresy just a few generations after they were proclaimed eternal revelations from the Gods. Even more frightening, the majority of contemporary Mormon members don't notice, remember or care. Church leaders are as secretive about Church history and doctrines as they are with the press about their tax-exempt financial activities. While talking with several young missionaries in recent years, I learned they don't even know Church history and doctrines. That the Church coaches missionaries to stir prospects' emotions, but avoid answering specific questions, is a testament to how Mormon leaders have perfected their mastery of cult techniques to grip members and deceive potential converts.

My first step toward spiritual and intellectual freedom came in grade school. I was only eleven when my family loaded all our possessions into the old, blue Studebaker and Uncle Cleo's cattle truck, and made a *Grapes of Wrath* run from our Mormon village for a new life in boomtown. As a former Utah homeboy, I was charmed when President Hinckley demonstrated his prowess at mumble peg to an *Associated Press* reporter, while his posse of public relations handlers winced and paced as he veered off script. Mike Wallace once stated that Gordon Hinckley is a good guy who means well, but Larry King was closer to the mark when he said he doesn't believe God talks to Hinckley.

Gordon Hinckley is a Utah farm boy who became a Church bureaucrat and then outlived the competition to become the Mormon Prophet. The Mormon management system of gerontocracy, which elevates the oldest, often most infirm person to Prophet Status is an uninspired and uninspiring way to run a government, company or church (the LDS Church has a history of serving in all three capacities). Because the Mormon Jesus doesn't announce his choice for prophet, and there's no vote by Apostles following earnest prayers, Mormons are stuck with a system where the really-old-guy automatically wins—often just before senility sets in or he dies. When Gordon Hinckley dies and Thomas Monson ascends to Prophet-hood, couldn't Mormons at least have a rumbling drum roll, some puffs of white smoke or Ed McMann say, "Heeeeres Tommy?"

In 1998, President Hinckley stated, "Individuals and thinking members can carry all the opinions they wish in their heads ... but if they begin to try to persuade others, they will be called to a disciplinary council." Peer pressure in the public schoolyard is used to intimidate thinking students to not achieve their full educational potential. In the Mormon Churchyard, it only takes a few words from the Living Prophet speaking for an anti-intellectual Jesus. In the secular world, scholarly research is the catalyst for improved civilization and scientific knowledge the foundation for our advancements, yet Mormon leaders "hardened their hearts" against modern science and the New Mormon History as if they could somehow stop progress and freeze time. At the same time, the LDS Church supports policies and beliefs that speed the doomsday clock, which now nears midnight.

The late Senator Daniel Patrick Moynihan would say Church leaders are entitled to their own opinions, not their own facts. Mitt, tell Church members that Hinckley doesn't know fact from fiction. Mark Hofmann, an obscure book dealer, exposed the foibles of the infallible Mormon Prophet and Apostles two decades ago by enticing them to pay him nearly a million dollars for forty-eight forged documents, so they could be squirreled away from the light of day. President Hinckley and other Church leaders were initially fooled, or at least unable to discern the authenticity of Mark Hofmann's "Salamander Letter," while the late Jerald Tanner of the Utah Lighthouse Ministry warned it was a probable forgery. LDS leaders paid a bundle to Hofmann and eventually looked ridiculous because Hofmann knew they suppressed many original documents for fear members would learn their content and lose faith.

Mitt, Jesus doesn't talk to Gordon Hinckley and Mormon Apostles aren't talking to Jesus. For Mormons, the real Gospel of Jesus Christ has been blown away like rose pedals on a windy day and replaced by a festering of dandelions. Tell Mormon leaders and their hired apologists it's immoral to advise members that sound scientific and historical analysis cannot be trusted. The best secular scientific and historical inquiry winnows out inaccurate ideas and concepts, while the Mormon leaders cling to an irrational, antiquated belief system not open for debate. Time and again, Mormon apologists have failed to employ care and professionalism in their scholarship, yet, year after year, the Church dispatches legions of public relations specialists and uninformed missionaries to confuse vulnerable people.

All the while, honest Mormon scholars and scientists are systematically punished for daring to divulge facts widely known in their professional fields. If they stand tall, they are excommunicated. If they repent and kiss the Priesthood ring, they are only sanctioned with disfellowship for a period of time. Add a promise to remain quiet about the truth, and wayward members are eventually reinstated to full membership alongside their family and friends. The Mormon Church's boundless benevolence is breathtaking.

The America envisioned by the Founding Fathers existed to protect freedom to think and act, but the Mormon Church stripped members of the ability to reason clearly. The Church's Living Prophets and Apostles admonish members to beware of their big brother Lucifer, who lurks everywhere just waiting to snatch their exaltation. That brave men and women who dare speak or write the truth about the LDS Church are tarred as the Devil's tools is a form of evil. Mitt, an honest debate about the Church's validity and credibility is long overdue, and you're the man who can lead it. If the LDS church doesn't humble itself and admit the truth, it will end up in the trash heap of history, and deservedly so. The Mormon Church has no prophets, living or dead, and was founded on distortions and half-truths now interwoven in its subculture's clay foundation. Above its soft foundation, Mormon leaders' punitive, holier-than-thou attitudes stand on rickety Nephite feet. What could be a greater calling than to knock this Christian caricature down and—once and for all—dispel the crazy stuff taught by our Prophets and their scriptures?

Several decades ago, Sandra Tanner, Brigham Young's great-great-granddaughter, began a professional pilgrimage to report why Mormon history, science and general doctrines don't pass the truth test. With husband Jerald, they started a small publishing company, which became the Utah Lighthouse Ministry, to expose Church dishonesty about history and doctrine. In 1960, Mormon Apostle LeGrand Richards sternly warned Jerald not to start anything against the Mormon Church. Unintimidated, the Tanners moved forward with their research and publications. Jerald passed away in 2006, but their humble ministry and bookstore still shines the light of truth into the heavens near the Salt Lake City Temple's long shadow. This medieval-looking monument to mysticism, ornate with Masonic symbols and adorned with the Angel Moroni perched in garish gold, houses secret chambers where Mormon actors guide faithful members through pagan rituals, veils and sacred oaths.

With limited resources, the Tanners reported (Sandra continues to report) the confusing magical and blusterous contradictions that prompted the imaginary Moroni to blow his horn and call the world to Mormon Zion. The Tanners discovered and disclosed copies of original church records hidden in the Church vault since the nineteenth century. Aided by scholars and scientists inside and outside the church, they peeked behind the Zion curtain and pulled back temple veils. Sandra's trek into the sunlight began even before she married. At Jerald's urging, she and her grandmother compared the original *Book of Commandments* with the official *Doctrine and Covenants* and discovered Joseph Smith began changing his prophesies between 1833 and 1835.

Mitt, did you ever take a class with BYU Professor Lou Midgley? Listening to him drone on for a semester about "what is" and "what ought to be" was laborious. Always full of himself, Midgley went to the Tanner's bookstore several times over the years to argue and perhaps pick a fight. A leading Church apologist and polemicist, he has a propensity to heckle and harass anyone with the courage to criticize the Church or BYU. Sometimes, I didn't understand what Midgley was talking about in his classroom, and years later I realized he didn't, either. Today, I have a much better understanding about what is and what ought to be. Sandra Tanner is a heroine, and Dr. Louis Midgley ought to apologize to her for his pompous behavior.

Thanks to inspired efforts by the Tanners and others, we know who Joseph Smith and the early Mormons really were. When referring to the boy prophet, it's no longer necessary to say, as did Fawn Brody, that *No Man knows my History*. Although there are still debates about whether he was mentally ill, a gifted con man or both, few dispute Smith's credentials as a master fabulist and fantasist. In his book, *The American Religion,* Harold Bloom said of Joseph Smith, "So self-created was he, that he transcends Emerson and Whitman in his imaginative response, and takes his place with the great figures in our fiction." Bloom caused Church leaders more consternation when he wrote, "The God of Joseph Smith is a daring revival of some of the Kabbalists and Gnostics, prophetic sages who, like Smith himself, asserted they had returned to the true religion."

Joseph Smith, who could read but not write, was a cool cat who definitely had his mojo working. Over a period of two decades, he created provincial Gods, who knew practically nothing beyond Nineteenth century New England, to suit his changing needs and desires. He developed a cult of personality around a group of converts—initially close family and shirttail relatives—who were superstitious occultists enthralled with magic and witchcraft. Early Mormons practiced palmistry, read tea leaves, and used divining rods and peep stones to search for buried treasures. Joseph Smith found a magic stone while treasure hunting with his father, had two stones he used from 1820–27, and acquired more over the years until his death. He placed two stones in a twin breast plated contraption he called the "Urim and Thummin" of the *Old Testament*, which he then used to translate ancient documents.

Students of history know about the War of the Roses, but few are aware of the Mormon Church's War of the Seer Stones. Several first-generation Mormon men also thought they were prophets, so they had revelations and made up their own stuff. Too many cooks can ruin a delicious stew and too many false prophets might ruin the witch's brew. Thus, when Hyrum Page started using a seer stone to receive his revelations in 1830, the Mormon Jesus reacted directly and decisively. In reference to Brother Page, as recorded in the Doctrine and Covenants, Jesus instructed his anointed Prophet Joseph Smith that, "Things which he hath written from the stone are not of me … Satan deceiveth him." The Mormon Jesus had to intervene because even Mormon children were honing talents as peeping stone users to find some buried loot of their own. Historical records reveal the next Mormon generation extended the occult traditions, and Church members used seer stones and other tools of magic well into the ninetieth century.

Mitt, the Mormon Church taught us Joseph Smith was a sweet, uneducated boy, chosen before birth to lead the end times. Despite being uneducated, he was intelligent and a skilled storyteller who studied numerous contemporary publications in addition to the *King James Bible*. This prepared him liberally to sprinkle the ideas and words of other men into the *Book of Mormon*, *Pearl of Great Price* and *Doctrine and Covenants*, which he either attributed to direct revelations from Jesus or said he was inspired to translate. Smith's mother, Lucy, said that as a teenager, Joseph entertained the family for hours with his fabulous fables about the early American peoples and their cultures.

Joseph Smith's imagination and story telling skills paid dividends years later, but, during those early difficult financial times, life required more than entertaining the family. A guy had to earn a few bucks, so young Joseph spun yarns for wealthy land owners, convincing some that treasures laid buried somewhere inside their fences. Of course, for a fee, he would take a peek. In the same way he later translated much of the *Book of Mormon*, Smith turned his hat upside down, positioned his seer stone inside, and covered it with his face. Then, with not much showing except his ears and unabashed aplomb, he revealed his character. Worthy of a Saturday Night Live skit, the creators of HBO's Big Love had fun portraying the hat trick in a power struggle between fundamentalist compound leaders.

The young Prophet's lifetime of hustling first caught up with him in 1826, when he cheated Josiah Stowell out of a sizable chunk of change. Original records found in recent years verified the tenacious assertion that "Joseph Smith, the glass looker" was arrested, tried and found guilty in a New York justice court. After admitting he used a stone to peep around peoples' property in search of hidden treasures, he was convicted of being "a disorderly person and imposter." At twenty, still a minor, the Judge gave Smith "leg bail," telling him to get out of Dodge, so to speak. In 1961, the leading Mormon apologist of his day, the late Hugh Nibley wrote, "If this court record is authentic, it is the most damning evidence in existence against Joseph Smith." When the original arrest record was recovered from the old court house basement in 1971 and reported to the public, the effervescent Dr. Nibley became quiet as a church mouse, as did the Mormon Prophet and Apostles.

Joseph Smith could have had a brain chemical imbalance that sent him into ecstatic states, possibly from the traumatic leg surgery he endured as a little boy, or he may have been simply a gifted charlatan. Whatever the explanation, he wasn't the Prophet you and I were indoctrinated to believe in from childhood. In truth, Smith made it all up as he went along. When Mormonism's founder wasn't in the company of occult treasure seekers, drawing magic circles, battling enchantments or diligently peering into his peep stones, he often dressed up in costume to impress the ladies. "Old White Hat," as Smith was known to many along the Mississippi River, was an egotistical womanizer known to kiss and tell. Mitt, for those who wanted to believe Joseph Smith was called to be the greatest prophet since Moses, it's sad to accept him as nothing more than a nineteenth century dandy dressed in military attire or strutting around in white beaver hats smoking a stogie.

By all reports, this dashing fellow looked sporting in his costumes, and the "Great Egotist" couldn't resist bragging in polite company. His tales of sexual encounters and female conquests, including details of the "degree of passion afforded by each of his favorites," were passed throughout the region. Physical attractiveness and personal charm fed outlandish behavior and spiritual misconceptions that led to his life of misperceptions and misbehavior. His questionable business dealings, multiple marriages, sexual liaisons, strange religious rituals, unorthodox teachings and political ambitions combined to create trouble for him and his followers wherever they settled. Joseph Smith was found guilty of various crimes on several occasions and barely stayed one step ahead of federal and state law enforcement officials until his death at Carthage jail.

Mormons weren't driven out of Ohio as popularly believed. Joseph Smith fled to avoid pending criminal charges and mounting debts. Visualize Joseph Smith, Sidney Rigdon and other leading elders high-tailing it out of Kirkland, Ohio in the dark of night to escape the consequences of their greed, speculation and counterfeiting, which led to the Kirkland Bank failure. Later found guilty of illegal banking activities in Kirkland, this great leader had already loped down the lane to create more economic and cultural pain. Still, he was thoroughly believable to our forefathers at first wooed by his charms and outrageous writings, then controlled by his cunning and comforting promises. Sad to say, many of our ancestors followed loyally along during those early years, and too many of their descendants still believe he was a persecuted prophet.

The 1820s First Vision is rudimentary to Mormonism because it coronets Joseph Smith a Prophet, seer and revelator. Considering that Joseph Smith had earned the great egotist moniker, this stupendous vision event embedded into our youthful psyches is even more remarkable. It may have been one of the rare examples of humility by Smith. He was out of character to behave so modestly about his 1820 heavenly encounter by waiting until 1838, in his third major revision of that vision, to disclose that both Jesus and God had appeared to him—hanging in the air as two separate beings. The Prophet's uncharacteristic reticence about reporting this momentous event is mind-boggling to me.

Can't speak for you, Mitt, but I'm an egomaniac and would have been so proud and excited at age fourteen, I would have run through the streets of Palmyra, New York breathlessly telling every bewildered person I encountered the stupefying news. I would surely have screeched, "Everybody; I'm chosen to change the world! God and my big brother Jesus just appeared to me in a vision and said the Christian churches are all wrong. I was called before birth to

straighten out everybody in the latter days." Beaming with eight grade exuber-
ance, I would have informed those lucky people I was selected to restore the true
Gospel, open the "Dispensation of the Fullness of Times," and save their souls. If
I had kept secret from the world until age thirty-two—that God the Father and
Jesus dropped in from Heaven to visit me—surely pride and concern would have
required I share the good news with family. As one of the greatest men to ever
wear a tabernacle of flesh and blood, I would certainly have warned the Smith
clan to stay away from all the abominable congregations waiting to lead them to
Hell.

Because Joseph Smith was so humble, and didn't alert his family, the young
prophet's Mother and three siblings joined the Presbyterians during the 1824
revival period. Even more weird, Joseph Smith himself, just informed by the
Gods that all Churches were an abomination, became involved with several
Christian denominations during the 1820s. In one recorded account, Joseph
Smith's father said young Joseph was baptized a member of the Baptist Church
in 1824. As late as June, 1828, the boy prophet sought membership in the Meth-
odist Episcopal class in Harmony, Pennsylvania, and was rejected because he
wouldn't renounce his previous money digging and occult activities.

In the exciting revival period of 1824–25, numerous aspiring prophets had
visions around the region. Records indicate it was at that time when Joseph
Smith claimed his first vision—which was only an angelic one. Then, he embel-
lished the tale each time told, making it more authoritative with each reciting.
The last revision of the First Vision was announced to placate several Church
leaders who were losing faith in his calling as a prophet. By 1838, the Gods themselves appeared in his majestic vision, then moved back to 1820 and a place in the
woods—or was it a grove?

President Gordon Hinckley said, "If the First Vision did not occur, then we
are involved in a great sham. It is just that simple." Ironically, it is just that simple
for those who want to know the truth. The First Vision didn't happen. Smith
later claimed suffering a severe persecution for talking about his 1820 vision
immediately afterwards, yet the historical record is blank on the subject of any
vision at all during the period when Smith was honing his skills as a teenage
exhorter for the Methodists. Mitt, like so many official Mormon documents, the
record of the First Vision was cobbled together long after the purported event,
and then tampered with repeatedly until formalized in its final form. President
Hinckley and the General Authorities should admit to a great sham so the Mormon people can move on.

Not only was Joseph Smith more humble than his critics credit him, he showed real courage, too. How else can Mormons explain his perennial reckless behavior? After speaking with Jesus and God the Father in a live appearance, he courageously behaved badly for the remaining twenty-five years of his life. Sarcasm aside, I've bet my Mormon salvation and promise of eternal progression that Joseph Smith never had heavenly visitations from God, Jesus, John the Baptist, Peter, James and John, Elijah, Moses, Elias, an angel named Moroni or Buzz Lightyear of Star Command. However, the boy prophet may have had Lucifer whispering the seven deadly sins in his ear and chose his favorites for daily pleasure.

Still, because of his carefully nurtured heroic legend, our uninformed people believe Joseph Smith was a great prophet who died a martyr's death. Church members don't know, or ignore the fact, that their Prophet was arrested and incarcerated at Carthage jail by Illinois Governor Ford after Smith felt so threatened, he sent members of the Mormon militia to crush the new Nauvoo Expositor newspaper and declared martial law. Armed with muskets, pistols, Bowie knives, swords and sledgehammers, they demolished the press, destroyed the type and burned existing copies of the newspaper.

Concerned Mormon leaders founded the rival press to expose recent changes to Church doctrines and express their outrage at Smith's dubious personal behavior. The reformers believed Brother Joseph's sacred new practice of polygamy blasphemous and were appalled by his revolutionary political plans for the Kingdom and America. Desiring only to return the Church to its beliefs before 1838, they announced polygamy's secret existence and reported Smith's endless licentious activities. Because of his bellicose bragging, Smith's multiple conquests were already widely known throughout the region and as information trickled back to the Latter Day Saints, disgust had grown in the membership ranks.

Opposition to plural marriage was the major issue, but the Expositor newspaper bravely reported the Prophet's stealing from gentiles and misappropriation of Church funds. The reformers also accused Smith of holding himself above the law and questioned his respect for separation of church and state. His elaborate secret plan to overthrow all earthly governments and set up an Old Testament version of the Kingdom of God was exposed, too. To further his theocratic monarchy, Smith had announced himself a candidate for U.S. President, and thousands of missionaries traveled the country to preach about his new gold Bible and beat the presidential campaign drums.

Outside the Church, the arrogance and extravagance of Smith's intentions aroused sensible people who resented the attacks on their Christian beliefs and viewed his political intentions as a threat to the fledgling nation. Smith's repeated failures in previous settlements and outlandish activities in Nauvoo, including polygamy, initiated new dissentions amidst a backdrop of swirling rumors. Confronted with this growing internal crisis, now fueled by men threatening to weaken his control, Smith perceived the Nauvoo Expositor reformers as traitors. Worse yet, they interfered with the Prophet and Apostles' polygamist plans for the girls! By that time, Smith was already secretly married to at least thirty-three women. Reportedly, several women bore his children.

The Expositor newspaper revelations were a major threat to Joseph Smith's plan to be President of America and King of the world. In defiance of the Bill of Right's basic tenant, he ordered the Expositor's press destroyed and then told the Nauvoo faithful, "It is thought by some that our enemies would be satisfied by my destruction, but I tell you, as soon as they have shed my blood, they will thirst for the blood of every man in whose heart still dwells a single spark of the spirit of the fullness of the Gospel." Historical records prove the Expositor assertions accurately reported, including the parts about secret lives and secret societies. The accusations weren't libelous lies, as contemporary Mormon apologists still argue. In spite of Apostle Dallen Oakes legal histrionics to justify Smith's behavior, he had violated the First Amendment when he ordered the Expositor destroyed. Joseph Smith's actions were comparable to a Utah Governor or Mormon Leader deciding to thrill the *Deseret News* staff by dispatching the Utah National Guard to destroy the *Salt Lake Tribune* offices.

Destroying the Nauvoo Expositor was a major miscue in Joseph Smith's career as a provincial man playing prophet. The gentlemen who founded this rival newspaper were disenchanted with Smith's religious and political policies and, along with Emma Smith and the Relief Society, only wanted to reform the Church and return it to earlier doctrinal positions. However, the Apostles and many other Church leaders were either away on missions or selling Smith's Presidential candidacy. No calming voices that might have saved Smith's life were present to counter his blundering behavior. Apostle Parley P. Pratt might have calmed him, but Pratt was returning to Nauvoo from a mission in Boston when the Prophet was killed.

Mitt, your great-great-grandfather Pratt was on a steamer headed for Chicago when he got word of Joseph Smith's death. In his autobiography, Pratt said, "there was a general spirit of exultation and triumph" among the people immediately after reports of Smith's demise. He compared it to "news of a great national victory" in time of war. Though depressing to Pratt, it was an understandable response considering almost everything Mormons represented was the antithesis of American freedoms and traditional Christian values. Your ancestor said he suffered "taunts and questions" about what the Mormons would do now their prophet was dead. Pratt answered that the Mormons "would continue their mission and spread the word he had restored to all the world."

Without Parley P. Pratt or any other Apostles present to possibly reason with him, the Prophet ordered the press smashed, initiated martial law and used fiery rhetoric to stir the saints into a fighting mood. Then, following a consistent behavior pattern, he did what he had done in several previous self-created crises. He ran from his mess and hid like a coward. He had fled Palmyra, New York, scurried from Far West, Missouri and high-tailed it out of Kirkland, Ohio. Now, perpetual promiscuity, illegal economic activities and other nefarious deeds placed him on the road out of Nauvoo with brother Hyrum and loyal bodyguard Porter Rockwell.

Joseph Smith was called a coward by many in Nauvoo, and Emma encouraged her husband to return and accept the consequences of his illegal actions. Not knowing where else to go, Joseph Smith returned to face arrest and, ultimately, his death. Even self-proclaimed living Prophets have to die and Joseph Smith went out in a blaze of gunfire in a fight with an angry mob. Someone smuggled guns in to Carthage jail for a pending jailbreak to once again rescue the man with a Messiah complex and a pair of stones. Incarcerated with brother Hyrum and his latest escape plan incomplete, the greatest prophet since Moses fought and killed two men.

According to John Taylor, at Carthage with him, before Joseph Smith was shot, he fired his pistol several times and "two or three were wounded by these discharges, two of whom, I am informed, died." Before Joseph Smith succumbed, he made the Masonic distress signal and spoke the first four Masonic distress words, "Oh Lord my God." I've known since childhood he cried out those words as he died, but no Church teachers, from teenage Seminary classes to required BYU religion courses, told me their Masonic origin. I thought he simply caledl out to God for help as he fell mortally wounded. Mitt, through independent research in the 1980s, I discovered the source and purpose of his death scream.

I hope Mormons some day share my sense of outrage, instead of pride, when the death of Joseph Smith is compared to that of Jesus. Not charged with any real crimes, Jesus Christ was turned over to authorities by Judas to die a martyr's death for our sins. In contrast, Smith was constantly running and hiding ahead of a litany of serious federal and state charges. Christ went quietly to his death, like a lamb to the slaughter, but Joseph Smith fought to the death and killed others. Considering everything we know about these two historical figures, it's heretical to mention Joseph Smith's name in the same breath with Jesus Christ. Mitt, Joseph Smith was a lot of things, but he was no Christian martyr.

The 2005 bicentennial movie to commemorate the 1805 birth of Joseph Smith elevated Mormon lying to a new zenith. My family watched the disgusting disinformation at Salt Lake City's Temple Square in June, 2007, and our four-year-old daughter asked twice whether Joseph Smith was Jesus. A young couple sitting near us was overcome by emotion as the great prophet and other leaders were jailed for no apparent reason. The only miraculous wonders the founding Mormon Prophet doesn't perform in the propaganda piece are raising the dead and walking on water across the Mississippi. No doubt, those feats will take place in the sequel.

The movie portrays Joseph Smith as a loving monogamist, constantly perse-cuted by devilish men for doing God's work. Following the presentation, we entered a lobby filled with Mormon preteens—too young to discern fact from fantasy—politely waiting for the next showing, lined up for the Library School Hour and expected to believe anything as long as it had appropriate fairy tale content. Mitt, isn't the indoctrination of innocent children even more abhorrent than immorally attempting to mislead adults? I seriously doubt this is what Jesus had in mind when he said, "Let the little children come unto me."

Had Joseph Smith not been killed at Carthage jail, creating a martyr for faith-ful followers, the Mormon subculture wouldn't have survived the nineteenth cen-tury and phony movies about Joseph Smith's life wouldn't exist to hold our people prisoners to the past. By 1844, this secretive religious organization of male selfishness was being exposed, and Mormonism showed signs of unraveling as growing internal dissention ripped at the Church's fraying seams. Joseph Smith said Jesus was leading the Church, but, although the Joseph Smith movie never explains why, calculation after calculation by the boy Prophet failed. Smith and his followers had not coexisted amenably with other Americans in several previ-ous settlements in Missouri and Ohio, and Illinois was no different. Mormons constantly collided with both Christianity and our Democratic Republic as local populations rejected their quirky religious beliefs and opposed their aggressive political plans.

10

"We Thank Thee of God for a Prophet"

Mitt, very devout Mormon should read the following statement by President Joseph Fielding Smith because the quote frames the basic question you and other members should ask and answer. After admitting Mormonism must stand or fall on the Joseph Smith story, he said Joseph Smith "was either a prophet of God, divinely called, properly appointed and commissioned, or he was one of the biggest frauds this world has ever seen. There is no middle ground." Mitt, the latter is true and there is not middle ground, so do your homework, walk out of the darkness and come over to the bright side. There's no room for error or wishy-washy behavior on the important question of Joseph Smith's status as a Christian prophet. Honest scholarship reveals Joseph Smith's prophecies and revelations, mostly unfulfilled or rewritten, were too convenient and self-serving to come from Jesus Christ or any other heavenly being. They are better characterized as the mutterings of an uneducated young man who, according to his father-in-law, Isaac Hale, had "want of sobriety, prudence and stability."

As he stared into his magical seer stones, Joseph Smith had far too many blurry head-in his-hat days. All in all, there are about sixty unfulfilled prophesies, and the *Doctrine and Covenants* is stuffed with many of them. An early and revealing Joseph Smith prophesy occurred after he failed to sell the *Book of Mormon* transcript. Before its publication in 1830, Smith was initially unable to convince Martin Harris to mortgage his farm for $3000 and give him the money. Impatient and broke, the Prophet had a revelation that his freshly transcribed *Book of Mormon* transcript could be sold in Canada for $8000. Upon returning from the trip north—tired and penniless—Oliver Cowdery and others confronted the young Prophet to ask why the plan hadn't worked. Smith responded that "some revelations are of God, some are of man, and some are of the Devil." This moment of candor in the life of a man destined to corrupt Christianity, con gullible men and seduce vulnerable women was missed by his early followers. They remained enthralled with the young prophet and loyal to his every word, no matter how absurd. Several more years passed before Smith's inner circle splintered, and men like Oliver Cowdrey left in disgust.

Mitt, it must be asked what good is a prophet if we never know whether his pronouncements will be his own, the Gods' or the old Devil's? According to the Bible, and even the *Doctrine and Covenants*, he isn't of much value. *Deuteronomy* states clearly that a failed prophecy indicates a false prophet. The 132nd Section of the *Doctrine and Covenants*, which introduced the doctrine of plural marriage, tells us, "behold mine house is a house of order, saith the Lord, and not a house of confusion." Notwithstanding, confusion is everywhere in Smith's prophecies and a river of unfulfilled prophecies flowed unabated during his lifetime.

By 1960, when it was apparent efforts to camouflage numerous alterations to Joseph Smith's revelations had failed, Mormon apologist Hugh Nibley admitted "revelations have been revised whenever necessary. That is the nice thing about revelation—it is strictly open ended." However, in 1966, Apostle Hugh B. Brown said that none of the revelations of the church have been revised. Apostle John Widsoe and President Joseph Fielding Smith made similar declarations during the 1950s. Clearly, despite the confusion, Nibley was correct. Church records were revised, eternal doctrines altered, and revelations previously declared direct from Jesus were ignored or buried without a eulogy, which is modus-operandi for the LDS Church. I have resurrected a few of Joseph Smith's choicest prophesies for their judgment day.

In 1831, Smith wrote that the nations of the earth shall bow to the Mormon Gospel or be laid low of power. One hundred and seventy-six years later, not one nation has bowed to the Mormon Church, although George Bush stops by Church Headquarters to glad hand the boys and pay homage to his loyal Mormon constituency. A year later, in 1832, "the Prophet Joe" said Zion would be built in his generation in Independence, Missouri. Apostle Orson Pratt reiterated the false prophecy in 1870, insisting the generation living in 1832 would still see it come to pass before they all died.

The Missouri Zion prophesy was obviously never fulfilled within the timeframe given by Joseph Smith, and reiterated by Orson Pratt and others, but the Mormon Church still claims the Latter Day Saints will gather soon in Jackson County, Missouri, home of the Garden of Eden, to build the New Jerusalem for the Second Coming of Jesus Christ. When Hannah Storm of CBS asked you about this belief in July, 2007, you bristled and told her to ask the Mormon Church about its beliefs. Mitt, she knows what the Church believes. She wanted to know whether, as you aspired to become President, you believed this nonsense, too.

While the Saints were still in Missouri, Smith prophesied by the authority of Jesus Christ, that not too many years shall pass away before the United States shall present such a scene of bloodshed as has not been paralleled in the history of our nation; pestilence, hail, famine and earthquake will sweep the wicked of this generation from the face of the Land. He raved on to declare the hour of his judgment has come and called for all who heard him to repent, embrace the everlasting covenant and flee to Zion. What a sales pitch! This guy knew how to put the fear of God in people. Of course, nothing of the sort ever happened in his lifetime or ours. Smith claimed all these things would happen because Christ was returning fifty-six years from 1836, which made 1891 the date for the Second Coming.

Joseph Smith was always ready with quick advice and guidance straight from the source of all knowledge to his followers in need of simple clarification or firm direction. Detailed accounts of Smith's failed prophecies have filled numerous novels that will never be sold in Mormon Church bookstores or found on members' recommended reading lists. Some have interesting twists. In 1842, prophesying about the newly-formed Relief Society, Smith said within ten years the Queens of the Earth would come to pay their respects to the Society. However, only two years passed before Brigham Young dissolved the Relief Society as payback to its members for voting unanimously to reinstate monogamy in Nauvoo. Joseph Smith formed this women's auxiliary to the Priesthood in 1842, just two days after he became a Master Mason. Over the next two years before his death, while Emma Smith served as its President, the Prophet made every officer in the organization his "spiritual wife." Needless to say, no queens came to pay their respects.

Even those with a stunted sense of humor find it hard not to snicker when reading many of Joseph Smith's predictions. On one occasion, he prophesied that David W. Patton was to go on a mission in the spring of the following year. In a spooky turn of events, the poor fellow died that autumn in the Battle at Crooked River, probably under a Halloween moon. On the subject of the moon, Smith said it was inhabited by very tall Quaker-type people. Even though that observation wasn't officially sanctioned as prophesy, it's one of my favorite tall tales.

Joseph Smith's comedy act continued when he prophesied his unborn child would be called David and would eventually preside as American President and the King of Israel. In a crazy turn of events, David Smith died in an insane asylum in 1904. Another belly laugher also came from Smith's mouth in 1844, when he announced that within five years the Mormons would live without cooking their food. By 1849, the Mormons were scrounging for food in the Salt Lake Valley to avoid starvation. Even today, Mitt, with our generation's capitalistic successes, few Mormons can afford to hire a live-in cook or eat out every day if they want.

We Mormons always took pride in one partially fulfilled prophecy. BYU professors referred to it and students reminded themselves that Joseph Smith predicted the Civil War in 1832. The comment was usually part of the "Hey, he got that right, and it's a really big one" argument. We would all nod in agreement, oblivious to the fact it was nothing more than a reflection of commonly held views in 1832 America. Smith prophesied a rebellion in South Carolina would lead to a war between the States at a time when South Carolina had declared its power to nullify any Federal Act, and President Jackson prepared to go to war to enforce federal authority. When the Civil War finally began almost thirty years later, there was no world war, famine, plagues or earthquakes, as he predicted, and the Civil War obviously didn't lead to the "end of all nations."

Always threatening our young nation, Smith prophesied in 1843 that the US Government would be overthrown if it didn't redress the Church grievances against it. He warned that if Congress did not grant his wishes, they would be broken up as a government and not much would be left except a grease spot. Church leaders incorporated this false prophecy into official Church history, although, in typical fashion, they edited out the grease spot part.

Another of Joseph Smith's famous prophecies always floated above the LDS Church like a halo. Smith supposedly said the Mormons would become a mighty people in the midst of the Rocky Mountains. The problem is, he didn't write it. Mitt, tell our pioneer families the original handwritten manuscript, which includes this 1843 prophecy, was found in the Nauvoo Visitors Center and published by the Utah Lighthouse Ministry decades ago. The Rocky Mountain Prophecy was squeezed in at the bottom of the page as an "interlinear insertion." It's an obvious forgery added later by a Church's scribe, probably Willard Richards or George A. Smith. Maybe one of Elmer Fudd's great-great-grandpas sneaked it in. Whoever it was, it wasn't Joseph Smith, who never wrote most of his "official" history anyway.

Even though Joseph Smith's prophecies could not be trusted, he had a quick answer for everything and was in constant need of easy money, shelter, and sexual favors from a steady stream of women as young as fourteen. With his lustful proclamations cleverly couched in heavenly authority, Smith told these prophet-stricken women, single or married, that submitting to his advances was the Lord's

Will. What a line! It's a worthy nugget for any drunken night at a singles bar when the bartender announces last call and a guy is desperate.

Even in my wildest days, when I could have benefited from more sobriety, prudence and stability, I never had big enough stones to prey like Joseph Smith! He had a revelation for all the girls, and any attractive woman was fair game. Mitt, when not making unwanted advances toward single women like Sidney Rigdon's daughter, Nancy, Smith lusted after married women like your great-great-great-aunt, Sarah Pratt. Regardless of his false prophecies and sexual misconduct, Mormons are expected to believe Brigham Young when he said Joseph Smith is the gatekeeper at Heaven's door and no one can enter without his approval. What will the Mormon Prophet, a known street wrestler and gunfighter, do? Will he pin surprised souls to the Pearly Gates—even if God has granted them grace? Maybe, he just plans to shoot them.

11

The American Bible

No reason to expect you to accept my challenge to free our people, or even believe I can test your loyalty to the Great American Cult. However, at the same time, I learned never to underestimate you. After all, as a Mormon Republican you got elected Governor in a Catholic Democratic state. If I do give you pause, hopefully with coffee in hand, consider the most glaring, obvious question anyone questioning Joseph Smith and the Mormon Church can ask. Why can't even one of the approximately thirty cities mentioned in the *Book of Mormon* be geographically placed in the Americas? We know where the Bible cities of Jerusalem and Bethlehem are located, but where are the *Book of Mormon* cities of Zerehemla and Bountiful? The answer smacks the giant Mormon Church like David's rock whacked Goliath. It's a cult killer.

Before my ex-communication in 1977, I had a lengthy phone conversation with Mark Cannon. He was concerned about my Church status because I had discovered the *Book of Abraham* had been discredited and stopped attending Church regularly. I told him original papyri discovered in the 1960s proved Joseph Smith had created, not translated, the script found in the *Pearl of Great Price's Book of Abraham*. As I explained my doubts about the Church, Mr. Cannon argued that I should ignore problems with the *Book of Abraham* and focus my faith on the *Book of Mormon*. This Mormon literary centerpiece was the topic of his Doctorial Thesis at Harvard and, like his Grandfather, Apostle George Q. Cannon, before him, he defended the book admirably and believed it adamantly.

Following that discussion over three decades ago, I remember thinking it interesting and confusing that Mr. Cannon could dismiss one of our four Standard Works of scripture and encourage me to keep faith in another. Should I continue following the teachings of Joseph Smith, the part time prophet? The last time we spoke, Mark still believed in the Mormon's flagship publication and directed me to the Church's premier apologist group, The Foundation for Ancient Research and Mormon Studies (FARMS). After reviewing a sample of their research material in disbelief, I now think of them as the Mormon FARMS boys. These men should be loading hay on a wagon, picking straw from their teeth and slopping the hogs.

Ending a few years of openness about history and doctrine—during Leonard J. Arrington's late twentieth century tenure as Church Historian—Mormon taskmasters formed the wagon train into a tight circle, as wheels began to splinter and fall off. Seeing their superiority threatened, Church leaders turned to the FARMS boys to conjure meaningless arguments over ancient Greek words or linguistic phraseology in an idiotic attempt to deflect attention from the obvious. Mitt, watching these paid polemicists defend the preposterous from well-meaning and well-informed researchers and historians insults the intelligence and offends the sensibilities of thinking people.

Few quotes about the *Book of Mormon* are more correct and humorous than those by Orson Pratt and Mark Twain. In 1851, Apostle Orson Pratt stated the *Book of Mormon* "must be either true or false. If true, it is one of the most important messages ever sent from God … if false it is one of the most cunning, wicked, bold, deep laid impositions ever palmed upon the earth." I assume not referring to the Mormon missionaries, Mark Twain once said a lie can be half way around the world before the truth can get its boots on. Twain read the *Book of Mormon* and observed it "seems to be merely prosy detail of imaginary history, with the Old Testament for a model; followed by a tedious plagiarism of the New Testament." Twain also described the *Book of Mormon* as chloroform in print. He observed the book was rather stupid, tiresome to read, and said Joseph Smith stopped just when he was "in danger of becoming interesting." A plain English version of *Book of Mormon* mumbo-jumbo is now available on the internet. How funny is that, Mitt? Well, it amused me.

Still, Church leaders and members exhibit zero tolerance for having any of their revered symbols or haughty claims questioned or ridiculed, particularly the *Book of Mormon.* Instead of admitting it's just a nineteenth century work of fiction; the General Authorities palm off the *Book of Mormon* as a legitimate one thousand year history of an expansive American culture. If they could review the literature today, I believe both your ancestors, Orson and Parley Pratt, would discount this work as the most perfect book on earth. Orson would agree with Mark Twain's conclusions and sadly admit the *Book of Mormon* meets his own false description stated above—it's a cunning, wicked, bold deception. Mitt, I woke up from the chloroform, escaped the bold deception and became an open critic of our strange heritage, which makes me as popular as a wasp at a Mormon wedding reception.

You and I were taught that the Church of Jesus Christ of Latter Day Saints would stand or fall on the validity of the *Book of Mormon*—this "second witness to Jesus Christ." The Church still claims it verifies Jesus came to the Americas after his resurrection to visit his "other sheep." At the 2007 spring conference, President Hinckley expressed frustration that mankind won't accept the *Book of Mormon* as proof Jesus appeared on these continents. "This is all recorded in detail in the *Book of Mormon*," Hinckley declared. He added, "I would think that every Christian would welcome this second witness of the reality of Jesus Christ. Strangely, they do not." Of course they don't, Mitt. The *Book of Mormon* is obviously a nineteenth century fictional creation. How strange, at this juncture, if Christians did embrace this book of bunkum and flock to the Mormon Church.

Church members are assured science has proved the *Book of Mormon* true, but it has proved the Book—and the Mormon Church—untrue. Unlike false prophets, archeology never lies, and cultures leave written records. The Bible civilizations are well attested in history and archeology, while *Book of Mormon* people and places are merely the product of Joseph Smith's imagination. The text is heavily laden with nineteenth century revival literature which Smith had studied and preached since his teens. The only truth about the *Book of Mormon* is nobody wanted to buy the original manuscript when Joseph Smith tried to sell it for eight grand.

Undaunted, the Church desperately clings to this work of nineteenth century fiction. In 1984, President Ezra Taft Benson said, "We do not have to prove the *Book of Mormon* is true. The book is its own proof. All we need to do is read it and declare it! The *Book of Mormon* is not on trial." In truth, the book was scrutinized closely by both historians and scientists in recent decades and found guilty of fraud. Now, it's time to dump it in the dust bin of history, along with the *Doctrine and Covenants* and *Pearl of Great Price*. Begin the process by allowing Biblical scholars to show you that Smith plagiarized large sections of the 1769 *King James Bible* into the *Book of Mormon*, word for word—along with its previous translation errors.

Neither was the *Book of Mormon* recently discredited. It was never accredited. Non-Mormon historians and scholars view the *Book of Mormon* as scarcely worthy of criticism or remark. No scholars or scientists outside the church ever took the book seriously, and many LDS scholars, scientists and historians have now lost their testimony in the face of overwhelming evidence. Some were punished when they spoke up too loudly. Even B.H. Roberts, a leading early twentieth century Mormon historian—and one of the church's greatest historical defenders—lost faith in the *Book of Mormon* at the end of his life. Roberts observed that two *Book of Mormon* anti-Christs, Sherem and Kohihor, were strikingly similar even though they lived 400 years apart and were recorded by Nephi and Mormon at different times.

Mitt, Roberts concluded those *Book of Mormon* bad boys and their followers were "all of one breed and brand; so nearly alike that one mind is the author of them, and that a young and undeveloped but piously inclined mind. The evidence I sorrowfully submit, points to Joseph Smith as the Creator." With reluctant resignation, B. H. Roberts documented examples of how Joseph Smith twisted biblical quotes and fictional characters together with nineteenth century Protestantism and occultism, all geared to play on our emotions and longings. The FARMS boys tried without success to mow down B.H. Roberts's final conclusions about the *Book of Mormon*.

After spending decades searching for evidence of the great *Book of Mormon* civilization, Thomas Ferguson, founder of the New World Archeological Foundation at BYU, also lost faith in the book. Fully expecting success, he led several expeditions throughout the Americas in the mid-twentieth century. Prior to his death in 1983, having found no cultural or architectural evidence in Mesoamerica or any corner of the American continents, Ferguson admitted there was nothing to be found. Heartbroken, he sadly accepted that the *Book of Mormon* great civilization in America never existed. Insights and findings presented by men like Roberts and Ferguson are ignored or undermined by the unenlightened Church intelligentsia today. Instead, Church leaders embrace the babbling by BYU-based FARMS boys parading as scholars in bib overalls.

In a 1976 letter, Ferguson explained he decided to keep quiet rather than destroy the faith of Mormons because he felt the "Myth Fraternity," the term he coined, was like a "placebo in medicine," that does no harm and can do some good—so enjoy! Although Ferguson's conclusion is understandable, he was wrong to decide it acceptable for our people to remain comfortable and smiling in smug ignorance. Speaking of the Church, an ex-member and returned missionary said in the 2007 PBS Mormon documentary, "Even if it's one of the greatest inventions of all time, it's still an invention." Mitt, clear your head of this fantasy so you and your team can expose the pseudo-scientist Mormon apologists masquerading as historians, linguists, archeologists, anthropologists and physicists. Tell devout members to stop listening to their Living Prophet's every utterance and accepting false assurances that the Mormon Myth machine is hitting on all cylinders.

Throughout the late twentieth century, Mormon propaganda led members to believe the Smithsonian Institute used the *Book of Mormon* to help find ruins from antiquity in the Americas. Mitt, tell out pioneer families there is no truth to this Mormon story. The Smithsonian Institute specifically stated it never used the *Book of Mormon* to search for any evidences of Mormon activities in Mesoamerica. *Book of Mormon* descriptions are too vague to help anyone find anything. *Smithsonian Magazine* wrote recently about Pompeii's ruins and treasures in the old world, and it reported about Fremont Indian sites on the Wilcox ranch in Utah, real people of early America. Concurrently, thanks to "Kennewick man," a new burst of scholarship occurred about ancient locations all over the Americas. The American continent is a treasure trove of historic antiquities, but none of it supports anything in the Mormon Bible. Somehow, thirty *Book of Mormon* cities have mysteriously disappeared into the ethers.

Mitt, tell our people no evidence exists outside the *Book of Mormon* that Jesus Christ visited either North or South America before or after his resurrection. There are only the accounts from *Book of Mormon* prophets, who themselves only exist in a shadow reality created by Joseph Smith. Conversely, biblical faith in Jesus can be built on a durable foundation of real history. In addition to the Biblical record, independent secular corroboration verifies both the Bible cities and Jesus existed. Many old world cities are still inhabited, and archeologists have located the ruins of others. Undeterred by reality, however, Mormons aggressively push their delusions on humanity.

Science systematically dismantling the *Book of Mormon* in recent years, and it crumbled as a book of anything remotely resembling real history. Mitt, you have more business experience than most former Presidents. Even if it requires layoffs at Church headquarters, won't you agree the *Book of Mormon* presents quality control issues, creating the need for a reorganization plan and internal restructuring? Tell Church leaders to halt production, recall the missionaries and stop their public relations pressroom from creating more propaganda to perpetuate the deception. Church members and prospective converts need to know it's an empty promise when Moroni assures readers the Mormon Holy Ghost (or Casper the Friendly Ghost) will manifest the veracity of the *Book of Mormon* to sincere truth seekers with a burning sensation in their bosom. That's just heartburn brought on by eating junk food to alleviate the monotony of reading the boring book.

Natural for Joseph Smith to have Moroni, his fictitious trumpeter, challenge *Book of Mormon* readers to approach the work emotionally, "with real intent," so they would learn the "truth of it" (Moroni 10.4). The trust-your-heart concept came from nineteenth century revival Protestantism, which played to emotionalism over intellectualism and found its way into Moroni's promise via Joseph Smith. *Proverbs* tells us, "The heart is deceitful above all things," and the *Gospel of John* says, "He who trusts his own heart is a fool." Mitt, now may seem an inopportune time, but finally and officially condemn the nonsensical teachings in the *Book of Mormon*. Unless Church leaders produce a shred of hard evidence, it's no longer acceptable for missionaries to tell people to merely trust their hearts about this purported second witness to Jesus Christ.

One piece of evidence would immediately change my attitude about the *Book of Mormon* and the Church. Seeing the Three Nephites would be a nice touch of realism. I'll beg for rebaptism if those old-timers, promised to live until Jesus returned, can be delivered to a press conference and share their 2000 year adventure. It would be righteous at last to see those ancient dudes we've read about since childhood. A quick bath, some Church talking points, and those fellows would be as valuable as the original gold plates. One internet wag suggested the Mormons hire celebrity bounty hunter Dog Chapman to bring them in.

Unbiased scholars know the greatest influence on the *Book of Mormon* was the *Old* and *New Testament*, including the idea for the Three Nephites. Yet, much of the *Old* and all the *New Testament* weren't written until hundreds of years after Lehi and his family miraculously left Jerusalem for America. It's truly a miracle they had these yet-to-be-written records to bring with them on their Jules Verne adventure in a wooden submarine. Even more miraculous because there wasn't enough wood in the Sinai desert to build an outhouse.

If that's not miraculous enough, it's a "marvelous work and a wonder" that Nephi's people possessed the *King James Bible* for direct quotes, parables and references to be recorded on gold plates Joseph Smith later found hidden in a hill guarded by angels. Imagine, a group of ocean traveling Jews arriving in America six hundred years BC who knew little about ancient Jewish traditions and astonishingly practiced a form of early nineteenth century New England Christianity. Mitt, that Church leaders and members remain mesmerized by this stuff completely blows my mind. When will you and other Mormon leaders accept the fact that Joseph Smith pieced and pasted together a new American Bible, which when objectively analyzed looks as hapless as Mr. Potato Head?

Historians know the *Book of Mormon* is a product of early nineteenth century New England. Scholarship reveals Joseph Smith put into it references to numerous issues discussed in upstate New York during the 1820's. Hard to believe contemporary religious controversies about infant baptism, the fall of man, repentance, atonement, fasting, the resurrection and other religious and civic issues were of great concern to Mesoamerican Jewish refuges. Thoughtful Mormons should question why the *Book of Mormon* discusses all these issues and says nothing about the plurality of Gods, the potential for men to become polygamist Gods, baptism of the dead or eternal marriages. Mitt, the answer is plain and simple. To serve his desires and maintain control, Joseph Smith created his theology as he went along.

A popular book published in 1823, *View of the Hebrews* inspired the Hebrew origins of the initial migration described in the *Book of Mormon*. Important to note that one hundred years ago, some Mormon leaders were still pointing to *View of the Hebrews* as strong evidence the *Book of Mormon* was true. The Church is quiet now the book has been proved wrong and merely one of Smith's plagiarism sources. Mormon scholar and hero Grant Palmer, disfellowshipped from the Church for writing the truth in his book, *An Insider's view of Mormon Origins*, describes how numerous motifs, descriptions and terminologies from E.T.A. Hoffman's book, *The gold Pot*, also found their way into Smith's writings. Prior to his official punished by the Church, Palmer was heckled at one of his book signings by bulldog Mormon apologist, Lou Midgley.

As further proof the *Book of Mormon* is a product of Joseph Smith's imagination, it speaks of cows, horses, elephants, chariots, steel, silk and linen, wheat, barley and gold and silver coins. In reality, none of these existed anywhere in the Americas before the Spaniards came. Metallurgy was unknown to Mesoamericans, and there were no animals to pull chariots or wheels to roll them into battle. No cows mooed in the fields, no horses dumped on the roads and no trumpeting elephant's lifted their voices across rivers. Revealing how desperate Church defenders have become, a FARMS affiliated Mormon anthropologist, John L. Sorenson, suggests Nephite chariots were pulled by deer or pigs. Behold Mormon, the great sword-welding Nephite warrior, standing stately in his mighty chariot and charging into battle against the evil Lamanites, pulled by a squealing pig.

Mitt, isn't it an "elephant in the room" for the LDS Church that there were no elephants in Mesoamerica, yet they somehow lumbered into the most perfect book on earth? The second Bible is the bread and butter of the LDS church, but there was no wheat or cows living in the Americas and no traditional farms. Unashamed, the FARMS boys persist in their defense of the Book of Mormon as real history. Anyone care for some cornbread and water before the hunting party heads out to look for a *Book of Mormon* city?

Laughably, the *Book of Mormon* is composed of various American colonizers called "Ites." There were the Jarodites, Mulakites, Nephites, Lamanites, Jacobites, Josephites, Zoromites, Lemulites and Ismaelites, and not one mention of "ites" that really existed in early America—termites and trilobites. The *Bible*'s "ites," like Midianites and Israelites fed Joseph Smith's fertile imagination and religious organizations called "ites" popped up like whack-a-moles in Joseph Smith's landscape. *The Book of Mormon* is an amalgamation of ideas meshed from Antebellum America, so it made sense for Joseph Smith to stuff his ludicrous creation with an array of "ites."

When reading the *Book of Mormon*, it's odd for thinking non-Mormons to encounter all those "ites." However, it's really quite logical when considered in context of early nineteenth century America. The Mormonism movement—also dubbed Mormonites—was just one of many new religions to sprout and bloom in upper state New York during the revivalist period. Intense religious activity, including George Miller's Shakers, caused the region to become known as the Burned-over District. Clearly influenced by the general milieu of his day, Mormonism's founding prophet constructed and reconstructed his private version of heaven and earth. Several groups in the region were then called "ites," and Joseph Smith cleverly used their example to create his primitive anthropology.

One revivalist group, called the Campbellites, saw themselves as a restoration movement, and reinvented Christianity under the leadership of Alexander Campbell and Sidney Rigdon. After Parley P. Pratt joined the new Mormon Church in 1830, he converted Rigdon, and they immediately raided Campbell's flock, giving the Mormonite movement its biggest initial boost. Jacob Cochran, whose followers became known as the Cochranites, developed a cult of personality and assembled a harem in early nineteenth century New England. When convicted on various sex charges and sent to prison, Brigham Young and Orson Pratt converted Cochran's flock and, in 1832, brought them to Kirkland, Ohio, along with their belief in "spiritual wifery." The foundation for Mormon polygamy, Joseph Smith secretly began practicing it and eventually shared it with trusted followers.

Intrigued with the idea of spiritual wives, as early as 1833 Joseph Smith secretly got involved with young Fanny Alger. Their relationship eventually became widely known and, when he found out about it, Oliver Cowdrey called it a "nasty, filthy affair." When Emma Smith discovered Joseph with Fanny and reacted violently, the Prophet expressed his remorse to both her and Oliver, but the damage was done. His empire again threatened, Smith quieted the flock and reasserted his authority by doing what worked in the past—he made a bold announcement. He gave his First Vision another major revision—this time to include Jesus and God the Father as two separate beings.

Just when it couldn't get any stranger, it did. Within two decades of publication, all eleven *Book of Mormon* witnesses lost faith in Joseph Smith and were excommunicated. Some became followers of another self proclaimed prophet, James J. Strang (Strangites), a natural transition for a collection of credulous, fanatical, unstable characters generally filled with superstition. They all believed in magic, and many had their own peep stones. Nearly all claimed "second sight" abilities, claimed their own visions, and admitted they only saw Joseph Smith's gold plates with their "spiritual eye." Of course, Joseph Smith claimed viewing the plates with the naked eye meant death.

The Church places great emphasis on the *Book of Mormon* witnesses, and we were taught that none ever refuted his claim to have viewed the gold plates. However, Joseph Smith's years of cumulative misdeeds caused the Great Apostasy of 1837–38 in Kirkland, when several powerful Mormon leaders and their families left the church. The three main witnesses to the *Book of Mormon*, Martin Harris, Oliver Cowdrey and David Whitmore, condemned Smith's un-prophet-like activities and numerous other prominent members lost faith in him as a prophet and respect for him as a man. Yet, I was told repeatedly during my youth that none of the Book of Mormon witnesses ever denied their testimony, wavered or changed their stories.

In his book, *Losing a Lost Tribe*, scientist and former Mormon Bishop Simon Southerton strips the *Book of Mormon* down to its genes. His work, for which he was excommunicated, reinforces what archeologists and anthropologists have known for decades—DNA studies prove Native Americans are descended from Asians, as are the island-hopping people of the Pacific, who are genealogical heirs of Southeast Asia populations. Mitt, the General Authorities should be honest and tell the Indian and Pacific Island Church members the truth about their heritage. Rather than building more new Mormon Temples in places like Guatemala, dedicated to the "Lamanite people," tell the Church to release Native American Mormons from the deception.

I believe it immoral for Church leaders to send naïve kids to proselyte Native Americans and Pacific Islanders with the discredited claim that they are of Jewish descent. A spiritual identity crisis awaits those who join the Church and discover the truth after baptism. The Mormon Church owes these brothers and sisters an apology and some long overdue honesty. Instead, the Church's missionary program has been changed to de-emphasize doctrine and play even more on peoples' emotions. Missionaries skip doctrinal detail and push prospects to seek Moroni's heartburn and quickly be baptized. Only after baptism are Native American converts sent to new member classes and eventually informed the Mormon Gods cursed them with dark skin.

Mitt, it is unconscionable and absurd for the Church to perpetuate the myth that Native Americans and Islanders are descendents of a cursed people. The *Book of Mormon* states repeatedly that the Lamanites were once a "white and exceedingly fair and beautiful" people who became "a dark, a filthy, and a loathsome people." Tell these trusting, misguided members there is no Lamanite curse making them historically evil or inferior because of their skin color. The real God is not tribal, vindictive, and didn't create an earthly caste system based on anthropology. He created and loves equally all his human children. The Church should discontinue its juvenile pageantries depicting the good Nephites in *Book of Mormon* battles against bad Lamanites.

The Mormon Church owes a formal apology for its role in the multi-generational cultural genocide of Native Americans, known as the Indian Placement Program. Mormons participated heavily in this program, which took Indian children from their families and placed them in Mormon homes. In the Mormon fantasy world, these children could magically become white and delightsome, and culturally correct by joining the LDS Church. Accounts by President Spencer W, Kimball and other Mormon leaders claim Indian children living with Mormon families actually started to turn white—reminiscent of Michael Jackson. An attractive Native American girl somewhat bitterly told me after a BYU religion class that she hoped someday to become white and beautiful. Though more mature than most students following my military experience, still I was too young, uninformed and unsophisticated to say anything meaningful that day. Hopefully, she discovered the truth and didn't spend her life carrying that weighty stigmatization around her neck like an albatross.

In 1981, without apology or explanation, the LDS Church quietly and conveniently altered the *Book of Mormon*'s white and delightsome terms, deleting the racial word "white" and replacing it with the word "pure." It was a reasonable organizational step in the ongoing Mormon program to recreate its past amid growing criticism, however, it's heart wrenching to watch Mormons treat there fellowmen so painfully in the name of their Gods and never feel a need to apologize or ask forgiveness. Then again, if the young Native American BYU student remained a devout Mormon throughout her life, maybe she's evolved into a Caucasian by now. If so, Mormon leaders should invite her to that press conference with the Three Nephites. The missionaries could convert some big name anthropologist in no time.

The future is blind, but I'm confident no prominent anthropologist will convert to Mormonism, and no credible linguist will seek baptism into the LDS Church, either. Language experts understand that it would be impossible, given the complexity and diversity of Native American languages—some 1500 were spoken by new world tribes—for them to evolve from Hebrew or "Reformed Egyptian" in the short historical period between the *Book of Mormon* civilization and the arrival of the European explorers and immigrants. Ludicrous to entertain the possibility not to mention there was never a language known as "Reformed Egyptian." It was another Joseph Smith creation.

Expanding on the initial deception about the origins of Native Americans, Mormon missionaries told Pacific Islanders they were also descendants of the *Book of Mormon* civilization. Anthropologists know these people descend from Southeast Asians and their languages have their own unique history. Their dialects are part of the Austrones linguistic family, traced back to Taiwan 5,000 years ago. Brigham Young was several years late in 1858, when he gave Prophetic Approval to the Mormon doctrine that the pacific islanders are from the house of Israel, of the seed of Abraham. Young George Q. Cannon and his missionary companions had already converted thousands of Sandwich Islands (Hawaii) natives when they preached this prattle in the early 1850's.

George Q. Cannon, the nephew of future Mormon President John Taylor, concocted the story that Pacific islanders were descendants of the *Book of Mormon* people. Elder Cannon and his missionary companions landed on this sales pitch after their efforts to convert British and Portuguese residents produced few successes. George Q. Cannon later became an Apostle, no surprise, and spent considerable time writing whitewashed, faith promoting Mormon literature devoid of empirical and historical analysis or perspective. Cannon had substantial influence on the Church's ongoing practice of directing members to avoid factual material and rely on their emotions to build and sustain faith.

Mitt, how can thinking Mormons still believe hundreds of thousands of *Book of Mormon* peoples, with their languages, great cities, huge armies, steel swords, wheeled chariots, agriculture and metallurgy simply vanished without a trace, along with their genes. Since thousands of warriors were supposedly slaughtered in a great battle at the Hill Comorah, suggest the Church excavate and search for artifacts so archeology can prove the *Book of Mormon* true. Clear it with Salt Lake City, and I'll grab my shovel and join the Mormon's Big Dig in New York!

Good to find a warrior's sword or a chariot wheel in the Hill Comorah excavation, but a Nephite coin would be especially invaluable to those who defend the *Book of Mormon* as real history and Christian scripture. Mitt, no artifacts will ever be found at Comorah or anywhere else in America because, while the Bible's peoples and prophets were real, the *Book of Mormon* peoples and prophets are fiction. Despite not a smidgen of evidence to support it and overwhelming evidence to refute its authenticity, devout Mormons accept their new Bible without question. Blindly, members believe the *Book of Mormon* prophets were real men and search their words for spiritual guidance more frequently than they reference Bible prophets.

We were taught as children that there is only one Hill Comorah, but, to save the *Book of Mormon* as real history, desperate Mormon apologists recently manufactured the theory that there were "two Comorahs." Contradicting everything in both Joseph Smith's teachings and the *Book of Mormon*, this second Hill Comorah supposedly now exists in some isolated, undiscovered location in the Americas. If the Church discovers it soon, faithful Mormons can swarm there to watch another annual pageant where play actors pretend to be Nephites and Lamanites and slaughter each other by the tens of thousands.

Like linguists and anthropologists, odds are no credible mathematicians will convert to Mormonism any time soon. Based on all known variables, it's not possible for Lehi's small family to have reproduced as quickly as the *Book of Mormon's* endless battles required. They could not have created a population base large enough to feed and sustain the constant wars and high casualty rates specifically described during that 1000 year period—unless they were really bloodthirsty rabbits who copulated like bunnies. Mitt, tell our pioneer families that Lehi and his offspring may have been bloodthirsty, but they were not bunny rabbits battling from chariots pulled by squealing pigs. Awaken millions of well-meaning souls from their strange *Book of Mormon* pipedream, give them a firm hand, and pull them out of their religious rabbit hole and back into the real world.

12

The Pearl of Great Price

While the *Book of Mormon* gave us bloodthirsty rabbit warriors and a "dark and loathsome people"—who were evil and deserved to be killed, the *Pearl of Great Price* casts Mormon Gods as even more bigoted. Joseph Smith used this large slice of boloney to give Mormonism the Curse of Cain belief. Mitt, do you really expect people to believe that in 1978 Mormon Gods relented to prayer pressure from Apostles in the Salt Lake Temple beseeching them to change their ways and lift this curse on Negroes? Well, sensible people will not accept it. When intellectually and spiritually blinded men and women pursue causes founded on falsehoods, the result will be ignorance and prejudice. Enlightened individuals know ignorance isn't bliss and God isn't prejudiced.

Voltaire warned that prejudice is the reason of fools, but it was a cornerstone of Mormon doctrine until changed only three decades ago. Mormons weren't the only religious group to hide behind the *Old Testament* curse as a cover for blatant racial bigotry. Joseph Smith simply institutionalized it in Mormon scripture, and the LDS Church held racial beliefs longer and more doggedly than most other sects. Consequently, the Church didn't officially change the doctrine until more than a decade after the great 1960s civil rights battles were fought and won. Finally, responding to intense social pressure on the LDS Church and State of Utah from various groups and organizations outside, the Mormon Gods revealed that Negroes can hold the Priesthood and share all rights and opportunities afforded other Church members. Mormon Gods recanted their racism, but Mormon General Authorities refuse to offer an apology.

Mitt, you've stated you consider yourself colorblind and don't distinguish people on race, ethnicity or faith. Based on my experience in the Mormon Church, I don't believe it's possible for any member to have evolved that far. As a boy, I felt innate racism, heard the acidic comments and witnessed the air of superiority Mormon adults held toward Negroes because of our Curse of Cain belief. When we moved to Las Vegas and I played sports with black teenagers, quickly I knew no curse existed. I knew skin shade is no more significant than eye color or the size of my big toe, yet childhood programming on race doggedly lingered. So it was refreshing, yet odd—considering the Church still discourages interracial marriages—to hear President Hinckley tell a recent Church conference that those who hold racial prejudices cannot call themselves disciples of Christ.

President Hinckley's proclamation must exclude all former Mormon Prophets, Apostles and Church members who died before 1978 from being Christ's true disciples. Brigham Young denied the holy priesthoods to all people of black African descent in 1852, and that LDS Church policy persisted for 126 years. Then, in a conversation with Horace Greeley in 1859, Young went beyond his 1852 announcement. Speaking of slavery, Brigham Young told Greeley, "We consider it a divine institution and not to be abolished until the curse on Ham shall have been removed from his descendants." Mitt, ask Church leaders whether the curse is permanently removed or devout Mormons will own slaves in the Celestial Kingdom.

As you know, this stinking racial garbage came from the *Book of Abraham* in the *Pearl of Great Price*, which has been exposed as a piece of fiction from the mind of Joseph Smith. For forty years, the Church has been remarkably successful at keeping vital information about the fall of the *Book of Abraham* from the Mormon faithful. Members don't know that once the Rosetta stone was discovered in the nineteenth century, Joseph Smith's ability to translate the Egyptian language became suspect at best. However, it was a real eureka moment, and one might say a blessing, when it was discovered the original Papyri that Smith used to create the *Book of Abraham* wasn't destroyed in the great Chicago fire as theorized. The greatest prophet since Moses was irrefutably finished forever as an oracle of the Christian God, except in The Church of Jesus Christ of Latter day Saints.

After the papyri was found in the New York Metropolitan Museum of Art and later gifted to the Church in 1967, Mormon leaders should have immediately reported the truth to members. Egyptologists, including a number of LDS members, translated the texts and found them to be pagan funeral rituals for a man named "Hor." They date to about 100 A.D. and bear no resemblance to Smith's self-serving concoctions in Mormon scripture. The Curse of Cain belief, which blocked African-Americans and blacks around the world from the Mormon Priesthood and Temple activities, was just one commonly accepted early nineteenth century folklore that found its way into Mormonism. Mitt, our people deserve to know the *Pearl of Great Price*, this book of purportedly Holy Scripture, has nothing more to do with Moses or Father Abraham than the Queen of Sheba.

The *Book of Moses* (7.22) says, "The seed of Cain were black and had not place among them," and the *Book of Abraham* (1.21) states that the Pharaoh was a descendant of Ham and "of the lineage by which he could not have the right of Priesthood." Obvious and atrocious racism coming from an uneducated man—or stuttering, befuddled Gods. Smith fictitious creations easily fooled our trusting ancestors because racism was deeply embedded in the popular thought of the day, and led some Mormons to claim black people represented the Devil's presence on earth. I was taught that Negroes were fence sitters cursed in the pre-existence for being unable to decide between the plans presented by Lucifer and Jesus. It's surprising that I didn't turned black in recent years. Brigham Young said, "But let them apostatize, and they will become gray haired, wrinkled and black, just like the Devil."

Today's residual racism, along with Mormons' unquestioning loyalty, allows members to accept the Church's decision to discontinue the policy as having come from heaven, yet still believe that it somehow remains part of their God's universal plan for humanity. It's intriguing to me that five or ten thousand African-Americans, including entertainer Gladys Knight, have joined the Mormon Church since the racist Mormon Gods repented. When missionaries tell black converts about "the white boy, a dead angel and some gold plates," as a women on PBS described her experience, they never tell the whole truth about Mormon doctrine, and black converts don't take time to research and understand the depth and breadth of racism in Mormon history. Many members of Genesis Group, the premier organization of black Mormons, would leave the church if they read Apostle Mark E. Peterson's 1954 racial diatribe. Peterson's harangue to LDS religion teachers epitomized the importance of institutionalized racism in the Mormon Church from its earliest days.

Apostle Peterson restated the old racist Jim Crow "one drop rule" used to deny Negroes the Mormon Priesthood—and blamed it on them. In part, Peterson declared "the Negro in the preexistence lived the type of life which justified the Lord sending him to earth in the lineage of Cain with a dark skin." Peterson went on to say that if Mormons intermarried with Negroes, their children would "all be cursed as to the Priesthood because there would be a drop of Negro blood in them." However, to show his magnanimous side, Brother Peterson added that he "would be willing to let every Negro drive a Cadillac, if they could afford one."

Though only-nine-years old when Peterson gave his instructions to religion teachers, I vividly remember my teenage aunt complaining that she couldn't go out with a boy she liked from Filmore, Utah because the word on the street was he had at least one drop of Negro blood. Though later ordered never to bring up religion around her again, I recently summoned the courage to question my aunt about that long ago event. She said ultimately, because he was fair skinned, blond and apparently had very little Negro blood, the Church allowed him "to do what he needed to do," which meant he was ordained to the Priesthood, allowed to do his Temple Work and didn't have to leave Utah in search of inclusion.

The Priesthood Authority Apostle Peterson addressed is a Mormon doctrine never mentioned in the *Book of Mormon* or discussed by Christ's Apostles in the *New Testament* Gospels. Scholars believe the idea to introduce this previously unsung *Old Testament* practice into the Mormon Church originated in the mind of Sidney Rigdon, the bright, highly educated former Campbellite who often influenced Joseph Smith's decisions during the 1830s. Records reveal the Priesthood was added to Church doctrine after years of baptizing converts without it, or even recording who had been saved. Mitt, Apostle Parley P. Pratt and uncountable others were baptized years before there was any mention of John the Baptist or Peter, James and John descending from Heaven to restore the Aaronic or Melchesidec Priesthoods to Joseph Smith and Oliver Cowdrey.

According to Oliver Cowdrey, the "Angel of God" that originally visited them was not identified as John the Baptist until Joseph Smith's calling as a prophet was challenged years later. No one knows for sure when Peter, James and John supposedly dropped in to ordain the boys to the Melchesidec Priesthood. Mormon Historian B.H. Roberts stated, "There is no definite account of the event in the history of the Prophet Joseph Smith or for that matter, in any of the Church annals." Mormon educator and author, Grant Palmer, described how the concept of Priesthood came into the Church by degrees, with each account becoming "more detailed and more miraculous."

Ignoring historical evidence, two statues at Salt Lake City's Temple Square pinpoint the month and year these miraculous Priesthood events occurred. One huge bronze statue depicts John the Baptist laying his hands on the heads of Smith and Cowdrey to bestow the Aaronic Priesthood, and another shows Peter, James and John ordaining them to the Melchesidec Priesthood. Inscriptions on these statues state both events occurred in May, 1829, a year before the Mormon Church was founded. If these priesthood events happened as the Church says, one could expect to find them recorded in the original *Book of Commandants*, predecessor to the *Doctrine and Covenants*. The *Book of Commandments*, which covers Mormon prophetic events during the early 1930s, contains nothing about either order of Priesthood.

Mitt, when you heard the news the Church changed its doctrine to allow Negroes to hold the Priesthood; you said you were so elated and excited that you pulled your car into a parking lot to recover. My experience was different. I had been excommunicated from the Church for about a year, and my Aunt said, "Now that Negroes can hold the Priesthood, you can come back."—as if that were the only issue involved in my decision to leave, and the policy change made everything hunky dory. Blacks being unable to hold the Priesthood was a major factor in my decision not to "repent" and avoid excommunication, but it was only part of a complex decision. Understandably, the Church's belated policy reversal was as pleasing to you as me, but while you were elated, the timing only increased my cynicism.

Mitt, as it did with Joseph Smith's First Vision, the Church added and altered revelations concerning the Priesthoods to deceive later generations about their origin and divinity. Joseph Smith and other early Mormons embraced and incorporated numerous *Old Testament* practices into their growing masterpiece of confusion, many of which were paternalistic, vindictive and unforgiving. The Priesthood certainly has served Mormon men well. A ruthless, sectarian tribal mentality persists behind Mormonism's *Old Testament* priesthoods, nurtured from inception by Joseph Smith, Brigham Young and other leaders. Mormon men became Gods-in-waiting to be admired and obeyed as such by their wives and children, and that foundational precedent still dominates the LDS Church's social structure today.

My bright, sensitive young son won't be programmed to believe that he is somehow superior to his sister because he will someday be ordained to hold holy ancient Priesthood titles, while she will only be an MIA Maid or Laurel Girl. My children will be taught the truth about the holy Mormon Priesthoods. Joseph Smith introduced the priesthood concept into the Mormon Church years after its formation to consolidate and increase power over his followers. Brigham Young later used the Priesthood in Utah to create a nineteenth Century theocratic kingdom filled with repression, darkness and cruelty. Today, Mormon men are told to honor their Priesthood so they can become Gods, and women are instructed to follow Priesthood guidance as their only recourse for celestial exaltation.

Mitt, Mormon children of pioneer descent should be reared to respect their heritage and proud of their brave ancestors who helped settle the American west, but they should be informed about what really happened. Rejected by the Methodists for a leadership position in the late 1820's, Joseph Smith started his own church and condemned all the others. They should understand that with the help of Sidney Rigdon, Smith plagiarized an obscure *Old Testament* priesthood structure to further consolidate his power and authority. Let our children know that after the Masons showed the door to Joseph Smith, he furthered his megalomania by forming more secret societies and introducing the temple ceremonies under these new priesthoods. Equally important, inform Mormon children the U.S. Constitution must never be undermined or destroyed by the Mormon Church's priesthood holders in a bogus guise to save it.

Besides the issues of curses and priesthood, additional *Pearl of Great Price* teachings have Mormon apologists and revisionists playing checkers while genuine scholars and scientists play chess. The latter balance their belief in God with an understanding of Einstein's theories, quantum mechanics and string theory. Einstein's fingerprints are all over today's technological advances, but Mormons remain marooned in a Newtonian/Copernican universe, where a polygamist God dwells on a really big planet circling a star called Kolob, which is supposedly nearest to the thrown of God.

Einstein was only twenty-two years old when he philosophized that a foolish faith in authority is the worst enemy of truth. However, it's human nature to become comfortably ensconced in old ideas and avoid the discomfort of changing thought patterns. Mormons behave typically when they choose to remain intellectual and spiritual couch potatoes and believe their Heavenly Father orbits Kolob in a nineteenth century constellation created by Joseph Smith. When reading the *Pearl of Great Price*, Mormons should be startled to see how much Father Abraham, during his life in ancient times, knew about nineteenth century physics. Equally disconcerting, Mitt, Mormon Gods knew nothing about twentieth century astrophysics when they coached Joseph Smith on the eternal nature of the universe.

In Mormon scripture, God's time and Joseph Smith's cosmology conformed to the laws of Galilean relativity and Newtonian mechanics. A relic, the *Book of Abraham* is full of common astronomical words and phrases from Joseph Smith's era. Unfortunately for the LDS Church, twentieth century discoveries superseded the limited nineteenth century theories that nourished the Prophet Joseph's scientifically primitive teachings. Einstein's theories dethroned Newtonian physics and established a vastly more complex universe than the one Joseph Smith plagiarized from Scottish theologian Thomas Dick's 1929 publication, *Philosophy of a Future State*. Mormon apologists argue the points, but it's hard to believe Joseph Smith didn't borrow Thomas Dick's notions that matter is eternal and indestructible, and our universe was peopled by intelligences that had the possibility of eternal progression. Snippets from Thomas Taylor's work, *The Six Books of Pro-*

clus on the Theology of Plato, are sprinkled liberally throughout Smith's writings as well. In retrospect, Joseph Smith's nineteenth century cosmology is no more useful in understanding our universe than nineteenth century phrenology is in understanding our brain.

Again making odds, there's not much chance Mormon missionaries will convert any astrophysicists with their emotional bleatings and primitive stories. These intelligent, highly educated men and women know that human reality exists in a complex universe. Scientifically trained individuals can't be converted to Mormonism with mystical tales about Gods (once just guys like us) who live on a Newtonian planet with the exalted right to spread DNA to "worlds without number"—courtesy of a huge hive of honey-bee wives. The belief is so illogical it makes excellent fodder for humor.

Mitt, envision a legion of Mormon Gods kicking back in the Kolob solar system, five starring it for summer school at Kolob Intergalactic University (KIU)—home of the Space Cadets. Each God brought along several of his best looking wives, and eye candy is everywhere. Those assigned to lower kingdoms of Mormon heaven aren't usually allowed to come up, but Einstein was given special dispensation to present enlightening instruction to these Celestial Beings. The Gods reluctantly enroll in Einstein's Special Relativity class. However, Mormon Gods don't appreciate challenge or being told what to do with their time and space—not even by God the Father. Some are in ungodly moods, particularly the youthful who think they already know everything. They came to KIU expecting easy classes and glorious days drinking sprite at the pool with their sprightly young playthings.

Ultimately, the Mormon Deities relent and attend Dr. Einstein's class, but most defiantly show up without notebooks and dressed only in bathing suits. Some are sporting T-shirts with "I'm a God" silk-screened on the back. When Einstein presents a few basic facts about the universe, several Gods arrogantly arise and prance out to the pool (even bigger and nicer that the new one at the Las Vegas Palms). Once poolside, they stop pouting and put on dark glasses to admire the view. Smiling and feeling frisky, one amorous Mormon God says, "Man, this is Heaven." Meanwhile, Professor Einstein's earnest instruction falls on deaf ears or floats past empty seats. Who needs Special Relativity when you're a Mormon God who garnered your own special laws of physics from nineteenth century New England?

Note: Modern planet hunters systematically searching the universe have found almost three hundred Exoplanets—no sign yet of Kolob or its solar system.

13

Go West, Young Mormon

When Joseph Smith was killed in 1844, in part because of his new plural marriage doctrine, the Church was divided between those few who secretly practiced polygamy, those who knew and found it repugnant and unchristian, and the majority of Church members who didn't know about it. In 1842, after some reluctance, Brigham Young was one of the first to follow Joseph Smith into plural marriage, and he wasn't inclined to give it up. For him and others who had accepted the Mormon Gods' exciting eternal program and begun assembling their concubines, it was too late for any other decision. Young, the Pratt boys and other Apostles, determined to keep their power and their wives at all costs, scurried back to Nauvoo following news of Smith's demise.

Brigham Young was President of the Twelve Apostles, and he arrived in Nauvoo just in time to fend off an assortment of claims to Joseph Smith's leadership position. During his sales presentation to be the new Prophet, Young is said to have experienced a transformation that made him sound and even look like Joseph Smith. Whatever happened that day, he roared like a lion, imitated Joseph Smith's speaking style and convinced the Saints he was the new anointed one. Our faithful ancestors, never able to see Joseph Smith as an imposter and his second bible a great hoax, needed someone to show them the way, and Young saved the Church from almost certain dissolution. Joseph Smith insisted he discoursed with Jesus regularly, but Brigham Young never claimed divine revelation. Still, he grabbed the reigns of power and, within a short time, was forced to forge the wagons forward into the western winter.

However, before Brigham Young convinced the flock to follow him, one of those strange "ites" jumped into the fray for power and glory. James Jesse Strang had joined the Church in 1844, and now he staked his claim as Joseph Smith's rightful successor. Brigham Young excommunicated Strang, who then set up his own Church of Jesus Christ of Latter Day Saints and convinced several prominent Church families to follow him to Lake Michigan and Wisconsin. Strang had metal plates of ancient writings, his own "Urim and Thommin" for translating them and witnesses to prove it. He eventually continued plural marriage, made himself King and practiced the Law of Consecration. Most Mormons who followed Strang left before he was assassinated to rejoin Brigham Young or become part of the Reorganized LDS Church.

The Mormons were as confused after the death of Joseph Smith as they are today. Most of those who knew about polygamy and didn't accept it stayed behind, while the Mormon polygamist crowd and their followers, unprepared, moved west earlier than planned. In 1845, the US Government indicted the Apostles for harboring counterfeiters, so the new King of the Mormons began the hasty exodus from Nauvoo into Iowa with the "bogus makers" loaded on the wagon train. On February 15th, 1846, Brigham Young and a large company of Saints, including Jefferson Hunt and his two wives and families, crossed the frozen Mississippi and began their migration west. Comments attributed to Brigham Young indicate he was clueless as to his final destination. California and the Oregon territory were two of several possibilities for the man still insecure about his calling but determined to follow Joseph Smith as prophet.

After Mormon leaders entered the Salt Lake valley, they continued counterfeiting and expanded the practice of polygamy. Why be Kings and High Priests if you can't print your own money and have first choice of the fresh young babes rolling into Zion? Members' property was again consecrated by the leadership and for real or perceived sins, people were killed in the violent practice of Blood Atonement. Brigham Young said some deeds are so threatening to one's salvation that sinners should be willing "to have their blood spilt upon the ground, that the smoke might ascend to heaven as an offering for their sins." Seems it was necessary to kill them to save them. Slitting throats was preferred so their blood could gush and make a mess in the dirt. The concept is foreign to the *New Testament*, which states: "If we confess our sins, He is faithful and just to forgive our sins and to cleanse us of all unrighteousness."(John 1.9).

Christ died to atone for our sins, but Blood Atonement was alluded to by Joseph Smith and taught well into the Twentieth century. Alternately asserted and repudiated by different Church leaders for more than a century, it was responsible for the Utah law allowing execution by firing squad. Scholars also believe it partly responsible for the culture of violence among members of the early Church. Some aggressive pioneer men helped reluctant young men part with the family jewels, allowing castration to make eunuchs of those men who were considered "obnoxious to the leaders." Translation: Mitt, these young men, in most cases, only wanted to marry their childhood sweetheart, as you did, but a powerful polygamist demanded she be assigned to him.

Nearly all Mormon pioneers remained in Utah to listen to the Lion of the Lord make his blood atonement speeches, praise polygamy, mock Christianity and attack the American republic. Most Saints simply endured the harsh living conditions, cowered to Young's cruel warnings and prayed they'd avoid the religiously sanctioned brutality. Until the transcontinental railroad was completed in 1869, they had few options. It was a long, cold walk back to Iowa.

The Saints arriving in the Great Salt Lake valley on July 24th, 1847 filled with anger and resentment. Brigham Young and other leaders, believing themselves free of the Union, used hate speech to incite members focused on their theocracy's natural enemy—the Federal Government. However, Brigham Young and the Apostles could run but not hide. After Mexico ceded the Great Basin to the U.S. at the end of the Mexican/American War, the government annexed the new Mormon Kingdom in 1848 and made it a territory in 1850. Subsequently, a decades-long power struggle ensued between territorial governor Brigham Young and several American Presidents. During those years, Mormon leaders preached that America was an evil nation, called it Babylon, and said the new republic was on the brink of destruction.

When Congress passed the Morrill Anti-bigamy Act of 1862, and Abraham Lincoln signed it into law, Church leaders' arrogant defiance reached a shrill pitch and profane comments continued unabated. Brigham Young attacked the man now considered the greatest American President, saying of Abraham Lincoln's Administration, "The whole government is gone; it is as weak as water." In 1882, the Edmonds Act put additional pressure on Church leaders, and the Edmunds-Tucker Act of 1887 unincorporated the Church and threatened, if Mormons didn't stop the practice of polygamy, to strip it of all political power and confiscate its property. The Prophet and Apostles didn't mind consecrating members' property, but they weren't keen on the idea of Uncle Sam grabbing their stuff. Just about time for the Mormon Gods to render a new earthly plan for their eternal order of plural marriages, and they conveniently obliged in 1890 in something called "The Manifesto."

Before the Manifesto officially discontinued polygamy, historical records reveal the 1870s and 80s were a wild and crazy time in Utah. Church leaders' repeatedly reaffirmed polygamy would never be discontinued and ranted against the US Government's efforts to stop it. Brigham Young and the Apostles had been gleeful about the distraction and destruction of the Civil War, having predicted it would lead to the country's collapse and the assent of Mormons to national power. The fact that it never happened didn't deter the Mormon leaders, even after Brigham Young died in 1877. New Prophets and Apostles preached the Union would be overturned as the world slipped into anarchy before the Second Coming. Basing their certainty on Joseph Smith's prophesy that the Second Coming would happen by 1891, Mormons expressed great confidence that Jesus would imminently deliver them from their last days' persecution and save their social order of plural marriage.

The 1890 Manifesto supposedly ended the practice, but plural marriages secretly continued well into the twentieth century. Defying both the Mormon Gods' new rule and the US Government's old one, records prove this primitive practice was continued for years by many of the Church elite. Mitt, review the early twentieth century congressional hearing for Reed Smoot, the Utah Senator and Mormon Apostle. Senator Smoot's hearing lasted three years and generated three million protest letters. Smoot is a hoot! The transcripts of lying, double-talking Mormon witnesses before Congress enlighten and entertain. Brigham Young had previously said, "We are the smartest people in the world and the best people who ever lived." However, when testifying under oath to members of Congress, those Mormon geniuses couldn't remember the names of their wives and children.

Lying before Congress was not new to Mormon leaders, but the Smoot hearings elevated it to new heights. Apostle George Q. Cannon had already lied for the Lord in 1873, when to retain his seat in Congress, he told the House Committee on Elections he wasn't a polygamist. Following the 1880 congressional elections, when Cannon responded to a flood of petitions from around the nation demanding his removal, he admitted to having several plural wives who lived with him. Even after the Smoot hearings revealed to a hostile nation the ongoing practice of plural marriage, the dishonesty continued into the twentieth century as Church leaders, including President Heber J. Grant, denied in an official Church statement that plural marriages were sanctioned after the 1890 Manifesto.

Mitt, while waiting for Jesus, some of your forefathers and mine migrated into Arizona and Mexico to avoid arrest and maintain their polygamist lifestyle. In his internet-posted *Work in Progress*, author Todd M. Compton asked whether you believe Joseph Smith was a Prophet, or whether your ancestors were wrong to practice polygamy after Smith introduced it. Compton said he wants to ask that question if he ever meets you, so I'll ask for him. What do you believe, Mitt? Were the Pratts, Romneys, and others—including the Moodys and

Hunts—right to accept polygamy as a righteous lifestyle on earth and the eternal order of heaven?

14

Polygamy and Temple Marriage

The Mormon Church has expressed disapproval of the HBO series, *Big Love,* and discouraged members from tuning in, but, of course, I enjoy watching the critically acclaimed hit. Americans need to understand that if the Mormons ruled America, there would be no HBO—not yesterday, today or tomorrow—it simply wouldn't be tolerated. The Church works diligently to influence and manipulate how the media and entertainment industry present Mormon history and doctrines, once successfully stopping a movie about the Massacre at Mountain Meadows. Given ultimate power, the LDS Church would censure all media. There would be no *Big Love* for me or millions of other Americans to enjoy.

Mitt, temple ceremonial activities are the heart of the Mormon belief system. Despite calling polygamy "bizarre and awful," evidently you still believed Temple Marriage and polygamist unions are the eternal order of things. Nevertheless, you made a special point to tell Hard Ball's Chris Matthews that marriage should be "between one man and one woman." On other occasions, you joked that marriage should be between a man and a woman ... and a woman ... and a woman. It's always good for a few laughs on the rubber chicken circuit, but it's not a joke. Chris Matthews let you off easy when you took a wild swing at his friendly softball and dismissed polygamy as nothing more than something the Church ended in "the eighteen hundreds." As your Presidential campaign intensified, the pressure from the press increased and their pitches came harder and faster.

Determined to minimize the plural marriage issue in your campaign, you hit a foul ball when you said, "There are caricatures that pick some obscure aspect of your faith that you never even think about and assume that it was the central element." Mitt, polygamy is integral to the Mormon theological ballgame, and you can't just stand in the Presidential batter's box and pretend it's trivial ancient history. So, in case the press doesn't—now or in the future—I challenge you on this issue, along with all the other blasphemous non-Christian doctrines Mormons espouse. Until you and the Mormon Church officially state differently, Americans and Christians must understand that Mormons still believe polygamy is the eternal order of Heaven. By the way, do you think my wife was just joking when she told me she had a heavenly visitation commanding her to marry additional husbands?

Christian theology clearly states that sex is not part of Divinity—darn it. According to Christian teaching, sexuality is for humans to enjoy in this life. Contradicting the Bible, President Joseph Fielding Smith paraphrased the 132nd section of the *Doctrine and Covenants* when he asked, "What is eternal life?" Then, he said it is to have "a continuation of seeds forever and ever." The faith of a tiny mustard seed can grow into a mountain of big love, and early Mormon prophets and Apostles felt men needed numerous female receptacles so their seed wouldn't be wasted. Join up now gentlemen and be baptized. Great sex happens through the only true Church, its priesthoods and exclusive temples ordinances. Mitt, the present Mormon Church has become so virtuous about traditional marriage and quick to indignantly disavow any connection to polygamy, terms like dishonesty and hypocrisy naturally drift through the consciousness of people still mentally engaged.

On the issue of plural marriage, it's difficult to tell where Mormon hyperbole ends and hypocrisy begins. How outlandish that after early Mormons defended polygamy and vilified monogamy, contemporary Mormons, including you as their emergent political leader, became crusaders against non-standard marriage in modern America. Not surprising or out of character. In the grand tradition of lying for the Lord, Mormons lied about polygamy from its beginning to the present era. The reason why is not in the stars or the Mormon Gods, it's directly related to the conniving mind of Joseph Smith and the evil he incorporated into his evolving cult. Simply stated, as young babe magnet Joseph Smith changed, so did his desire to sleep around and justify it.

Over two decades, Joseph Smith created provincial Gods that suited his needs and yet knew nothing beyond nineteenth century New England. When necessary, our prophet created polygamist Gods in his lustful image and presented them to America and the world. One of the most glaring contradictions in Mormon literature is a byproduct of his growing sexual appetite. The *Book of Mormon* (Jacob 2.27) states, "For there shall not any man among you have save it be one wife; and concubines he have none." Jacob 2.28 adds that "whoredoms are an abomination before me, thus saith the Lord of Hosts." It's pretty clear, Mitt, one Mormon host is to have only one hostess. Yet, in the polygamy sanctioning 132nd section of the *Doctrine and Covenants*—written years later—Joseph Smith quotes God saying the ancient polygamists were justified because "David's wives and concubines were given him of me."

Polygamy contradicts the *Book of Mormon* and early versions of the *Book of Commandments*, yet, while being publicly denounced by the mainstream LDS Church, is still privately incorporated in Mormon doctrine as the eternal order of Heaven. Church behavior on the polygamy issue is religiously disgraceful, but politically understandable. The early Republican Party regarded polygamy as one of the twin relics of barbarism, along with slavery—and modern Republicans want no part of it, either. So, as when Joseph Smith and a few chosen leaders practiced plural marriage and hid it from the general membership, the lying continued over the generations. For much of the nineteenth century, the LDS Church lied to the world about the existence of polygamy, lied about when the practice ended, and Church leadership lies about it now.

Joseph Smith, Brigham Young and others secretly practiced polygamy before the 1843 revelation formalized it, yet Brigham Young didn't publicly admit its existence until 1852. Introduced to elite members by Joseph Smith in 1841, by the time of his 1844 death, at least 29 other men, including your famous relatives and mine, had married a second wife or more. Not to forget that Joseph Smith had been indulging himself sexually since his early 1830s affair with Fanny Alger. The Prophet philandered so much that Emma considered leaving him and returning to her New York family. Still, as late as 1850, future Mormon President John Taylor (twelve wives and eight children at the time) said, "Insomuch as this Church of Jesus Christ has been reproached with the crime of fornication and polygamy, we declare that we believe that one man should have one wife."

Joseph Smith taught that men should be honest in all their affairs, but he lied about his own sexual intrigues and multiple marriages. The current Prophet Gordon Hinckley has continued that dubious tradition by lying about plural marriage, too. On Larry King Live, September 8th, 1998, Hinckley said, "I condemn it, yes, as a practice, because I think it is not doctrinal. It is not legal." Then, he told another tale when he said polygamy, on a restricted scale, was permissible only after the Church moved west. In reality, numerous Mormon men were polygamists before the trek west and later practiced it in far greater numbers that the 2–5% figures the Mormon Church teaches members. Analysis of nineteenth century census reports shows the number of male member polygamists was more like 20–30%. Never a Church welfare program for widows and orphans, as Mormon apologists have claimed, polygamy was encouraged, even mandated although according to Apostle John A. Widsoe, there always seemed to have been more men in the Church than women.

As you know, Mitt, the principles of polygamy and Temple Marriage for time and all Eternity were given together in the 132nd Section of the *Doctrine and Covenants*. If Joseph Smith is a prophet, then those two fundamental doctrines must walk hand in hand. In 1880, Apostle Orson Pratt said, "If plural marriage is not true or in other words, if a man has no divine right to marry two wives or more in this world, then marriage for eternity is not true and your faith is in vain." Ever since the Prophet Joseph gave this revelation, Mormon temple marriages and polygamous relationships have been united in holy—or unholy—matrimony for time and all eternity. Verily, I asketh of thee, Mitt, which of the Mormon Prophets and which scriptures are members supposed to believe? Hopefully, with your help, it will cometh to pass that they doth believeth none of it.

Polygamy and Temple Marriage must unquestionably stand or fall as one. Along with other self-serving revelations created by Joseph Smith, these obvious cult rituals have crumbled together. Unfazed, the Church reveres Temple Marriage as its eternal centerpiece for heaven and teach that eternal life can come only through celestial marriage in a Mormon temple, while scrambling to distance itself from polygamy as if it came straight up from Hell. According to Prophet John Taylor, polygamy indeed came from the Mormon Gods. On several occasions, Taylor stated that polygamy is a divine institution handed down from heaven. Mitt, face it. Our ancestors followed divine orders directly from the Gods, or they were misled by a lecherous Joseph Smith. Plural marriage in Mormon doctrine is about eternal sanctification and exaltation, or it's about human lust and sexuality. Mimicking early Mormon leaders, Fundamentalist LDS leaders today claim plural marriage is about living "The Principal" and not about sex. In reality, it always was and still is about sex.

While you continue to repeat the line that Mormons stopped practicing polygamy in the eighteen hundreds, evidence tells a different story. Your great-grandfathers, Miles Park Romney and Helaman Pratt, men of stature in the Mormon Mexican colonies, engaged in the Post-Manifesto era of polygamist marriages. Though officially banned by the Salt Lake Church leadership worldwide—even Mexico—Miles Park Romney had multiple wives and "married his fifth wife in 1897," almost seven years after President Wilford Woodruff, officially ended the practice with the 1890 Manifesto. General Authorities visited the Mexican colonies and knew the men there continued to take plural wives, but the practice continued. Leaders of those polygamist Mormon colonies were not punished for defying the Manifesto, and many of their descendants, including your father, had substantial influence on the twentieth century Mormon Church.

Excommunication for practicing polygamy didn't begin until 1904, and genealogy records reveal many polygamist unions endured for decades into the twentieth century. Joseph Smith's nephew, Joseph F. Smith, served as Prophet until 1918, along with several wives. Then, with no evidence the marriages to any of his three wives had been annulled, Heber J. Grant remained the prophet until 1945. Ah, the webs we weave. In *Hebrews*, Paul says Jesus defined marriage as being between one man and one woman, and the *New Testament* offers advice on marriage and celibacy—both acceptable—but says nothing about polygamy. Roman law permitted polygamy, but it was never part of Christianity. Unimpressed by the *New Testament* teachings of Jesus and Paul, Brigham Young stated in 1866, "The only men who become Gods, even the Sons of God, are those who enter polygamy."

Brigham Young's Second Counselor Jedediah M. Grant once proclaimed that "A belief in the doctrine of plurality of wives caused the persecution of Jesus and his followers." Not wishing persecution like their Mormon Jesus, whose traveling ministry included a bevy of polygamist babes, Mormons now resort to a shameless public display of dishonesty. I was stunned to learn that Church leaders have distributed erroneous literature in recent years portraying Joseph Smith and Brigham Young as monogamists. Even for an organization conceived, weaned and nourished on falsehoods, it's dumbfounding that Mormon decision makers can rationalize this deception or be so disrespectful of the people they are increasingly desperate to deceive. Does the end of retaining members and supposedly saving gentiles justify the means of lying about a doctrine so eternally fundamental to the LDS Church?

Instead of embracing monogamy, current LDS leaders should be crusading against it. In 1869, Apostle Orson Pratt stated, "This law of monogamy, or the monogamic system, laid the foundation for prostitution and the evils and diseases of the most revolting nature and character under which modern Christendom groans." The only groaning Orson heard came from a multitude of plural wives wondering when their old man would get by to see them—or worrying that he would. Busy early Mormon leaders were frequently away from home on Church duties, and much of that work included keeping their other wives from feeling totally neglected or prospecting for pretty new ones.

The Prophets Joseph and Brigham shamefully played their polygamist rolls. Most descendants of Mormon pioneers know Joseph Smith was "sealed" to scores of women, and Brigham Young had many more than the official twenty-seven our generation was taught. My Mormon religion teachers said Joseph Smith's unions were merely "spiritual wives" who chose to be with him for eternity, and the Prophet never consummated the relationships. Records from the period indicate otherwise. Many women in Smith's large cadre of well-documented wives stated that they rolled in the hay with this larger-than-life stud muffin. After all, little spirits wait impatiently in the preexistence for their earthly tabernacles of flesh and blood. One major purpose for plural marriage—so the Church claims—was to bring those eager souls to earth quickly so they could continue their eternal progression to Godhood.

Contrary to Joseph Smith's assertions in his New and Everlasting Covenant revelation in the *Doctrine and Covenants*, no Angel of God drew a sword to threaten him into polygamy. That claim was simply doctrinal justification for his conniving actions. To seduce his next conquest, the Prophet would sometimes promise women Goddess status, declaring they would pass by the Angels and go straight to heaven. More likely, the angels of Christian heaven viewed Smith's lustful lying through tear-stained eyes. Besides at least thirty-three wives, one-third of them teenagers, researchers verified Brother Joseph sealed himself to eleven women already married to other men, and who continued to live with their spouses. The Prophet was not only a philanderer and polygamist, he practiced polyandry! Clearly, this man had a pair of stones, which were much more useful finding hidden treasure in the bedroom than riches buried in the ground.

Yes, Mitt, the rules and fees of the Church are indeed demanding, but mostly for our women, who have paid a dear price. Please tell contemporary Mormon women it's acceptable to stop training themselves and their daughters for Stepford Wife status on earth and in heaven. Plural marriage was never a Christian doctrine, and *Genesis* reveals that Abraham's wives, Sarah and Hager, didn't warm to each other—to say the least—and Jacob's wives, Rachel and Leah, were "torn by bitterness." Personal diaries of Mormon pioneer women are replete with accounts of their heartbreaking experiences with the New and Everlasting Covenant of plural marriage. Surely you're aware that Hannah Hood Hill, your great-grandmother, recorded in her autobiography that she walked the floor and shed tears of sorrow over her husband's multiple marriages. Numerous other devastated pioneer women also recorded their loneliness, misery and emotional pain.

I remember several conversations with college girls on the sensitive topic of plural marriage. Most were at BYU to get their Mrs. Degree, and none wanted to share her future husband with another woman, not in this world or the Celestial Kingdom. Unfortunately, Mormon women engage in wishful and naïve non-doctrinal thinking when they hope polygamy will magically disappear forever. Brigham Young pontificated on the subject countless times, and multiple quotes in the *Journal of Discourses* by early Mormon leaders support Joseph Smith's and Brigham Young's claim that only polygamists can become Gods in the Celestial Kingdom. General Authority Bruce R. McConke reiterated the importance of plural marriage in 1958 when he wrote, "Obviously the holy practice of polygamy will commence after the Second Coming of the Son of man and the ushering in of the Millennium."

Several years ago at a high school reunion I quipped that I was waiting for polygamy to be reinstated before marrying, and a childhood friend piped in to assure me one wife is enough. Heads nodded and he got more laughs than I did. That said, every Mormon man should read more of Brigham Young's sermons before he seeks to convince his wife or fiancé he won't take other wives in eternity. In another of the innumerable harangues during his thirty year reign, Young made it clear that this man "will perhaps be saved in the Celestial Kingdom; but when he gets there he will not find himself in the possession of any wife at all." Referencing the *Parable of the Talents*, King Brigham declared this sexual loafer, who didn't want additional wives, had a talent he hid up when he refused to build even a mini concubine.

Based on several Prophets' prophesies and General Authority pronouncements, the Mormon man who refuses plural marriage can kiss his one-and-only wife good-bye at the end of this life. He will watch the Mormon Gods assign her and his children to some eternal stud that either built a harem on earth or promised to do it in Heaven. Not very reassuring for contemporary Mormon couples who want to continue their monogamist marriage in the Mormon Celestial Kingdom, and particularly bad news for the faithful Mormon man who believes he found his soul mate and refuses to compromise his principles. That heart-broken chap will watch righteous characters like Joseph Smith, Brigham Young, the Pratt boys and Bruce McConke whisk the love of his life away to another celestial concubine.

I recall BYU professor Hyrum L. Andrus fielding student questions about why the *Book of Mormon* condemned plural marriage, Joseph Smith's New and Everlasting Covenant and the Patriarchal order of the Gods. Andrus made excuses and seemed sincere but never got it right. The answer is that Joseph Smith expanded his reading material in the early 1830s and completely capitulated to his carnal nature. So, he presented the *Book of Mormon* as the most perfect book on earth and then contradicted it later to seduce the tempting young women surrounding him. Even if he knew the truth, Professor Andrus couldn't have given us that explanation—unless he wanted to find a new job outside the only true school.

When Joseph Smith realized faithful followers would believe almost anything he said, he used revelation and charm to seduce other men's wives and daughters, while denying it with a straight face. The Prophet, along with Brigham Young and the other young men he quietly convinced to join his lechery, also had no qualms about taking advantage of dirt-poor immigrant girls. Attractive and impressionable young women were led upstairs to a small room at the Prophet's Nauvoo store where Church leaders pressured them like timeshare salesmen. Scores of vulnerable women were threatened with loss of eternal salvation if they didn't marry Smith or one of the brethren.

If they refused to cooperate with Smith or any leader, the women were warned that to disrespect the Prophet's council was to disobey the Gods and invoke their wrath. Joseph Smith introduced plural marriage into the conversation when he couldn't seduce women without it or to help another fellow with the girl he fancied. If a woman resisted and defied the threat of eternal punishment, the great Prophet said, "Be silent, or I will ruin your character. My character must be sustained in the interest of the Church." Then, the men besmirched her reputation in neighborhood gossip groups. This atrocious behavior is known today because some victims didn't cower, cooperate and keep quiet.

After the Saints arrived in Utah, Brigham Young's First Counselor, Apostle Heber C. Kimball, developed an immense passion for polygamy—known officially as the Law of Abraham—and immersed himself in its considerable pleasures. Ostensibly, he drew vitality from serving the Gods' will, accumulating forty-five wives during his life. Kimball said, "I have noticed that a man who has but one wife and is so inclined to the doctrine, soon begins to wither and dry up, while a man who goes into plurality looks fresh, young and sprightly ... for a man to be confined to one wife is small business ... I do not know what we would do if we had only one wife apiece."

Apostle Kimball and the other leaders grew frustrated by the mid-1850s because there were so few fourteen-year-old girls in Utah who weren't married or about to be. As the supply of new, young companions dwindled, missionaries were instructed to bring back single females to replenish the pot. Kimball became even more frustrated when he realized "the brother missionaries have been in the habit of picking out the prettiest women for themselves before they got here, and bringing the ugly ones for us." He issued instructions to the missionaries, "Here after you have to bring them all here before taking any of them, and let us all have a fair shake." Imagine old Heber shaking a leg and telling cute chicks he was tighter with Jesus than any young roosters.

After aggressively defending polygamy for much of the nineteenth century, I am disgusted to watch recent generations of Church leaders attempt to distance themselves without asking for absolution. Mitt, do you and the General Authorities believe you can have it both ways? Are people supposed somehow to forget Mormons created this festering American social problem? Even today, the Church still practices a limited form of polygamy. If his wife dies before him, a faithful Mormon man is allowed to enter a temple and marry a second, third or more wives for eternity. One of my Mormon friends since childhood has done it. After his childhood sweetheart died, he married his current wife for eternity in the temple. When I recently asked him about it, he said, "Yes, I'm a polygamist."

Fundamentalist LDS members and various polygamist splinter groups, which remain more faithful to the teachings of Joseph Smith and Brigham Young than the LDS Church, believe your mainstream Mormon Church is in apostasy. These secretive sects follow the plural marriage teachings that Joseph Smith started by revelation, the next six Mormon Prophets practiced, and more recent Prophets have reaffirmed as the order of Heaven. Masters of obfuscation, deceitful LDS leaders now send public relations cats to cover up polygamy's fetid odor, and you say, "I don't think Americans care about what brand of faith someone has." American voters care, Mitt.

Although no reference to the "eternal family" exists in the *Book of Mormon* or *New Testament*, Joseph Smith introduced this tangled mass of interfamilial unions into the early Church, including the curious practice of sealing men to men. When Joseph Smith suddenly declared all gentile marriages "null and void" in Nauvoo, some of the "very best women in the church ... were seduced under the guise of religion." During what was called the "great promiscuity" in that period of Church history, "all sense of morality seemed to have been lost" and some women later said, "they did not know who the father of their children was." Over the next several decades, plural marriages became a cause of tremendous anxiety, anguish, anger, sorrow, loneliness and fear of abandonment for our pioneer woman, and it continues in the fundamentalist groups that perpetuate it.

In a game of who's your daddy, genetic tests on Mormon pioneer families would be both interesting and embarrassing. Mitt, maybe you got your height, good looks and political ambition from Joseph Smith, and I got my short stature, nasty temper and controlling personality from Brigham Young. The early Church leaders traded wives like playing cards, so genetic fingerprinting could be scandalous. And who is my mommy? How can my earthly mother be my Mother in Heaven when the Church taught me I already have a Mother in Heaven? Although it's strictly forbidden to address her in prayer, Mormons believe this Heavenly Mother exists on a celestial planet somewhere in a nineteenth century universe.

Adding to the consternation and confusion about heaven, will my grandma Kelly be my grandma in Heaven or will she be her grandmother's granddaughter? Will Grandma be there to pamper me for eternity, or will she want to sit on her grandma's lap for a while before running outside to play? In Mormon heaven, both my grandmas will be so busy birthing new worlds on some celestial planet that they won't have time for their grandchildren from this world. Following that line of reasoning, even with two mothers in heaven, neither would have time for a brunch. Mormon women believe they will become goddesses in the Celestial kingdom, but according to previous prophetic proclamations, they will be reproductive polygamist wombs.

Considering my status with the LDS Church, there's no need for me to worry about grandmothers and mothers in Mormon heaven. Then again, there's no need for you or anyone else to worry about the complications of the Mormon Celestial Kingdom. It doesn't exist. The Mormon's stated eternal condition for men and women—past, present and future—is preposterous. Original Mormon scriptures and statements made by several Mormon Prophets and Apostles about the nature of God, the structure of the Godhead, the state of the universe, Jesus, Jehovah, Adam, and men and women are so confusing and contradictory, a sane person must conclude that Mormon Prophets were intergenerationally ignorant on the subject of life after death. Still, Church leaders know most people feel good when they think of having family with them in Heaven, so missionaries are trained to stir these emotions when hustling prospective new members. Unprincipled, but it has served LDS interests for decades.

The late Owen Allred, former patriarch of one of Utah's largest polygamist congregations, acknowledged a tragic plural marriage lifestyle flaw when he admitted child abuse in polygamist communities is a "stinking mess." Mitt, help our pioneer families realize that the Colorado City/Hildale community we knew as Short Creek as children is a microcosm of what life was like in Brigham Young's nineteenth century theocracy. Granted, coercing young women to "keep sweet" and dutifully marry powerful polygamists is less misogynistic than burning them at the stake, but who's comparing? Today, criminal men continue to mount trapped schoolgirls before they have a chance to grow up, and if they try to leave young girls are sometimes dragged back.

On the other hand, teenage males in polygamist communities are mistreated until they leave or are simply dumped off in places like St. George and Las Vegas. These "lost boys" are isolated from their families and left to fend for themselves. Brigham Young's polygamist theocracy, like Warren Jeffs' contemporary world, was energized by sexual desire for young playmates—jailbait in today's world—and had little to do with serving God, finding a soul mate, or rearing a new generation of quality children. Polygamy was and remains all about sexual desire and the lost boys are merely cultural baggage discarded by older men to pursue their addiction to young women. Hopefully, the recent conviction of Warren Jeffs on accessory to rape charges will begin the end of this lingering travesty.

First generation Mormon women made a courageous effort to end polygamy in 1844. The athletic beauty Emma Hale Smith, first president of the Relief Society, introduced a resolution denouncing the practice and reaffirming the "traditional Christian standard of marriage." Members of this newly formed organization for women voted unanimous support. Their action created so much consternation in the men's councils, Brigham Young smeared Emma as a tool of the Devil and, contrary to official Church history, ended the Relief Society for ten years because of the incident. Emma was marginalized after Joseph Smith's death and mostly written out of LDS Church history. Emma's father, Isaac, bitterly opposed to her marriage to Smith, watched helplessly as his daughter suffered years of indignation.

Emma Smith was uprooted and dragged from place to place, subjected to Joseph Smith's constant promiscuity, and buried four of her first five children along the way. Because of her strong willed defiance of plural marriage, she was threatened with destruction by the Mormon Jesus in the 132nd Section of the *Doctrine and Covenants* "if she abide not by my law." However, some justice prevailed. The Prophet was destroyed within a year of his self-serving revelation, and Emma lived until 1879. Mitt, I think Mormon men were dealt a grievous injustice, too. The Mormon Jesus, stingy in his New and Everlasting Covenant, told Joseph Smith that worthy Priesthood holders only get "ten virgins" given unto them. Muslim men are promised seventy-two stunning virgins. Maybe that's why Joseph Smith, irritated, defied the Lord and secretly married so many non-virgin wives.

One of the Ten Commandments is "Thou shalt not covet thy neighbor's wife." However, Jedediah M. Grant acknowledged wife swapping occurred in Nauvoo and Utah and it's also reported in the *Confessions of John D. Lee*. As in North Korea today, where the Great Leader, and now the Dear Leader, can never be wrong, in the Mormon Kingdom of Joseph Smith and Brigham Young, wife swapping, polygamy, polyandry and other non-Christian practices were acceptable if Church leaders were involved. In addition to being traded, numerous women arrived in nineteenth century Utah as happy new brides only to discover their missionary husbands already had other wives there. Mitt, too many women were isolated in an incestuous, paternalistic world where one powerful Bishop claimed his nieces at three and married them at thirteen.

A Mormon pioneer woman was chattel, a commodity like cattle, existing to satisfy a man's lust, boost his ego and elevate his status in the Church. She was akin to livestock that existed for compulsory reproduction. Apostle Heber C. Kimball once remarked that he didn't think any more about taking another wife than he did buying a cow. Mitt, I have no confidence in a belief system that allows lustful men to dictate God's eternal plan to teenage girls and the wives of other men. Today, thanks to multiple federal interventions in the nineteenth century, Mormon women's suffering has diminished, but they will never be free until the LDS Church admits Joseph Smith and Brigham Young were false prophets, and Fundamentalist LDS characters like Warren Jeffs stop perpetuating their teachings. FLDS groups all believe they are the true restored Church and claim the mainstream Mormon Church is in apostasy. If Joseph Smith and Brigham Young were truly prophets, then the FLDS Churches are correct, and the Salt Lake City Church has lost its way.

Mitt, tell our people polygamy is an unworkable social order and condemned in the *Book of Mormon*. Since pioneer days, our women have been told their primary purpose is to follow the brethren and birth all those intelligences eagerly waiting in primordial life for their earthly tabernacles of flesh and blood. Heaven's very elect were held back until now to be born in the Fullness of Times and build the Gods' kingdom on earth. A Mormon women's priesthood bearing, polygamist husband was to help his dutiful wife fulfill her part of the designated plan. If the concept of women as baby factories has a familiar ring, it's because it was later part of the Third Reich.

Hitler cleverly mixed Christianity and the occult to amass power, and Heinrich Himmler programmed German women to believe their bodies and blood belonged to the nation for reproductive purposes. To create a superior race, young German women were to sacrifice and sexually avail themselves only to pure Aryan men. Blood their Holy Grail, the brown shirts believed they were marching down the path to Godhood. Since Jesus Christ supposedly talked to Joseph Smith, Mormon men believe they will become Gods through their holy priesthood, and the primary purpose for Mormon female existence is sperm receptacle, on earth and in Heaven. Not in my God's Heaven—or on His earth! My daughter will never be told to prepare for eternal queen bee status in an orgasmic heaven where animal behavior is deified. Instead of sending her to BYU in search of a returned missionary destined for polygamist godhood, we will encourage her to pursue whatever career she chooses.

Unlike you, Mitt, apparently virtuous all your life, I understand the polygamist pioneer men and how they thought. Being no better, I would have sought my share of the female bounty, too. Joseph Smith found a way to use the concept of God to legitimize lustful behavior, and now the Church has significant doctrinal capital invested in his huge, lingering lie. In denial, or uncertain what to do, LDS leaders have tried to hide it and hope it will become the man on the stairs who wasn't there. Mitt, the man on the stairs has stood there too long and grown too big for the LDS Church to simply send its clever public relations people to convince the press and public differently. Current Church leaders, trapped in a multigenerational anachronism, can only make the man who wasn't there disappear for good by telling the truth. Help them find the right words.

During his long tenure as Chairman of the Senate Judiciary committee, Senator Orrin Hatch never made a serious attempt to hold hearings on polygamy. Instead, he was more interested in turning Bill Clinton's brief affair with an intern into the crime of the century. At the same time, Mormon political leaders for decades chose to ignore the ongoing polygamous outrages in Utah. Mitt, tell Senator Hatch and all Utah politicians that polygamy is a form of human bondage hiding behind false revelation and religious freedom. It needs to be vigorously renounced at the same press conference where the LDS Church's General Authorities appear in mass to apologize to women and Christians. Polygamy and its related social ills were introduced into American culture by our Church founders as an eternal ordinance rudimentary to the Mormon belief system. LDS leaders should admit it, disavow it and work harder to stop it in Utah and elsewhere. Mitt, chastise the paternalistic Mormon leadership and free our women.

Based on historical observation and personal testimony, polygamy is an earthly enslavement of women. According to writer and polygamy expert, Susan Mazur, most countries now view polygamy as a human rights violation under the United Nation's convention on the elimination of all forms of discrimination against woman. For Mormon women, the discrimination has been earthly and eternal. The social pressure is particularly intense, because women can't hold the priesthood and therefore are permanently subservient. Never have they bowed low enough or worked hard enough. Being a Mormon Mom makes being a Soccer Mom a stroll through the mall. It is time to empower our contemporary women and stop mentally imprisoning them as mythical harem girls-in-waiting.

Mitt, accept this calling to once and for eternity separate Christ's sheep from old Mormon goats. The primitive social order of polygamy, where male animal violence results in the banning, maiming or killing of other males, is part of the evolutionary order of earth, but it's not the heavenly promise of Jesus Christ. It sounds like hell to me. Still, Joseph Smith and Brigham Young determined to impose this socially regressive order on the faithful, in this world and for eternity. In closed religious circles, Mormon leaders continue to teach the eternal order of heaven awaits reinstatement during the Millennium. Despicably, the Church missionary program deliberately misleads the general public, and converts are baptized before the truth about plural marriage is revealed in new member indoctrination classes.

Shortly after arriving in the Salt Lake valley, Latter Day Saints started a forty year project to build another Temple, where they continued sealing the living and saving the dead in eternal rituals commanded by their Gods. Maybe what happens in Vegas stays in Vegas, but what happens in Mormon Temples has been leaking like a faulty baptismal font—the pagan kind decorated by pioneer oxen. Details and descriptions of ever-evolving temple ceremonies paint a fascinating slice of plagiarism, paganism and paternalism. For centuries, Masons had known how to use secrecy effectively, and Joseph Smith studied their ceremonies before commandeering symbols and secret handshakes for his Mormon Temple ceremonies. Plagiarized Masonic rituals became LDS prerequisites to meet their Gods and reach the highest level of Mormon heaven.

Joseph Smith repeatedly condemned secret societies in his early writings and ramblings. Then, after his brother Hyrum had joined the ancient group around 1826, Joseph joined the Masons in Nauvoo and became a Master Mason in 1842. Mormons followed their prophet into the Masonic organization in droves, and the Nauvoo Lodge became bigger than all the other Illinois Lodges combined. Nonetheless, here were basic differences between Masons and Mormons. Masons disavowed suppression of the people and believed in a Divine Providence that transcended religious denominational boundaries. Within a short time, the Masons officially disassociated themselves from the Nauvoo Mormons.

Masons severed their ties to Joseph Smith and the Nauvoo Mormons over matters of separation of church and state, democratic election of leaders, tolerance, equality and freedom of thought. With members ranging from George Washington to Benjamin Franklin and John Hancock, the Masons introduced a new way of thinking into the U.S. Constitution that challenged ignorance, tyranny and fanaticism. Joseph Smith's desire to build a kingdom based on theocratic principles was obviously contrary to the principals famous Masons helped legislate into the American governmental system.

Mormons tried for generations to ignore the obvious similarities between the Mormon and Masonic ceremonies by declaring Joseph Smith had successfully restored the Masonic ceremony to its perfect eternal form. Most current Mormons would be startled to hear that as late as the turn of the twentieth century, Church leaders still stated that Mormon temple rituals embodied true Masonry, a remnant of the ancient priesthood dating back to King Solomon's Temple. However, recent generations of Mormons leaders sought to minimize the Masonic connection and instructed Mormons not to join the Masons. Conversely, Masons who visit Salt Lake City are often surprised to see their symbols on the old granite Temple building in Temple Square.

LDS Church leaders remain sensitive and defensive about comparisons of the Mormon and Masonic Temple rituals, but the evidence is irrefutable. After close examination, even Dr. Reed Durham, who once served as president of the Mormon History Association, admitted the parallels. Dr. Durham stated, "I believe that there are few significant developments in the Church that occurred after March 15, 1842, which did not have some Masonic interdependence." Durham went on to say, "there is absolutely no question in my mind that the Mormon ceremony which came to be known as the Endowment, introduced by Joseph Smith to Mormon Masons, had an immediate inspiration from Masonry."

Though temple rituals have no foundation in the *New Testament* or Christianity, Mormons are deadly serious about these comical little plays. In yet another distortion of biblical teachings, Joseph Smith announced in 1844, "The greatest responsibility in this world that God has laid upon us is to seek after our dead." Joseph Fielding Smith, the Tenth Mormon President, later declared, "The greatest commandment given us, and made obligatory, is the temple work on our own behalf and in behalf of our dead." According to Biblical scripture, Jesus actually said "Let the dead bury their dead," (Matthew 8.22), and Timothy 1.4 says, "Neither give heed to fables or endless genealogies." It almost sounds like Timothy knew the fabulist Joseph Smith was coming to murk up the Christian Gospel by introducing secretive, childish rituals as a rite of initiation to a special new heaven.

Until removed by modern Mormonism after 1990, the temple ceremony included several bloody oaths required of devout members. If members wagged their tongues about what occurred in the temple, they were to have them ripped out by the roots. Bodies were to be torn asunder and the bowls sent gushing. Earlier parts of the ritualistic ceremony also included violent statements about breasts cut open, and hearts and vitals torn from bodies to feed the birds. No wonder sensitive Mormons were repulsed by the throat slitting and disembowelment gesturing that occurred in what they thought was the holiest place on earth. Mitt, tell out people the temple ceremonies never were dictated and sanctioned by Jesus Christ. Over the decades, numerous members have divulged what happens there, and it's all for the birds.

Jesus Christ never mentioned baptism for the dead or temple marriages for time and all eternity, and no evidence exists that His personal life and public ministry included either of those Mormon doctrines. The Christ to whom I cling made it clear that the first of all commandments did not include dead ancestors or multiple wives on earth and in heaven. He said, "Love the Lord with all thy heart," and He extended on that admonition, "Love thy neighbor as thyself." Mitt, have you ever wondered how the Mormon Jesus found enough hours in a day to service all his wives, build a sophisticated religious bureaucracy and still had a few minutes to hang out with the boys over a bite to eat?

It's arrogant, insulting and presumptuous for the Mormons to do baptisms and marriages for dead Christians, Jews or any members of the human race. Undeterred by fact or reason, the Church claims only its Priesthood holders have the keys to Christ's kingdom, and only they have the authority to provide for mankind's salvation, but the process isn't working. Countless human births, lives and deaths went completely unrecorded in both pre-history and recorded history. Mitt, how can non-existent genealogy be traced to do these peoples' temple work, now or during the Millennium? Rituals depicting Adam and Eve in the Garden of Eden, secret handshakes and the Five points of Fellowship borrowed from the Masons, must somehow be completed for every human being who ever lived. Mitt, shouldn't it have been Adam and Eves in the Garden of Eden? Ten virgin Eves should have bantered with the snake. I know, I know, Adam came from another planet and only brought one of his wives.

The Mormon Temple endowments are completed for only a few hundred million people out of the billions who live or have lived on the earth. What's to become of countless humans who have died and supposedly wait miserably for redemption in the Mormon spirit prison? We were taught that they are given an opportunity to hear the missionaries' final call for salvation in this Mormon holding tank, but their baptismal and marriage ordinances must be done by authorized priesthood holders here on earth. Since there's no record these people lived, how can their genealogical records be recovered and completed so they can be saved by my relatives and other Mormon temple workers? Are more gold plates or secret records hidden in hills around the world with the names of souls who lived tens of thousands of years ago?

Mitt, we displayed or referenced our family's genealogy sheets from time to time as I was growing up. It was fun and interesting. I'm proud my children are sons and daughters of the American Revolution, the Texas Republic, and the Utah and California Pioneers. I haven't seen the genealogy yet, but my wife swears her family traces to the Mayflower. However, genealogy fun is far different than the Mormon claim that it's vital to their role as saviors of humanity.

Even the *Book of Mormon* says nothing about baptisms or marriages for the dead, and it appears to contradict those concepts in its *Book of Alma*. Mormon leaders blame early Christians for removing these vital temple ordinances and doctrines from the *New Testament*, but early Christian sects and the Catholic Church never had the *Book of Mormon* to alter, change or delete any of its material. Ancient writings about early Christianity discovered since the late Nineteenth century don't support Mormonism's outlandish claims either. Still, the Church spends billions on endless genealogies and spiky temple buildings, claiming it's the Gods' eternal plan, and only the LDS Church has the power and authority to save the human race.

Joseph Smith said, "Ordinances instituted in heaven before the foundation of the world, in the priesthood, for the salvation of men, are not to be altered or changed," and then Mormon temple ordinances were repeatedly changed. The most recent known alteration to the ceremony came in 2005, when the LDS Church changed the way men and women are bathed and oiled, thus ending some of the groping that bothered women. More remarkable, a major deletion occurred about 1927 when the Prophet and Apostles convinced their Gods to strike the Oath of Vengeance from the secret rituals. The oath was issued by Brigham Young a year after Joseph Smith's death and recited in the Endowment ceremony for years, before being quietly removed when someone leaked it to the non-Mormon press. The vengeance oath required all members to seek revenge upon America for the death of Joseph Smith and his brother Hyrum. Previous to the change, faithful temple travelers were instructed to teach their children vengeance, too.

As the Twentieth century progressed, vengeful Mormon Gods were persuaded to show compassion and forgiveness toward America. Then again, Mormons believe the Trinity is composed of three separate and distinct beings, with God the Father and Jesus in resurrected tabernacles of flesh and blood. Mitt, is it possible the big three LDS Gods are all strong-willed guys who disagree a lot? God the father and Jesus begin to formulate a policy, and the Holy Ghost chimes in to haunt them with his two cents worth. Maybe, Mormon eternal ordinances are decided and later changed on a 2-1 vote by a raucous, squabbling Godhead. If so, prayerful LDS Apostles in Salt Lake City would only have to change one vote—and bingo—a new eternal plan is decided and announced. It's just my theory, but it would explain a lot of the confusion and contradiction found in Mormon history and doctrines.

As part of their recurrent sanitation of Church doctrines and rituals, Mormon leaders also convinced their Gods to delete the black devil from the Temple ceremony. As you know, until a few decades ago, a Mormon play actor dressed like the devil and hired a sinister Christian minister to lead the people astray. This audacious Mormon accusation was obvious, petty and vindictive. Christian Churches had changed almost every ordinance of Christ's plan, were controlled by the devil, and their leaders were morally and spiritually lost. Mitt, tell our people the temple ceremony was created by Joseph Smith, and the deletions and changes came gradually and reluctantly to make them more civilized and socially acceptable to sensitive members and new converts.

The same can be said about the temple garments you and all dedicated Mormons wear. Nineteenth century Mormon leaders repeatedly said the endowment garments, with their mystic signs, squares and underside flap hatch for the outhouse, are sacred and never to be changed. With sleeves to the wrists and legs to the ankles, the faithful could only quickly jump out of them to bathe, and then put on a clean pair. Almost eighty years ago, under pressure from the evil modern world, President Heber J. Grant quietly allowed modifications to begin. Mitt, tell members these undergarments are valueless, and now the butt of jokes. Comedian Bill Maher, known to some as the bravest man in America, has dubbed Mormon temple garments "magic underpants."

Temple garments were designed as shields to protect members from danger and evil, yet changes came to Mormon funny underwear despite dire warnings of serious consequences. Joseph F. Smith, the sixth Mormon Prophet, reaffirmed over a century ago the garments of the holy priesthood are the most sacred of all things and should remain "unchanged and unaltered from the very pattern in which God gave them." Apostle J. Reuben Clark and other Church leaders also stated blessings promised for wearing the garments could not be realized if changes were made to their form or the manner of wearing them. Mormon Temple garments have been adulterated by repeated alterations, rendering them valueless except as cleaning rags. Mitt, tell our women its okay boldly to walk into

Victoria's Secret—where no devout Mormon woman has gone before. Assure them it's acceptable to slip into something sexy and appealing to their future Gods.

Clearly, Mormon temple ceremonies and garments didn't come from the Christian God. Still, the Church continues to build temples and pressure members to do temple work, wear their lifesaving underpants and complete their family genealogy all the way back to Adam. Forget about the cave men. They get no respect in auto insurance commercials or the Mormon plan for salvation. Some time ago, my big sister/aunt informed me she planned to fill her retirement time doing genealogy work for the Thorstensons, the last branch of our pioneer family to arrive in the United States. After Mormon missionaries found him in the early 1880s, my great-great-grandfather, Chris Thorstenson, sailed from Norway to Boston, found work and sent money home for his wife and five children to join him. They traveled to Salt Lake City and down to our central Utah valley a year later.

My aunt sounded unenthusiastic about the Thorstenson genealogy research, as though a job to which she was duty bound. Since limited genealogical work has been completed for the Thorstensons (who changed their name to Thompson), my aunt reluctantly decided it her responsibility to hitch up her undergarments, put her shoulder to the wheel and push along. I resisted the urge to stir trouble by encouraging her to dedicate precious retirement years to something more beneficial in the living world. Was not something more worthwhile—and fun—than trying to trace the Thorstenson clan back to the Vikings and beyond to save them in the Mormon Celestial Kingdom? However, I decided auntie would only be angered by ideas from my demon-addled brain and kept quiet.

Mitt, I know this aunt won't be deterred from her genealogical and temple responsibilities unless you, Gordon Hinckley or Jesus Christ Himself tells her it's unnecessary. Saving dead people is a Mormon obsession, and she is only one of my relatives busying themselves with this waste of time and money. Mormons believe Jesus Christ traipses through each new temple after its completion and dedication. Reportedly, He's pleased as punch with his Church's efforts to gather genealogy records and perform phony ordinances for dead people, while hundreds of millions of living humans wallow in abject poverty. Mitt, these beliefs and actions helped me conclude the LDS Church is a parasite cult determined to take over the Christian host.

I have another aunt, expressive and outspoken, who spends Fridays at the Las Vegas Temple doing ordinance work for the dead. Following her successful Mormon deprogramming—that exists only in my daydreams—I imagine her snarling, "I can't believe it. I just can't believe it! I spent my whole life swallowing this damn crap!" This same aunt posted a yard sign in 2004 supporting a Nevada constitutional amendment to prohibit gay marriage that was strongly supported by local LDS Church leaders. Once a semi-independent spirit, sadly she's become an elderly woman, loyal to the Church, content to dwell on the wrong side of religion, history and science until she dies.

Mitt, it's now time to run the temple builders out of the Mormon Church so our people can become Christians again. Opportunities exist to turn these temple structures into useful properties. Why not following the model established by Tiger Woods and transform them into learning centers for disadvantage children? Another possibility is for them to become shelters for battered women, abused children or the homeless. Instead of continuing to insult Native Americans with all these outrageous lies the Church has spread for generations about their origins, the temples in Central and South America could serve as cultural arts centers, where they would learn more about their real heritage.

15

The Little Woman

My wife once asked me how Mormon women tolerate their subjugation to Priesthood paternalism and defend an organization that for generations has kept them subordinated and relegated to second-class citizenship. It's a fair question without a simple answer. A logical place to begin is to understand that Mormon women, from the Church's founding, have been systematically stripped of strong female role models

Joseph Smith's teachings and writings were heavily influenced by the Methodists, who had significantly reduced the role of the Biblical Mother Mary. The early Catholics had made her an icon, but the Methodists, for whom Smith was a teenage preacher, diminished her as a significant Christian figure. In addition, Brigham Young further dismissed the other women who followed Jesus as merely his train of wives, and male Mormon Prophets made it clear to generations of women that their ticket to the most prestigious heavenly feast is marriage to a male Priesthood holder—preferably with several other wives.

Mormon leaders also accepted Pope Gregory's 581AD claim that Mary Magdalene was a pathetic reformed whore. Constantine paid for the comprehensive biblical work done in the fourth century, when numerous translations were made from Hebrew and Greek into Latin. At that time, certain books were canonized while other early Christian writings were excluded from the Bible. Centuries later, Gregory used his authority to denude Mary Magdalene and effectively all Biblical women in the process. Pope Gregory, known as Gregory the Great, transformed Magdalene into a pitiful person—Christian history's "Penultimate Penitent."

All ancient scriptures considered, including those newly discovered, Mary Magdalene emerges as a confidant of Jesus with near Apostle Status. Now, she shines as a powerful leader in Christ's inner circle. Evidence shows that, like you, Mitt, she even went to France as a missionary. Concomitantly, Jesus is remembered as one who treated women as respected equals in his ministry. He refused to reduce women to sexual objects and never mentioned polygamy as an earthly Christian condition or heavenly directive. In a perversion of Christ's teachings during the first centuries of Christianity, women were generally disempowered and subjugated. This gender prejudice is firmly embedded in the Mormon sub-culture in the insidious form of polygamy and *Old Testament* priesthood subser-vience.

Mitt, the LDS Church taught us the Mary Magdalene myth. Yet, Joseph Smith told his followers the Gods instructed him to restore Christianity to its original structure at the time of Christ's ministry. If Smith's monumental procla-mation were true, Jesus would have instructed him to correct Mary Magdalene's role and restore her to her rightful place as a confidant and leader in His ministry. After all, Jesus chatted with Smith almost daily on a variety of trivial topics. It's unreasonable to think Jesus would allow his great latter day prophet to spread misinformation about the importance of Mary Magdalene. Far more reasonable to conclude they never spoke.

Mitt, from childhood, we were taught that several ancient prophets and apos-tles also descended to Joseph Smith, creating numerous opportunities to correct the Magdalene mistake. The Mormon founding prophet claimed Jesus commis-sioned him to edit and correct the Bible. Hard to imagine Christ didn't inform Joseph Smith that Mary Magdalene—one of His closest confidants and possibly most beloved—had been for centuries unfairly maligned. Since that apparently didn't happen, why was not one of our twentieth century Living Prophets wor-thy? Instead, Christian scholars garnered bits of information about Mary Magdalene from recently translated ancient records—not living or dead Prophets in Salt Lake City.

Add the above historical negatives to Emma Smith's Devil status for trying to restore monogamy to Mormonism and the answer to my wife's question crystal-lizes. Mormon Priesthood paternalism, from inception in the first generation, created a religious cast system based on sex. Our pioneer women never had a chance at meaningful lives, and nothing much has changed in the Church today. Nearly all prominent Mormon women gained notoriety for standing up to Church leaders—and were eventually excommunicated for their heroism.

The historical Mormon practice of denigrating women continued into the mid and late Twentieth century, when Sandra Tanner and Sonia Johnson were smeared and mocked for daring to confront Church leaders. Linda King Newell and Valeen Tippets Avery also received a dose of Priesthood punishment when they wrote their revealing book, *Mormon Enigma: Emma Hale Smith*. While

Emma Smith and Sarah Pratt led Mormon heroines in the first generation, Sandra Tanner and Sonia Johnson earned the title in the latter twentieth century. Sonia Johnson courageously supported the Equal Rights Amendment even though the Mormon General Authorities and their political pawns chose to fight it. Laughably, Church leaders claimed they opposed the ERA on "moral grounds." Alongside other selected fabrications and prejudices, the Church said it "would not dignify women, but would put them down."

When Sonia Johnson refused to back down on the ERA issue, Mormon men turned the big dogs loose. To protect the empire, the boys chased her down and dragged her around, eventually forcing her out of the Church as part of the infamous 1993 Mormon Purge. Mormon men acted quickly and with authority because the ERA was dangerous for the Myth Fraternity Empire. The Mormon Church's Special Affairs Committee concluded early that Mormonism's structural inequality between the sexes made the ERA a threat to their coveted tax free status. Mormon Public Relations staffers manufactured a list of self-serving, boogieman reasons the amendment should be defeated, while marshalling loyal Mormon women to help fight the newest war on evil. Mormon girls didn't need trouble-maker Sonia Johnson filling their heads with silly notions about social equality. Loyal Mormon women believe their eternal exaltation is tied to Priesthood paternalism and they must obey their husbands and fathers, who know best. Priesthood Studleys and Dudleys pulled the puppet strings on the ERA matter, and most Mormon women danced to the High Priests' tune.

Senator Orrin Hatch, boorish Mormon water boy and political assassin on capital hill, did his job superbly. He sneered at Mrs. Johnson when she appeared before a Senate subcommittee to support the amendment. Difficult to refute a sneer, but Johnson held her ground against a vain man who, in frequent self-righteous moments, easily transforms himself into hyperventilation mode. As a political scientist and former Mormon, I have watched Senator Hatch explode indignantly over the most trivial matters—when he could have provided positive leadership on issues vitally important to America and humanity. I'm curious whether Senator Orrin Hatch is named after Orrin Porter Rockwell, a real assassin.

Rockwell namesake or not, Senator Hatch has been blindly dedicated to the Mormon vision of Heaven and earth. This single minded Mormon warrior once played the organ in a Hildale Sunday school class, and instead of standing up for their women and children forced to live in polygamy, gave his stamp of approval to the lifestyle by saying polygamists were good people. On other occasions, he attacked gay rights with a look of pious disgust on his face. Senator Hatch and

Church leaders have pushed hard for a constitutional amendment to block gay rights and protect traditional marriage, yet they do little about their sacred polygamy. Hatch's political behavior is not surprising because he obviously swallowed the Mormon hook deep into his gut long ago. A confused old man and product of his environment, it's natural that he simultaneously accepts or seeks restrictions on civil liberties and ignores the criminal behavior of contemporary polygamist cults.

Certain he's destined to spend eternity in a polygamist theocracy makes Senator Hatch a dangerous man on earth and in Mormon heaven. Righteous LDS men like Hatch and you, Mitt, will become polygamist Gods and corner most of the women in concubines up Heaven's celestial stairs. Some male losers in the Mormon eternal game will be castrated, like the old polygamist goats did to losers in Brigham Young's era. Other losers will become homos in Mormon Heaven or perhaps slaves in female-dominated concubines. Heaven will be hell for any man assigned downstairs to lower kingdoms alongside the strong-willed women who refused polygamy's charms. If by chance I get into the Telestial kingdom, just neuter me. Otherwise, I'll figure a way to sneak out of Heaven's basement, creep up the back stairs, and peek around master suite doors to see what's going on in there.

The good news is we drones-in-waiting aren't stuck in the Romney-Hatch version of heaven and earth just yet. My God says I can come to his Heaven and there's still a fighting chance against those who oppose civil rights on earth. In future years, resurgent supporters of equality and free speech will be victorious over those who opposed the Equal Rights Amendment, but want constitutional amendments against gay marriage and flag burning. Polls showed a majority of Americans supported the ERA, yet professional observers believe Mormon opposition tipped the scales for the entire nation by changing votes in a few key States. As a result, women remain unequal, and socially repressive Mormon leaders remain safe from secular legal intervention.

With the ERA conquest notched on the bedpost and Mormon women firmly in their place, an unrepentant Mormon Church continues to stand on the dark side of history and oppose equal rights. Negroes and women were the traditional scapegoats for our regressive monolithic Church, and Mormon views on race and gender are still caught in a time warp. Mitt, your record on appointing minorities and women to the bench in Massachusetts was atrocious until the very end, when you were criticized by the State Bar Association. Homosexuals are the latest minority to pursue equal rights and, like Negroes and women, face Mormon leader's self-righteous wrath. Predictably, the Church holds that gays who come out of the closet must be legislated against, counseled to forsake their evil ways, or told to deny their nature and be quiet.

16

Theocratic Socialism to Capitalistic Fascism

One morning in San Diego, drinking gourmet coffee and watching hungry seagulls dive-bomb Mission Bay, I remembered the Miracle of the Seagulls and considered the precarious situation of our ancestors newly settled in the Salt Lake valley. According to Mormon lore, in 1848 the pioneer's first food crop was saved when seagulls flocked to eat hordes of crickets, proving God answers everyone's prayers or nature will take its course. Reflecting on the Mormon social structure of that time, I was struck by the magnitude of Mormonism's march across the economic and political spectrum.

In the Nineteenth century, the LDS Church experimented with attempts at Karl Marx-type communalism and socialism, when the Church tried to control almost every aspect of members lives. Now, it's a hopeful sign that in just a few generations the socialist Mormon Gods learned there is value in economic liberty and free markets, and passed their new knowledge to earthlings. Discouragingly, however, the pendulum has swung so far right that the Church supports politicians who accept fat campaign contributions in return for ripping off government (and taxpayers) for crony capitalism. Lobbyists and politicians call it privatization.

American founders shared a belief in the individual's right to hold property, at least for white men, yet Mormon founders institutionally stripped members of their property and economic individualism. Even as current members embrace economic liberties on earth, the Mormon Church still claims socialist and communal concepts are the order of Heaven. Communalism in the Mormon Church began in 1831, when Joseph Smith introduced it by revelation in the 92nd section of the Doctrine and Covenants, and it was practiced in sputters and spurts after the Saints arrived in Utah. In the early 1870s, Brigham Young made a major push universally to institutionalize communalistic practices. Young emphasized that the Law of Consecration was not a new revelation. He reminded the Saints that consecration is the order of the Kingdom where God and Christ dwell, and has been from "eternity to eternity." I don't know how many eternities there are, but that's a long, long time to live like nineteenth century hippies with a slew of wives to service and kids to feed.

While Brigham Young gathered a personal fortune and the Mormon elite lived economically comfortable lives off membership labor—similar to political leaders in late twentieth century Communist Russia, Young directed the Saints to organize in the Order of Enoch in the new and everlasting Kingdom, according to the order of Heaven. Zions Cooperative Mercantile Institution (ZCMI) had been established by Brigham Young to drive out non-Mormon merchants in Salt Lake City and across the territory, and the United Order was organized to manage the Law of Consecration. While Young may have seen returning to an even more communal economy essential to prepare for the imminent Second Coming, the Panic of 1873 had brought depression to Utah industries and money was desperately needed to publish more Church books and tracts. Some Brethren, including Apostle Orson Pratt, were also concerned the recent completion of the Transcontinental Railroad diminished Church control by enabling Church members to become more individualistic and capitalistic.

In response, over the next twenty years, 200 United Orders were organized in LDS Communities, but most never got very united. The Order of Enoch is the Mormon Gods' plan for our eternal lifestyle, but the 80,000 Utah residents rejected it in favor of their frail but functioning capitalist economy. The Saints of Orderville, Utah, the only ones to show real success with the Gods' plan, took it even beyond Brigham Young's proposals. Those gung-ho folks ate in common dining halls, wore uniform clothing made by Orderville manufactures, and lived in cookie-cutter apartments. Reading about it again recently almost made me homesick for the Army.

Orderville only succeeded in honoring the Gods for a few years. The communal community became mostly deserted when polygamist residents fled into Arizona or Mexico to avoid arrest. Brigham Young, by then an old man, was bitterly disappointed when the Saints rebelled against the Gods' Law of Consecration. He said, "He could not get the Saints to live it, and his skirts were clear if he never said another word about it." Today's Mormons don't all eat at one big table, although their thoughts seem trapped in the same Orderville mentality. Dean L. May, in the *Utah History Encyclopedia*, stated the principals of the United Order remain central to present-day Church governance. For those who choose to live in reality, the growing, maturing scientific and economic systems of today rendered the pop culture economic and social structure implemented by Joseph Smith and Brigham Young quaint and obsolete.

LDS Church leaders should be shamed for filling members' heads with these mind numbing thoughts. They turn our people into automatons programmed for a seat at the Orderville communal table in the Celestial Kingdom of Heaven; while at the same time control them socially, economically and politically on earth. Mormons need to know the Church's steady move from nineteenth century experimentation with communalism—its Law of Consecration—to contemporary affairs with materialism and the Bush Administration's economic Fascism wasn't done under the auspices of Jesus Christ or any other Gods. Fortunately for Joseph Smith and Brigham Young, gullible followers accepted any excuses given when prophecies went unfulfilled, policies were changed or their property confiscated. Mormon pioneers gave up all earthly possessions to Church leaders when prophetically instructed, and even today their gullible descendants swear similar allegiance in secret temple rituals.

Thousands of deceived Mormon pioneers needlessly perished across the American heartland because they faithfully followed Brigham Young and his Apostles to wherever the hell they were going. Present day members and prospective converts also seek transcendental assurances in all things, so they defer their emotional and economic interests and, to sooth their souls, succumb to some phony oracle's earthly wisdom. Members accept the Mormon Church's authoritarian rule, are taught that communalism is the heavenly order of things, but still want modern capitalistic creature comforts in earthly life. Mitt, you were willing to spend a portion of your quarter billion dollar fortune on the Presidential campaign. Would you title everything if Gordon Hinckley or a future Mormon Prophet said your resources were needed to build the kingdom? Would you do it if the Prophet said Jesus commanded it?

My children will be renaissance men and women, not workers in the culture-killing Mormon beehive. As children, they won't be enrolled in Mormon Sunday School and Primary, or inculcated with the Mutual and Seminary programs as teenagers. Being indoctrinated to believe the Law of Consecration is the sacred financial order of Heaven or unbridled capitalism is the answer to current human needs, is unacceptable. Mormonism remains a nineteenth century pop cult quest to rule the world from America, the Promised Land. The Church's economic and political goals persist despite public relations claims that a brick wall exits between the Church and political campaigns like yours.

The LDS Church claims political neutrality, but in the latter twentieth century, Mormon leaders tightened their grip on members and again demanded allegiance to their all-encompassing agenda. After the Democratic Party championed the Civil Rights movement and later supported Women's Rights, Church leaders joined with southern Yellow Dog Democrats and ushered the faithful Mormon flock into a socially threatening new Republican alliance. Salt Lake City's white grandpas reminded Church members that they are to be adored and blindly trusted, because they will never lead the Saints astray. This resurgence in the Church's political control led to the Mormon voting block once again being developed to near perfection. Las Vegas news reporters discovered a "Mormon mailer" was sent in the 2006 gubernatorial race, specifically targeted at Mormon members in Southern Nevada, yet a local Church spokesman and former political joker—nicknamed Ace—claimed the Church wasn't involved in compiling or disseminating the mailer.

In another lying for the Lord moment in Church history, it remains an official mystery how a Mormon primary candidate for Nevada Governor got a mailing list of Mormon members. That candidate, Jim Gibson, the son-in-law of the man who gave me my Patriarchal Blessing, didn't win the Democratic primary because he's more Republican than Democrat. However, while you proceeded on your course to become the first Mormon President, Nevada got its first Mormon Governor in 2006—sort of. A flyboy named Jim Gibbons, a Protestant in previous Nevada and Congressional records suddenly became a proud Mormon when he needed their votes in Southern Nevada.

Despite getting drunk and hitting on a cocktail waitress at a local hangout three weeks before the election and being tagged on the front page of the Wall Street Journal in a major ethics scandal, Gibbons was elected Nevada Governor. In addition, it was disclosed he had hired an illegal alien nanny and then lied about it when exposed by the media. Jim Gibbons even became joke fodder for Jay Leno, but Nevadans elected him anyway, thanks in part to the Mormon vote. Gibbons is a Republican and Nevada remains a red State with the help of Mormons and red neck "cow county" Republicans. The election of "Shallow Jim" Gibbons was a feather in your cap, Mitt, even though as Chairman of the Republican Governors Association you lost twenty out of the thirty-six gubernatorial races, you won this one. Now, embarrassed Nevadans endure his legal entanglements, generally bumbling behavior and poor leadership.

Nevada Mormons pretended to be proud as peacocks of their Mormon Governor. LDS legislators held a celebratory ceremony honoring his governorship, and missionaries camped out at the Governor's office praying for prey. According to media reports, the missionaries have occupied his office more than Gibbons himself. A majority of Nevadans are unable to share the glee that the State is stuck for years with an ideologue lacking depth and vision. Gibbons can be characterized as Bush lite—if that's possible. The man, who should be a candidate for excommunication from the Mormon Church, was instead presented with a personally inscribed book of scriptures by seven Mormon legislators. When he accepted the gift, Gibbons asked, "Does this mean I'm going to have to go to church?"

It's fascinating to watch the Mormon Gods-to-be work in mysterious ways, their wonders to perform, tax status to protect and powers to increase. In addition to illegally providing membership lists to favored candidates and denying it when caught, Church leaders' candidate and position choices are whispered at election times in conversations surrounding Priesthood and Relief Society meetings. They want to make sure members like my aunt get anti-gay signs posted in their front yards. Granted, some old time Democrat Mormon members ignored the whispering or, figuratively speaking, didn't get the memo. Some members still don't realize the Mormon Gods have become economic conservatives, changed political parties and now strongly support only traditional marriage. These fallen faithful remain loyal to the Democratic Party and still cast their secret ballots against the Gods and their new political allies. Nevertheless, they represent a minority, and many probably have a guilty conscience.

Mormon leaders demand loyalty at all costs and developed the social tools to enforce it. Like loyal Republican leaders, faithful Mormon men are rewarded with earthly riches in business and rarely fired or forced to resign their Church leadership roles. Those members who dare to dissent, or openly question policy, are quickly punished. Just as the Bush cronies rarely showed the integrity to resign and apologize for their political ineptitude or deviousness, Mormon Apostles can't admit the Church is founded on falsehoods and resign on principle. It's frightening how many men in key political and religious leadership positions see themselves indispensable to God's plans for mankind. Lies mean nothing to religious and political characters who feel they are invaluable and justify their contempt for the secular rules of law because they answer to higher religious ones.

17

Political Reinvention

Mitt, only a few years ago, you said you would remain a moderate force in the Republican Party. Today, you're an instant champion of contemporary Christian conservatives and pander to right-wingers who despise our secular system of government. Just as the Mormon Church reinvented itself in recent generations, you conveniently changed your personal and professional positions on key social and economic issues to garner support from religious conservatives. Painful to watch you dart around like a windblown kite in this contemporary political storm, willing to pay any price for power. Thomas Carlyle asked, "Can there be a more horrible object in existence than an eloquent man not speaking the truth?"

I do not suggest this is your lying for the Lord moment in American history. During my years in politics and business, I met several good salesmen, and the best were those who believed their own propaganda. Maybe, you convinced yourself you've been wrong in the past and your sudden conversion to conservative social positions is an honest correction. Paul Weyrich, a founder of the Moral Majority and the Heritage Foundation, believes you're sincere. Endorsing you for President in November, 2007, he told the Boston Globe, "I believe that he has flip-flopped in the right direction, if you will—the direction of value voters—and I think he will stay there." Mitt, only you know whether you are "an ambitious square-jawed opportunist" or a repentant moderate progressive. If merely an opportunist, you're not the first man to put principles in mothballs when Potomac fever intensified, and you have had the fever at least since our college days. That said, award winning columnist John Brummett wrote that you are "vulnerable to the charge of unprincipled expediency."

Passing judgment is big business in America's tax-free, right wing world. In the late twentieth century, Mormons joined this misguided alliance that wallows in hate and blames their behavior on the teachings of Jesus Christ. You switched positions on numerous social issues and appear ready to cater to those in the hate business. Is it fair to say you and the LDS Church locked arms with people who

distain our nation's constitutional authority and persistently vent moral indignation at fellow citizens? In 2007, you said, "You don't change your principals, but
your view on a particular issue may change." Mitt, what should Americans think
when you change positions on almost all the social issues? Where is the integrity
or the principals?

In 1947, Erich Fromm wrote, "There is perhaps no phenomenon which contains so much destructive feeling as moral indignation" because it "permits envy
and hate to be acted out under the guise of virtue." The current Mormon
Church, like a sexually repressed Puritan, fears somewhere some soul might enjoy
his free agency and have some fun at the same time. Mormons label people evil,
while they endorse and sponsor those who enhance their Kingdom's organizational goals. An American proverb posits that men are blind in their own cause
and as a past member of the Mormon Church, I saw, felt and heard it first hand.
Now, I ask you not to sacrifice your conscience to political ambition and become
a national and international advocate for the religiously incorrect Mormon
Church and their fundamentalist Christian allies.

The LDS Church is opportunistic and disingenuous when it proselytizes on
traditional family values and presents itself as a monogamous Christian church,
and it is superficial when you change your political positions to please Christian
evangelicals, campaign operatives, special interest groups and donors. I realize
these Americans, who refer to themselves as values voters, are now the Republican
Party's political base, but does the end justify the means when you behave like a
politician straight out of central casting? Had you stuck to your tolerant, moderate positions, you would be immune to political theatre. Throughout his career,
your father, whom you idolized, stuck to his core beliefs. Mitt, you disregarded
what you believed and now say you are an "Evangelical Mormon"—whatever the
heck that is. I scratch my head, because Mormons traditionally have been theo-
logically further away from contemporary Christian evangelicalism than the
Catholics or mainstream Protestants. Even if Mormons and evangelicals are ready
to somehow overcome their core religious differences and work collectively to
enact and enforce their repressive social agendas, do you really want to champion
those who assume their destiny is to rebuild America in a Mormon theocratic or
Falwellian image?

I could have warned you that moving your political position to the far right
would surround you with an outrageous cast. No surprise that Ann Coulter,
whom Mad Magazine called "Queen of the vile," has dumped her endorsement
on you. Chagrinned, I watched you begin a political love affair with Coulter and

shuddered when she crossed those skinny legs in the middle of your Presidential campaign and said you tricked liberals into voting for you. Later, she added that she likes a guy who hoodwinks the voters so easily. Of course, Rush now loves you and, who knows, since you went hunting to bond with Republican donors, Dick Cheney may invite you to borrow a gun and join him in a field to relax and talk strategy.

Mitt, are you really happy being the marquee political fighter for Mormons, Ann Coulter, Dick Cheney, or Bob Jones III? Wouldn't you rather be the man who secured the title of great statesman in history? Socrates would advise you to be a great citizen for the ages not the leading political citizen of Mormonism and the other narrow minded Americans of our time. Continue your present course, and I predict you'll be left standing in the waiting room to greatness with a folder full of Republican talking points and Mormon religious spin. Or worse, if Americans are duped into electing another Republican any time soon, you could be appointed to serve in his uncompassionate Presidential Cabinet.

Voters deserve to know whether you really have core values and, if so, what they are. Once, you declined a public service commercial for Massachusetts, saying you would leave the acting to actors, but now you are putting on the acting performance of your life. In a humorous vein, your redefined positions on social issues earned you the monikers Flip Romney and Slick Dancing Mitt. More seriously, Massachusetts Republicans for Truth were concerned enough to launch a web site in March, 2007 to begin a Mitt Romney educational campaign. A spokesperson said, "We can't elect an unknown quantity to be President of the United States." Maybe it's all sincere, but over the past few years, you starred in a national spectacle that, at the very least, makes you look like a desperate political actor in a campy melodrama.

Abortion and stem cell research are good examples of flip-flopping. Before his death, Gerald Ford told Presidential historian Michael Beschloss that George H. W. Bush sold out to the hard right of the Republican Party with his phony position on abortion. George W. Bush continued the process, and now it's your turn. In the past, you said we should protect the woman's right to choose, then, as the issue alternately simmered and burned, you had an epiphany and declared yourself pro-life. You previously believed abortions should be safe and legal and now claim to be in a "different place" with views that "evolved and deepened." Congressman Rahm Emanuel amused at the 2007 Gridiron Club shindig when he described you as a pro-choice Governor of Massachusetts now running as a pro-life candidate from Michigan.

A supporter of stem cell research during your 2002 run for Governor, you vetoed a stem cell research bill and now support banning the creation of new human embryos for the purpose of research. "It is Orwellian," you philosophized. All that political maneuvering, Mitt, when the Mormon Church, despite numerous restrictive positions on social issues, hasn't expressed a problem with embryonic stem cell research. Your presidential campaign cleverly muddied the stem cell debate, so it's difficult to know where you stand. Still, you once were open to stem cell research and now, like President Bush, you support serious restrictions—to the detriment of scientific progress. New Massachusetts Governor Deval Patrick believes life sciences should be guided by science not politics. Research breakthroughs allowing scientists to reprogram ordinary human skin cells to behave like embryonic stem cells could end the controversy, but probably not. Those who object will find a similar issue to protest and continue the social upheaval.

Your change of heart on abortion came after a comment by a Harvard scientist concerning the morality of using embryos for research. The reinvented Mitt stated, "It struck me very powerfully at that point that the Roe v Wade approach has so cheapened the value of human life, that somebody could think it's not a moral issue to destroy embryos." In his book, *Letter to a Christian Nation*, Sam Harris writes, "A three-day-old human embryo is a collection of 150 cells called a blastocyst. There are, for the sake of comparison, more than 100,000 cells in the brain of a fly." A fourteen-day-old embryo has more cells than a three-day-old one, but that doesn't make it a moral issue. Since human embryo cells don't have brains or neurons, it should be a non-issue morally—unless we also plan to stop killing flies. It sounds like a corny argument over how many devils can dance on a doorknob.

Mitt, your flip-flopping positions on abortion and stem cell research cheapen the national discussion and subvert the real moral issue. Most Americans, including you, have family members or friends who will benefit from advances in embryonic stem cell research. In an attempt to please the moral indignation crowd (never placated) you missed the real moral issue—all the good that will come with this research. Your position on abortion has also morphed into something more politically expedient, and confusing. Referring to Roe v Wade, the old Mitt Romney said, "You will never see me waiver on that." Now, claiming taxpayers shouldn't pay for something that ethically troubling, you want Roe v Wade reversed and support a constitutional amendment to ban abortion nationwide. At least that's what you said the day before you told another audience abortion should be left to the States to decide.

I served at the US Supreme Court in 1973 on scholarship from BYU when Roe v. Wade was announced. Dispatched to the offices of the "Grand Old Man" of the Court, Justice William O. Douglas, I helped his staff open thousands of pieces of hate mail. The ordinarily hushed and solemn halls of the Court had not seen the equivalent since 1954 when Brown v The Board of Education struck down the separate but equal precedent. As with Brown v The Board, the Roe v Wade decision inundated the Court with hate-filled and threatening correspondence. Abortion is heart-wrenching and can be personally devastating, but I agreed with the Justices' decision and drove to my Virginia apartment each night tired and depressed after reading vicious mail and looking at gory pictures clipped from the *Saturday Evening Post* all day.

Justice William O. Douglas, son of a Presbyterian minister, had served on the Court since the Roosevelt administration and was a major target of the correspondence—a large percentage form letters orchestrated by the Catholic Church. When introduced to Douglas, a staff member explained I was on loan from Chief Justice Burger's office. Douglas glared at me, then turned and walked into his office. I never knew whether his behavior resulted from the pressure of an institution under siege, or because I came from the Republican side of the Court. He simply may have been exhausted, worn down by the venomous onslaught. Douglas had a stroke in 1974, and retired from the Court a year later. I'd wager he now rolls in his grave as you, and those you represent, seek to reverse the privacy precedent he and his key colleagues set.

The current Bush Administration appeases its conservative base by attacking judicial precedent and suppressing or rewriting scientific analysis that doesn't suite their preconceived agendas. Mitt, you adopted Team Bush's social positions, and now stand against a woman's right to privacy, and seek to block other scientific research efforts as well. As President, would you serve our secular society and support scientific issues or advocate for the agenda of the Mormon Church and religious right? Since Mormons are masters at rewriting and suppressing information, and you're their new potitical front man, it's fair to question your intentions and ask where your loyalties reside. Your recent comments and constant political positioning raise much doubt.

The Mormon position (your new-found position) on homosexuals is particularly vexing—and not because I'm secretly gay and live in fear Ann Coulter will add me to her list of faggots. Watching you and the Mormon Church join misguided Christians to judge and punish other Americans is frustrating because I have gay friends. The LDS Church has spent millions in recent years to lead the national business of gay rights suppression. It's understandable, but hypocritical to the extreme, for Mormons loudly to advocate for traditional marriage when their Gods are polygamists. Nevertheless, Utah Senator Orrin Hatch rides shotgun on the Church's homophobic garbage truck, and you recently climbed on board and grabbed a seat.

Mitt, during your 1994 Senate run, you assured the Massachusetts Log Cabin Republicans you would provide them more effective leadership than Ted Kennedy. Then, at the 2004 Republican Convention, you likened the threat from same sex marriage to Islamic terrorism. Never mind gay marriage isn't even on the short list of threats to America or the heterosexual family, you believe same sex couples should be denied hundreds of federal benefits available to heterosexual couples. Unwilling to support civil unions, hospital visitations are the only privilege you'll grant this beleaguered minority. Contradicting recent campaign statements, you said in 2007, "I am opposed to discrimination against gay people." Mitt, your positions reveal embarrassing contradictions that can't escape scrutiny in our in-the-moment world of cyberspace.

Founded in Provo, Utah, the gay Mormon support group, Affirmation, just celebrated its thirty year anniversary amidst concerns about the unusually high suicides rate among gay Mormons. Although the Mormon Church still believes homosexuality is a "temporary condition," leaders modified their position in recent years, magnanimously allowing gays to remain in the Church—if they reject a sexually active gay lifestyle. Apostle Dallin Oaks said thoughts are no longer evil, just actions. According to Oaks, the sin is yielding to temptation. Does Oaks believe anyone would simply chose to live a gay lifestyle in the same way he would chose to rob a bank? Mitt, the real sin occurs when LDS leaders punish members for being themselves and render God's creations unwelcome in their cultural community and disrespected by their families. A former homosexual Church member said being a gay Mormon, living a closeted life or punished for not doing so, was beyond hell.

The hostile Mormon position on homosexuality begs the question; why does the Church choose this issue for such a strong stand when there are many more pressing problems in our nation and the world? Neither the Mormon Jesus, speaking in the Book of Mormon, nor the Biblical Jesus said a word about homosexuality. Opposition to homosexuality really has no solid basis in Christian teachings and theology at all. The LDS Church's antigay policy travels under the guise of protecting the family and marriage, yet Mormons have done more to corrupt the family structure, traditional marriage and our western cultural value system than gay couples who simply want a legal, committed relationship, to enjoy equal property rights and to possibly adopt a homeless child. Why do the Mormon leaders remain determined to make life difficult and dangerous for gay citizens? Does the Church so adamantly preach homosexuality is a grievous sin because a gay person epitomizes the antithesis of Mormon reproductive beliefs about eternity?

It's preposterous to hear Mormon leaders sounding the trumpets for preservation of traditional marriage, a hollow, toneless sound, because Mormons believe in polygamy and refuse to denounce it as an eternal ordinance fundamental to their faith. Mormon men missed their chance to return to traditional marriage when in 1844 Nauvoo, Emma Smith and other Relief Society women unanimously voted to restore it. Mitt, a youth movement towards gay acceptance will make today's anti-gay Americans and their political leaders look like hate peddlers in history. How sad that Mormons again chose sides with those who fought against earlier civil rights movements, and you made a sharp right turn to please those waving placards for repression.

Science provides evidence that sexual orientation is innate and linked to biological conditions. Homosexual men and women are influenced and guided by genetic and hormonal differences. It's neither a personal choice to live an evil life in defiance of the Creator, nor an effort to infuriate and incite insecure heterosexuals. Homophobic activism by right wing Christians and Mormons is a poisonous side-show diverting attention from more important conversations on the national stage. Mitt, this regressive policy position reveals the only truth Church isn't divinely inspired, benevolent or scientifically informed.

As my children's favorite sea critter, SpongeBob SquarePants, would say, Mormonism is "just imaginaaation." To circling religious barracudas like Focus on the Family founder, James Dobson, he is also known as SpongeBob Queer Pants. Not long after Pat Robertson attacked the purple Teletubbie, Tinky Winky, for packing a purse, Mr. Dobson, another self-designated moral guardian, squeezed the sponge for financial contributions to support his crusade. Mitt, I'm deeply disappointed the Mormons, and now you, joined forces with those who include homosexuality with real vices like the lust for fame, fortune and power—or an obsessive/compulsive desire to drive a huge yellow hummer.

Your father was an early supporter of the civil rights movement, and you appeared an early advocate of gay rights, until you realized that stance might impede your Presidential aspirations. I believe your ancestors—still in their graves awaiting Mormon Resurrection—would fidget uncomfortably if they heard you defend a "federal rule on marriage" over that of a State or territory. Apparently, if it helps you win political support, you're willing to change and defend any position. When your boundless political ambitions placed you in the middle of the Gay Rights debate, you expediently adopted the uncompromising position of those who would amend the US Constitution to block civil liberties for yet another besieged minority. After the Massachusetts court ruled in favor of gay marriage, you said, "We don't want Massachusetts to become the Las Vegas of same sex marriage." Mitt, Las Vegans don't want to become the Utah of plural marriages, yet polygamists work and live in Las Vegas, bring corporations here and earn money to support Warren Jeffs' world.

You were quoted in the *Washington Post* saying, "Who is going to tell us what a civil right is and what is not? Well, the people will." Mitt, you know if the majority of voters decide what a civil right is, due to the "tyranny of the majority," Americans would have few minority rights. Besides, Americans don't vote on all matters; our government is a Republic if, as Ben Franklin said, we can keep it. We chose elected officials to speak for us and rely on Constitutional checks and balances, including an independent judiciary, to protect minorities from politicians pandering to insensitive people impossible to please. You made a decision to morally digress for the support of right wing bigots instead of proposing vanguard positions which will lead our nation into its future.

Presumptuous for a former, part-time community college instructor to lecture a Harvard law graduate on Political Science 101 concepts, but I take the liberty. Mitt, the real test of a democratic society is not whether the majority rules, but how the government protects the rights of the most unpopular minorities. The Founding Fathers established an appointed federal judicial system to provide politically unencumbered systemic oversight and protect the rule of law. Often the last bastion of freedom, our quasi-independent courts defend controversial civil rights from grandstanding candidates and elected officials seeking votes from intolerant, judgmental types waving family values banners and insisting they're uniquely qualified to dictate societal norms for all.

Observing the current Bush Administration's policies, author and columnist Maureen Dowd wrote, "Checks and balances are now as quaint as the Geneva Convention." Pleased with illegal torture, the pinched-faced crowd who wants homosexuality punished also seeks to silence appointed men and women they call "activist judges." Mitt, you stated, "I believe our laws ought to be written by the people, and not unelected judges." Should we overthrow the Republic, forget representative democracy, discard separation of powers and ignore the rule of law? Judges don't write laws. Roe v Wade, for example, only overturned laws written by the peoples' representatives found to violate our Constitution. James

Madison, wisest of the founders, understood a separation of powers was needed, or the majority could impose intolerant and perhaps illegal positions on society.

After sectarian Mormon theocrats spent the nineteenth century belittling and defying American principles of equality and democracy, their successors were dragged kicking and screaming into the twentieth, battling modernity all the way. The church scowled and snorted through the 1960s civil rights movement, and then railed against the Equal Rights Amendment in the 1970s. Now, Mormons must be pulled—huffing and puffing—into the twenty-first century and through the gay rights movement as well. But there's good news. Gay Rights are being embraced by the majority of more tolerant young Americans, products of diversity education received in our constantly criticized secular public school system.

Mitt, public opinion polls reveal the vast majority of Americans believe in family values, a concept not exclusive to fundamentalist Republicans and Mormons. In fact, polls also show divorce rates are just as high, and in many cases higher, in red states than in blue states. A simple and reasonable resolution exists for those who really wish to stop the divisive battle over legalized gay unions The solution to the horror of gay marriage is to have civil marriage authorizations issued by the government and religious marriages performed, sanctioned and supervised by the church of the couples' choice. Civil marriages can then legally be performed and dissolved in secular environments, and those who believe in the "sanctity of marriage" can honor their vows or deal with the functionaries of their religious affiliation. It's a practical solution that fits nicely under the separation of church and state umbrella.

Mitt, you further enhanced your reputation as a political opportunist by changing your position on gun control. In 1994, you favored a waiting period on assault rifles, and once stated "I don't line up with the NRA." That was before you suited up like Elmer Fudd and accompanied several white bubbas to shoot semi-tame critters on a Georgia game preserve and, in August, 2006, joined the NRA. Mitt, killing-for-fun spectacles should disgust you. Our families of pioneer Utahans hunted wild game to put food on the table. My Grandma Kelly shot deer for food for the family and neighbors. After hearing you portray yourself as a life-long rabbit hunter, *Boston Globe* columnist Joan Vennochi, observed, "Leave it to Mitt Romney to shoot himself in the foot with a gun he didn't own."

On your reinvention roll to please conservatives Republican voters, you took a harsher stance on immigration than even President Bush and Senator McCain. How can you callously cater to immigration hysteria and ignore the personal cost to millions living and working in our country? Actions based on rigid ideology have consequences for real people. Remember, Mitt, immigrants built America and the Mormon Church, and, over the past three decades, immigrants, some illegal, helped to rejuvenate dying cities from Marshalltown, Iowa to New York City. This sudden, obvious pattern of scrambling across the political spectrum (including the global warming issue) raises an important question thinking Americans need answered. At this critical juncture in history, do you really want to lead a regressive crowd of right wingers or do you only pretend to support their causes for cynical political purposes? Your actions raise issues of trust, integrity and strength of character.

Defending your political reinvention, you said, "In the style of Mark Twain, I would suggest rumors of my changes in positions have been greatly exaggerated." Mitt, your position changes are obvious, not exaggerated. Your ideological acrobatics deserve an Olympic medal. Granted, all politicians change their political stance to some extent during their careers. As you pointed out, every politician does it. However, the difference is that your peers didn't politically retool themselves in a year or two and hope the voters wouldn't notice. On a kinder note, comedy writer, Ben Alper, thinks you deserved credit for seeking the support of evangelical Christians without changing your name to Billy Joe Romney or sponsoring a NASCAR team. I wonder whether Mr. Alper knew you were called Billy as a little boy.

No Mormon can lead this nation into the twenty-first century with his mind and heart captivated by a nineteenth century cult focused on keeping its members uninformed, fighting civil rights for minorities and lobbying to suppress scientific development. Mitt, the unfinished pyramid on the nation's dollar bill awaits completion by future generations. America will survive as world leader led by politicians who offer hope for a better tomorrow, not individuals and groups who support a bigoted world—or fear a bleak earthly future and have faith in a primitive heaven. Americans should be concerned that your value system is based on the Mormon mélange, and those muddled beliefs justify your expedient political behavior.

Mitt, you have unfinished business before you're ready to be President of the United States. Our Mormon generation, along with its children and precious grandchildren, needs you to enrich their lives. Help them accept what many suspect but don't want or dare to know. Stand up to those puffed up popinjays at Church headquarters—with their six-figure incomes and corporate perks—and let your legacy be that of a great warrior who articulated principled positions and restored vision to the Mormon people. If we fail publicly to refute the Church falsehoods, our generation will be designated the generation of shame. How much more courageous to do the right thing than to pursue corrupt Republican Party politics alongside Karl Rove, mendacious Mormons and right wing evangelicals.

In late 2006, you invited nearly every evangelical leader except Ted Haggard to your home in Belmont to break bread and seek endorsements. I understand your motivation for pandering to all these opportunistic Billy Sundays for Jesus. Almost unbelievable to me, a recent Gallop poll reveal 53% of Americans are creationists. These folks believe the cosmos was created six thousand years ago, which, as author Sam Harris points out in *Letter to a Christian Nation,* is "about a thousand years after the Sumerians invented glue." A cadre of courageous scientists is presently locked in a renewed battle with creationists and intelligent designers crusading to relive the 1920s monkey trial and dumb down our children's school curriculum.

Mitt, as you pursue your presumed destiny, your political repositioning is understandable. The majority of Americans tell pollsters they think the earth is younger than glue, and millions accept as fact that all the species, including the dinosaurs, marched onto Noah's ark two by two. At age four, my son knew dinosaurs became extinct sixty-five million years ago. I agree with Sam Harris when he observes that "our country now appears, as at no other time in our history, like a lumbering, bellicose, dim-witted giant." Sadly, you felt you had no choice but to scamper to the right and bow to this harebrained thinking. Do scientists and historians have to battle with the religious right's nonsense and be challenged by politicians like you, too?

It should be unnecessary to even say it, but the *Old Testament* ark, even if as big as a modern aircraft carrier, couldn't have held all the earth's species. Breaking my word not to resort to potty humor, even if those critters safely boarded, a great many would have slipped on slick piles of poop and slid into the Bible's famous flood. Predators that kept their footing during Noah's big adventure would have feasted on trapped prey. Interestingly, the glue-inventing Sumerians also had a flood myth recorded in their ancient records that predates the Israelite's *Old Testament* account and featured a hero named Ziusudra. Mitt, I'm relieved you have admitted the possibility of evolution and a world older than six thousand years—at least that was your last position in the issue.

Compassionless religious ideologists, Mormons and other calculating interests groups live in a simplistic world, which, by definition, requires them to despise many of our liberties that anger their *Old Testament* God. As money rolls in to feed their cash-hungry organizations, their success at influencing foreign policy make the world more dangerous. They strive to rob us of freedoms at home and believe a preordained, catastrophic climax to human events is inevitable. Worse, they support foreign policies that could turn their fantasy based universe into a self-fulfilling prophecy. Cock-sure simpletons and single-issued bigots send money to finance those sanctimonious entities and are instructed to vote Republican on election day.

Republican political manipulation of Christian fundamentalists is cynical and ironic. According to inside sources, Karl Rove never cared about this croud or their social causes. He merely tolerated their positions because their presence created a majority coalition for the Republican Party. So far, the right wing evangelical's social agenda remains mostly unfulfilled, but they won't be satisfied until it's politically implemented. Mitt, after determining you couldn't win the Republican nomination without the support of the religious right, you callously reinvented yourself to achieve your political goals. Freedom-loving Americans should be concerned that you want to champion these repressive crusades—or pretend to.

18

"Bogged down in Bushistan"

Mitt, growing political differences took us both to New York City in 2004. You arrived to play a starring role at the Republican convention, while my destination was Democratic National Committee headquarters. Your testimonial speech for President Bush excited cheering conventioneers waving flip-flops, and I joined Iowa Governor Tom Vilsac, General Tony McPeak and others as Nevada Republicans for Kerry coordinator. We reminded Americans the Iraq mission was not accomplished. After our presentations to the national press, a staff member told me I should be the Kerry campaign's national spokesman. Flattered, but not as pretty as spokesman Terry McAuliffe, I returned home and continued the political fight to defeat Bush as we tried desperately to alter history.

Directly and indirectly, the Republican Party spent one hundred million dollars in its sickening Swift Boat attacks to turn John Kerry, a decorated American war hero, into a perceived liar and traitor. I handed Senator Kerry a note in early September, 2004, urging him to ignore the focus groups and more assertively defend his character. General Wesley Clark personally assured me they would counter the Swift Boater's charges aggressively, but it was too little too late. The attacks had done their damage. In a letter mailed to thousands of Nevadans in October, 2004, I said Kerry was a double hero for serving with distinction and then telling the truth about the Vietnam War when he returned home. Mitt, you aren't a fan of Senator Kerry, but to me, Kerry is a triple hero for also working with Senator John McCain during the 1980s to restore diplomatic relations with Vietnam.

One of your top early Presidential fundraising supporters was a Houston home builder named Bob Perry. Perry was a major donor to the Swift Boat Veterans for Truth, before joining your campaign to raise money for future political attacks and dirty tricks. When word reached Senator Kerry's office that Bob the builder had enlisted in your campaign, spokesman David Wade responded "it was appalling but not surprising a Texas tycoon famous for funding lies would now bankroll a Presidential campaign built on flip-flopping and fiction." Fair to say Senator Kerry isn't one of your fans, either?

Politics has been described as the art of the possible, yet President Bush squandered our military resources and international prestige in actions at least in part motivated by the fact that Saddam threatened his daddy. Driven by ideology and vengeance, the Bush Administration destabilized the Middle East following 9/11, instead of exploiting international good will and building intelligence networks to fight terrorism. Rather than focus on Afghanistan, Bush and the neocons unleashed conventional warfare in Iraq, created dangerous instability and increased hatred of our country. Later, the White House wrapped failed foreign policies in altruistic notions about democracy to justify their obstinate blundering, and you, Mitt, supported them through it all before hedging your bets in late 2007.

President Bush could have learned from Vietnam, but he didn't go. In recent years, Mitt, you rarely missed an opportunity to praise the President's fortitude, but "bring-it-on" Bush, like Cheney and other administration warriors, was never inclined to bring it on in Vietnam when given the chance. Nonetheless, the Bush administration sent young soldiers to fight and die in the misdirected, misbegotten Iraq war. Now, you lamely tell voters Team Bush has kept us safe all these years, and we're left with no viable options in a place we never should have gone.

One crushing result of our bungled foreign policy maneuvering since 9/11 is our substantially diminished influence in the Middle East. The Administrations action's handed our enemies more trump cards than The Donald has. America isn't even trusted when we attempt to do something right. In a late 2006 report, *The Economist* stated, "So entrenched is the idea of an American led assault on Muslims that virtually any new development is immediately enlisted as further evidence." In these circumstances, even "high-minded western initiatives" like placing a stronger peacekeeping force in Darfur arouses suspicion and skepticism.

While still not obvious to some, the only mission accomplished in Iraq was to squander our international goodwill, destroy human lives and to waste hundreds of billions of dollars (or trillions) our grandchildren must repay. Mitt, I love this country as much as you, and pray the American Republic didn't peak in the prosperous Clinton/Gore years and begin its decline under Bush/Cheney. Historians will tell us in the future whether 9/11 began the end of our role as world leader. Bush and Cheney predict history will vindicate their Iraq policy, which you endorsed with little reservation. For years you defended the Bush administration and the Iraq war, only recently admitting "mistakes were made." Understandable since you had strong political support from Jeb and other Bush family members.

As we progress into the twenty-first century, more Americans see through the façade and recognize the real traitors. A well-worn truism is old men start wars and send young men to fight them. In the Iraq war, draft-dodging, combat-avoiding old men started the wrong war and sent thousands of young men and women to die or be maimed for life. George W. Bush once hid in—and from—the Texas National Guard, and when his administration's Iraq failures became politically overwhelming, he started hiding behind his generals. Dick Cheney received several draft deferments because he had "other priorities," and numerous key players in the Iraq war fiasco also never served in the military. Had you served a tour of duty in Vietnam instead of a Mormon mission, I wonder whether you would now recommend expansion of our armed forces as a cornerstone of your foreign policy.

The Catholic Church has opposed the Iraq war and called for an end to the suffering, but LDS Church silence implies tacit approval. Former National Security Advisor Brent Scowcroft is the only prominent Mormon to speak against the Iraq war. Though Mormon President Heber J. Grant was a pacifist and voiced reservations about America entering World War II, we were reared in a Church which emphasized its Restored Gospel must be preached to the entire world before the Second Coming. Mormons believe all nations and peoples must hear and respond to the only true Christian Church's message, so wars are necessary to open new markets for their missionaries. In my lifetime, I don't remember a war the Mormon Church didn't support, so long as missionary deferments existed for children of elite LDS families.

It was natural for Mormons to view the invasion of Iraq as an integral part of their religious goals. If the Soviet Union hadn't fallen, today, missionaries wouldn't be allowed in Romania and other eastern block countries. The Gospel of John (5.9) says, "Blessed are the peacemakers, for they will be called the children of God." In our contemporary American culture of war, supported by Mormons, those who disagree with the Iraq war are children of a lesser God—the one called the Prince of Peace. The last bastion of scoundrels is patriotism, and it didn't take long for Mormons and others to hide behind the "support the troops" slogan or use "cut and run" as a weapon against those who opposed the administration's Iraq policy. Mitt, many Americans simply wanted to support the troops by bringing them home and saving their lives.

As a counterpoint to the Bush/Romney position on Iraq, former Rhodes Scholar and Senator Bill Bradley said Iraq is a more horrendous error than Vietnam and the worst foreign policy mistake in our lifetime. History will prove Bradley correct. By the end of 2007, Senator Chuck Hegal and several other

Republicans finally became disenchanted with the Bush debacle, too. The Bush administration's decisions wore out our military equipment, ripped service families apart with constant redeployment and maimed or killed thousands. America squandered enough money to rebuild its crumbling infrastructure, fund a tax-subsidized program for alternative energy sources and provide health insurance for all Americans. In the process, this cast of characters you supported displayed a blatant disrespect for American political tradition and reckless disregard for the international community.

Mitt, the fact that the axis of evil countries was never directly implicated in the 9/11 attacks mattered little to our arrogant, stubborn President with his inevitable end-days beliefs. However, Bush is now partly humbled. For most Americans, it's less embarrassing to see him hide behind his generals than dress up like a candidate for the Village People. Bush smirked on a flight deck, strutted on the world stage and flailed away at the straw men he created. The dangerous result was the axis of evil developed muscle and resolve. Americans who opposed the Iraq war, particularly any who dared challenge policy, were labeled "morally confused" by Secretary Rumsfeld, who said dissenters appeased the new Hitlers of the world. Times changed. Rumsfeld is gone, and protestors became part of what Garry Trudeau of *Doonesbury* called the "treasonous mainstream."

As America nears the end of what Maureen Dowd labeled the "macho politics of marshmallow men," the Iraq disaster will linger for years, if not decades. Retired General John Batiste said, "We did this to ourselves. We might as well call it Bushistan." From 2001 until its undeniable failure, the Bush Doctrine was for recycled cold war warriors—the so-called Dream Team—to misapply old school ideas and strategies to fluid new crises. As a result, to paraphrase John Kerry's statement about Vietnam, we're still waiting for the last American soldier to die for the Bush Administration's blunder in Iraq. An unjustifiable mistake magnified by a basic unfairness that the large majority of soldiers killed in Iraq have been from poor rural areas, while elite Americans and their children made no sacrifice. Later, all our grandchildren will pay.

19

The New Grand Old Party

Mitt, this Republican administration has taken unprecedented steps to abridge American civil liberties. President Bush and his supporting cast defecated on the Constitution, but God forbid any of us show disrespect for Old Glory. How sickening to watch Bush and his bristling neocons remain defiantly determined to pursue the Iraq lost cause, not admit their multiple foreign policy disasters and endlessly wage cultural war to secure their conservative support. Bush and his cronies stirred hate to hold power and continually legislated against feminists, homosexuals, the poor and environmentalists. In the fall of 2007, while requesting a short-term financial fix of another forty billion dollars for his Iraq war, President Bush vetoed health care for poor and working class American children, despite strong national support to expand it.

Joseph Smith claimed a calling directly from Heaven, and Bush had major hallucinations, probably lingering from his party days, which lead him to believe he too was called by God. Meanwhile, back at the ranch, his "brain," Karl Rove had Bush hypnotized for decades. I don't know what hypnotized Rove—maybe money and power—but he has proved a skilled political tactician. Rove the manipulator organized political campaigns around "poisonous trivia" and successfully convinced rock-chucking Christian pretenders to vote against their economic self interest. Fortunately, the 2006 midterm elections revealed Rove, the "evil genius," was overrated and not bright enough to understand what he arrogantly called "the math." As much hype as heavy hitter, Rove limped out of Washington during the 2007 August break, one step ahead of congressional subpoenas. He fired a few parting shots, and then hit the road for Texas to spin history in a memoir or regroup for new political attacks in other campaigns.

Now, Mitt, you want to be the next leader in the new Republican Party that spearheaded cultural wars at home and the culture of war abroad. Traditional conservatives and moderate Republicans have been pushed aside by aggressive social reactionaries determined to control the party, believing it's their God-given duty to legislate morality. Right wing religious groups can always find something "detestable to the Lord" that requires immediate attention, and the Bush crowd is ready to oblige—or cynically pander to them. Although these religious policies perpetuate a zealous tribal culture, the Mormons have adopted the tactics, and you have reinvented yourself to promote the divisiveness and diversion. This strange coalition is not the Republican Party I joined thirty-five years ago. I belonged to the Grand Old Party of Rockefeller, Goldwater, George Romney and Reagan, now sentimentally remembered by columnist George Will. Little room remains for the legacies of Abraham Lincoln, Teddy Roosevelt or Dwight Eisenhower.

Having plowed under its great conservative principals of limited government, States rights and balanced budgets that won a congressional majority, the new Republican Party has alienated or ignored deficit hawks in favor of issues like gay rights and abortion. Western Republicans advocate States rights and want the federal government's role limited, while southern Republicans want more federal intervention and faith-based initiative money. Westerners think government should stay off our backs, and southerners want it to impose a legislated national morality. Thomas Jefferson said, "The natural process of things is for liberty to yield and government to gain ground." Mitt, this occurred under the Bush Administration you supported.

Barry Goldwater wanted government to stay off our backs, out of our wallets and out of our bedrooms, but today's white evangelical Republicans scale the wall between church and state to pry open bedroom doors for a morality inspection. Adding to the disappointment, the Bush Administration tossed the Party's past affinity for limited government, State rights and deficit reduction off the Republican platform. The federal government, staffed with inexperienced, incompetent ideologues, ballooned in size and scope under George W. Bush and six years of Republican Congressional control. Another fact that draws tears, 70% of our nine trillion dollar national debt was incurred under Reagan and the two Bush Presidencies.

Decades ago, Senator Goldwater predicted his views would appear liberal someday. Although wrong on civil rights, he despised the religious right and warned of the dangers their growing influence presented. Politics indeed makes strange bedfellows, and the Republican Party traded in its political pup tent for a bigger one to gain a governing majority. The bigger tent created uneasy sleeping arrangement between Western economic conservatives, who like to sleep naked, and Southern social conservatives, who sleep in jammies. Political merger created a schism that has each faction flashing a political infidelity finger at the other.

While the party floundered, Mitt, you delivered impressive but simplistic stump speeches to rally the new party base.

Neoconservatives changed the national debate from economic justice and the Bill of Rights to noisy, inane wars on social issues, constantly repackaged and replayed, to force restrictive legislation positions on a traditionally prudent, pragmatic American electorate. Karl Rove encouraged cultural combat on religiously oriented social issues and ultimately, the present Bush administration failed both the nation and the refreshing ideas that attracted me to the GOP in my youth. Thankfully, religious conservatives' long term success has been limited, but calculated actions like attacking the press, frightening judges and impugning the patriotism of liberal Americans were short term political winners.

Mitt, abandon religious conservative's efforts to undermine our freedoms at home or to advocate abroad for what former Soviet leader and Nobel Peace Prize winner, Mikhail Gorbachev, calls America's "winners complex." Instead of promoting America's economic and military imperialism, put away that neoconservative saber, draw your enlightenment sword and lift it to free the Mormon people. Do the right thing and rebuke the right wing, along with Mormon leaders, who endorse tiresome social tirades and major global military miscalculations. Only then can you secure a truly righteous position in American and religious history.

Though our founding fathers wanted separation, politics and religion have never been more closely intertwined than in American politics today. A struggle rages between those who seek draconian principles of religious dogmatism over the secular American experiment initiated by the founders. Little more than a generation passed from the late eighteenth century epoch, when America's founders created the modern world, until Joseph Smith and his followers tried to unravel their dream. Today, although God and Christianity are not mentioned in the Constitution or Bill of Rights, persistent fundamental religionists use the Republican Party to dictate repressive policies. The Mormons, after their nineteenth century failure to overthrow and control the Republic, have become their political allies.

Mitt, if Americans don't reject foolish, short-sighted foreign and domestic policies, apocalyptic prophecies could become self-fulfilling on our nation and the world. One understandable but frightening slogan floating around today is, "America is a Christian nation." In 2004, a Mormon cousin came over to pick a fight after learning I was working in the Kerry campaign. During our family get-together, I refrained from mentioning my involvement with Kerry to avoid any potential confrontations. My discretion ended when she said that she and her husband walked out of a Linda Ronstadt concert because Ronstadt paid tribute to her friend, Michael Moore. Being a fan of both Ronstadt and Moore, the war of words was on.

I refused to back down and tried to talk sense, but this high school educated cousin, who birthed almost enough boys to field a football team, followed us out to the family van. Flashing self-righteous anger all the way, she informed me that America is a Christian nation. Nothing resulted from that silly situation, except that we haven't spoken since. Truth be told, and it's getting harder over the emotional din, the Vatican is a Christian nation, but not the United States. Our system was founded on Judeo-Christian principals, but we live in a nation that allows citizens to be Christian, Jews, Buddhists, Hindus, Muslims, pagans or whatever they choose. My cousin was not aware that a group of remarkably enlightened men founded America as a secular nation to operate under the rule of law. No interpretation of the Constitution establishes or creates a Christian nation.

My cousin isn't the only one confused. A "State of the First Amendment 2007" national survey discovered that 65% of Americans believed the U.S. Constitution established a Christian nation. Mitt, the American Constitution and Bill of Rights need protection, and the President has a legal and moral obligation to defend the unalienable rights the founding fathers declared our human birthright. We can't allow gifts from our Creator to be circumvented or dismissed by Mormons, Christian fundamentalists or any group of misguided, uninformed citizens. My cousin's arguments and conclusions are built on a foundation of ignorance and confusion too prevalent in our country and the Mormon Church today. Ironically, she is faithful to the Mormon Church and, thus, isn't a Christian.

According to early twenty-first century public opinion polls, the new Republican Party's hate-pedaling, liberty-attacking policies won't work long term. These polls show a "youth-quake" coming on social issues, and the generations behind us will provide a healthy stir to the American melting pot. The divisive strategies of social conservatives and Mormons may not even work in the short term. Evaluation of the 2006 midterm elections clearly shows Americans of all ages are both weary and wary of those attacking social liberties at home and applauding military-oriented policies abroad. Mitt, the trend lines are moving against your newfound positions in our country's cultural and military wars. Most Americans are unhappy with the country's direction, and more call themselves liberal than at any time in a generation. As you campaigned for a bigger military, and suggested that we handle Iran with a "bombardment of some kind," fewer Americans wanted to spend money on wars abroad at the expense of needs at home.

Polls show the majority of Americans are hungry for sensible, moderate leadership in domestic and foreign policy. They want a President sworn to uphold the constitution, not another quick-trigger President eager to fight the forces of evil at home and abroad. Like other western cultures, most Americans view religion as a personal choice and not the most vital issue for government to address. True patriots don't claim their religion is the eternal and literal truth and don't want it imposed on others by government fiat. The midterm elections made millions proud to be Americans again. Voters rejected a same sex marriage ban in Arizona, defended abortion rights in South Dakota and endorsed stem cell research in Missouri. Mitt, could we be on the brink of turning our current American hate debates into thoughtful discussions on important social, economic and environmental issues facing America and the world?

There's more favorable news for freedom lovers. While moderate young Christian evangelists emerge in America, core religious right leaders are quickly becoming irascible, dying old men. Still, change won't come easily. The Christian Coalition, founded Pat Robertson, persists in pursuing a negative course. However, recently, it's newly elected President Joel Hunter realized the organization was unwilling to take on the issues that Jesus would have cared about and stepped down. Those issues—poverty, AIDS, pollution, serving the poor and climate change—don't incite people to send money. The Christian Coalition and many other so-called Christian organizations financially cater to a base more motivated by the inflammatory issues that divide and distract us.

Over the last few years, Pat Robertson's causes and comments have become more even asinine than his 1982 prediction that when all the planets aligned, their gravitational pull would tilt the earth on its axis and create havoc—just punishment for an evil world, of course. I listened to Robertson's 700 Club frequently back then, and the blabbering blowhard made me nervous before I realized obsessive men like Robertson get their snoots in a snit over priggish issues every few months. Like Jerry Falwell, Robertson and others will die not understanding that tens of millions of Americans are tired of religion used to attack our liberties, divide us as a nation or simply frighten us for manipulative purposes. Their negativity continues while they pass judgment on one or another minority and plead for money.

Most recently, Robertson said God informed him terrorists will succeed in a mass killing of Americans in 2007, possibly nuclear. Misguided, insecure Americans surely spend sleepless nights fretting over Pat's predictions. God told Pat that He's bringing mayhem and destruction to an American city near you very soon, and we'll deserve it because our people are so darn evil. Mitt, you hitched up your magic underpants, cinched up your Bible belt, and altered your moderate political ways to please the likes of Robertson, Coulter, Christian fundamentalists and the prevaricators in Salt Lake City. Then, Pat Robertson endorsed Rudy Giuliani.

Religious Right wedge issues, which feel like "wedgies," are generational issues caused by old fuddy-duddies with their underwear in a wad. Over time, even more freedom-loving Americans will move to the political center because they resent having their skivvies yanked up by the Republican's war-oriented, division-driving, privacy-stealing policies. The recent midterm elections renewed my faith in the majority of Americans who won't loyally go along with the Republican Revolution. The revolution began with Newt Gingrich needlessly shutting down the federal government over a decade ago and continued with promises to balance the budget and limit federal government growth. Then, the Party allowed partisan purity and religious dogma to supersede common sense, scientific facts and fiscal responsibility.

Forty years of corruption dismantled the Democrats power base, but, courtesy of Team Bush debacles—and Republican money and sex scandals—the long anticipated Republican Revolution ended with a whimper in little more than a decade. Ironically, just when fiscally conservative and socially moderate Republicans decide it time to destroy this new, radical Republican creation, Newt reemerged to offer his services to the party again. This hypocrite sought redemption by admitting that while he attacked Clinton for abusing a good cigar, he had an adulterous affair with a young staff member—now his third wife. After grabbing headlines for months by toying with a Presidential run, Gingrich decided instead to pontificate from a non-profit soap box.

More than ever, America's looming financial, energy and environmental crises create the need for a focused President who faces problems and tells the truth. From his wide-eyed little seat on Dick Cheney's lap, Bush never really developed his own voice. Even before President Bush told columnists that America may be having a Third Great Awaking, I was praying that he would have his first. On complex problems ranging from his Axis of Evil to oil independency, he couldn't articulate or integrate a consistent leadership strategy. His foreign policy decisions were disastrous, and *New York Times* Columnist David Brooks observed,

"The GOP has become like a company with a great mission statement, but no domestic policy products to sell."

In his first six years, President Bush put the veto pen behind his ear and let Republicans run wild through the congressional pigpen. He had fewer vetoes than any President in more than a century, and then used vetoes mostly on social issues. Republicans went on a spending spree like they had a tap in Paris Hilton's trust account, and outspent the Democrats they replaced. With a Democratic Congress back in power, Bush had a chance to act like a real fiscal conservative and stand against obscene political pig outs. Instead, in May, 2007, he vetoed his first spending bill, not because of appropriation levels, but because the supplemental budget bill contained a timeline for withdrawing our troops from Iraq. Only with his Presidency failed, and with Democrats in control of Congress, did Bush finally act like a fiscal conservative and veto spending bills.

While in control of both Congress and the Executive branch, the Republican Party betrayed its political trust and become reckless and corrupted by power. The Bush administration undermined agencies that generated information conflicting with their neocon goals, seeded government with appointees chosen for ideological affinity and blind loyalty and pushed outsourcing of services, which created scandal and runaway costs. Adding to their disgrace, Republican lack of concern for the middle and working classes has threatened to push the nation into a new gilded age. Despite 650 Nobel Prize winners supporting an increase in the minimum wage, including five who won their prizes for economics, the Bush administration remained opposed. Its version of a social safety net was another tax cut for the wealthiest Americans. In 2007, ignoring boogieman arguments by trade association lobbyists, for the first time in a decade a Democrat Congress finally passed a minimum wage bill. Why? Because civilized countries set minimum wages to protect those at the bottom of the economic food chain with the least leverage in the marketplace.

Uncontrolled spending on the Iraq war and the tiresome "no new taxes" mantra have combined to create a staggering long-term national debt. U.S. Comptroller David Walker warned that unfunded budget deficits are a "fiscal cancer" growing in our nation. Even former Fed Chairman Alan Greenspan finally criticized Bush for his "unwillingness to wield his veto pen against out-of-control spending." Author Garrison Keillor said "my college kids are graduating with a 20-pound ball of debt chained to their ankles. That is not right, and you know it." The Prairie Home Companion legend's solution, "cutting health care to one-third of the population—the folks with Bush/Cheney bumper stickers, who still believe the man is doing a heck of a job—will save enough money to pay off the national debt."

The GOP made its political priorities clear in recent years, and they don't include budget, energy policy or environmental issues. Religious Right "nut jobs," the tail that now wags the Republican Party dog, are more interested in thwarting what Bill O'Reilly calls the secular-progressive movement, as if free-thinking Americans are barbarians at the door. According to religious right wingers and Mormons, "secular humanists" have a secret deal with the devil and only conservative Christian evangelicals and the LDS Church can save America from evil "liberal" conspirators who want to prevent the Bible or *Book of Mormon* from superseding many constitutional concepts and the guarantees found in the Bill of Rights.

After working through their self-righteous Senator Hatch to impeach Bill Clinton, the Mormon Church's current political missions are to dish our social punishment to homosexuals and unwaveringly support George W. Bush's persistent effort to be named the worst President in U.S. history. Bush faces stiff competition, but may still prove he's just bad enough to dip below President Warren G. Harding. Whether Bush eventually is labeled our worst president, history will never view him as he sees himself. In a world begging for stability and diplomacy, Bush always tried to prove he's the man and as Maureen Dowd put it, "not some wobbly, wavering, multilateral metrosexual." The disastrous results of his Administration have left Bush out of touch with independent voters, discouraged moderates and fiscal conservatives in the Republican political coalition, and imperiled our nation's future.

It's not the nature of most governments to be responsive to the will of the people. However, day to day, balanced systems serve men best, and ultra-conservative ones are the most difficult to hold accountable. The Bush Administration has so insidiously pandered to its big business and religious allies that both our financial and personal freedoms are at risk. If doomsday is pending, it will more likely be caused by Bush Administration policies bankrupting our grandchildren and weakening our leadership role in the word, than the harsh actions of an angry God who likes to chat with special souls like Joseph Smith, Pat Robertson or George W. Bush.

Mitt, America's financial strength deteriorated more in the first six years of the Bush Administration than any similar period in the past fifty. In addition to a weakened dollar and mounting national debt, Republicans used tax cuts as bribes to retain the favor of the wealthy, while the middle class shrank and gaps between the economic classes grew. Historical evidence reveals two social negatives of unfettered capitalism are poverty and corruption, and the resulting imbalance of personal wealth blocks the emergence of a middle class. So, while President Bush and his allies sought to privatize the Social Security safety net and pushed policies that widened income inequality, Tony Blair's government attempted to reverse the surge in poverty and inequality that occurred under Prime Minister Margaret Thatcher's ultraconservative leadership.

American worker productivity increased dramatically during the past two decades, and today we lead the world in hourly output. However, data compiled by Boston's Northeastern University shows the growing economic disconnect between CEOs and working Americans continues to grow. From the years 2000-2006, labor productivity in the non-farm sector of our economy rose by 18%, but during the same period, worker's inflation-adjusted weekly wages increased by just 1%. Quite a contrast from the productivity gains in the decades following World War II, which were broadly shared and enhanced the living standards of all American families. This upsetting economic data apparently doesn't concern core Republicans, who historically have not supported wealth redistribution policies and programs. Nor does it appear to concern today's economically conservative Mormon leaders, so different from those in the first two Mormon generations and their stated financial order of heaven and earth.

20

President Mitt Romney

For the Mormon Church, the 2008 Presidential sweepstakes stacked as tall as eternity. Church leaders claim political neutrality, but your value in the White House is undeniably significant. Mitt, not only would you be a poster boy for the missionary sales team, Mormon financial assets could grow like weeds on steroids and help Church leaders further legitimize and expand their empire. Your Presidential power position could expand the Mormon holdings in real estate, stocks, news and entertainment, agriculture and various other business ventures. At present, the Church uses political influence to support minor figures that chip away at our constitutional corners. Given the opportunity, Mormon leaders will do much more, and what better place to begin than to have you parked in the Presidency?

The Mormon Myth machine raised millions for your campaign to be king as a wide swath of members' donated significant amounts across Utah, Nevada and other western states. LDS business and member contributors to your Presidential bid will desire more than mere access. If you become the most powerful man in the world, the brothers and sisters expect a devout Presidential response. The Mormon elite place a mob-like premium on loyalty. The Brethren will come to call and, as leader of the western world, you will be perfectly positioned to advance the Church's worldwide goal—total theocratic domination.

President Bush, who believes himself chosen by God to be President, and Dick Cheney, who believes himself God and President, used national security to reconsolidate power in the executive branch beyond what was lost after Watergate. From a man who would be free to the man who would be king, is it not fair to ask if a Mormon President could give even more depth and meaning to the term Imperial Presidency than Bush/Cheney? Remember, Joseph Smith and Brigham Young believed in a convoluted version of the Divine Right of Kings. Gods tell the kings what they wants done and the kings tell the people. Past Mormon Prophets had themselves anointed king, but now the Church wants its own

President. Joseph Smith and his followers were determined to control America by electing him President and, until it specifically indicates otherwise, the LDS Church continues a religious manifest destiny with national and worldwide designs.

Our Mormon pioneer families see you aspiring to the highest office and it confirms everything we were taught for generations. It's perfectly logical to have a Mormon President with the millennium finally here. After all, Mormons know they belong to the only true church and the Prophets' teachings must be fulfilled. Now, you have emerged as the LDS Church's political leader and your loyalty has made you the national pride of the Mormon Myth Fraternity. Aided by your native talent, birth position and proven abilities, you have achieved remarkable financial and political success. Your problem that won't magically disappear is the Mormon Church, which was founded on falsehoods and perpetuated by calculated corporate conspiracies. You can't be elected President as the political leader of an aggressive cult that reveres simplistic science fiction and aggressively pedals religious heresy, can you?

The U.S. recently celebrated the 40th anniversary of the Freedom of Information Act under an imperial administration with a despotic predilection for secrecy to rival any in our nation's history. Team Bush, adroit in the art of information suppression, has used the nebulous War on Terror to justifying its unconstitutional behavior. For this administration, information is guilty until proved innocent, leaving the burden on American citizens to pry loose government documents that in a truly free society would be readily available to the public. Mitt, Mormons mastered the art of secrecy and document suppression generations ago and your family has accepted leadership positions in the Church since generation one. You continued the family ecclesiastical participation by serving as a Bishop and Stake President, yet you regularly distance yourself from Mormonism when speaking before certain groups. In one breath, you state you aren't running for President as a Mormon and then bristle defensively if someone questions whether you're a devout Mormon.

Mitt, you are a devout Mormon, a true believer, married in the temple—and your freedom to dissent or ignore council from the General Authorities is limited. In the Law of Sacrifice portion of the Mormon Endowment Ceremony, you and other faithful members knelt in the temple and agreed "to sacrifice all that we possess, even our own lives if necessary, in sustaining and defending the Kingdom of God." Former First Presidency member J. Reuben Clark, whose name is emblazoned on the BYU Law School, said of the Church, "This is not a democracy, this is not a republic, this is a Kingdom of God." Mitt, you have sworn allegiance to another power! If elected President, would you uphold the rule of law or prepare America for the Millennium and the Mormon version of the Kingdom of God on earth? With no foreign policy experience except a Mormon Mission, would you, as President, be more inclined to help export Mormonism than to develop an integrated international vision that prioritizes policies to solve current and future problems for our secular nation?

Mitt, you swore the Mormon oath of the Law of Consecration. You knelt at the temple alter and covenanted to consecrate yourself, your time, talents, and "everything with which the Lord has blessed you, or with which he may bless you, to the Church of Jesus Christ of Latter Day Saints, for the building up of the Kingdom of God on the earth and for the establishment of Zion." The term "the Church" has always been synonymous with "the Kingdom," which since inception, pursued the goal of a one-world government under Mormon paternalistic priesthoods. That hasn't changed to my knowledge. American values and Mormon values never coincided because a democratic republic and free enterprise system were historically too messy for Mormon leaders. Regardless of contemporary economics and policies, a socialist theocracy better suited Church leader's earthly objectives historically and is the stated order of their multi-tiered heaven.

Joseph Smith and Brigham Young created a Council of Fifty, replete with special robes and secret signs closely resembling Freemasonry. The Council of Fifty anointed Smith King and actively pushed him for President before his death. This secret organization was the pattern for governing the future Mormon theocratic kingdom that would set aside the laws of the United States and all other secular governments. Does the Council of Fifty secretly wait to take control of America? Does the old Ghost Government of Deseret still exist to assume daily management of American and global cultures? Probably not, but if the day ever comes that Mormons achieve their ultimate goals, say goodbye to a citizen's rights to little pleasures like watching HBO, having a cup of coffee in the morning or a glass of wine at dinner. I take small solace knowing you sneak a cup of tea now and then.

The unrelenting, unrepentant Mormon organization goose-stepped into the twenty-first century, and you embraced the religious right in pursuit of your lifelong goal to win the Presidency, or, if not successful, the Vice Presidency or a Cabinet position while you prepare to run for President again. Theodore Roosevelt, whom you hold in high esteem, said aggressive fighting for the right is the noblest sport the world affords. Unquestionably, Roosevelt's idea of "the right" was neither a future Mormon socialist theocracy nor the agenda of religious fundamentalists.

Despite his pathetic performance at home and abroad, you have referred to George W. Bush as a strong President who stands his ground. As President, would you stand your ground against those who faithfully push the false Mormon agenda? You swore to give your time, talents and money to Mormon hokey and as part of your devotion, subscribe to horrible and supposedly inevitable end days scenarios. Generations of Mormon leaders have assailed our nation as evil and getting progressively worse. Mitt, can you focus your management and social skills and serve America's best interests in the real world if you remain blindly loyal to Mormon mythology? At best, you would be inclined to perpetuate the LDS Mission Statement. Certainly, as President you would serve under constant pressure from the Mormon Church to support policies that further its organizational causes.

Mitt, the polls indicate most American voters are hungry for moderate leadership that can bring us together, not another polarizing President on a religious mission. Still, many people uneducated in American constitutional concepts and the international rule of law believe governmental secularism and religious tolerance are anti-religion. One thing that makes your candidacy look dangerous is how willing you are to indulge their ignorance and confusion. Does an educated man like you really want to continue the regressive Bush agenda at home and abroad, or did you become an accomplished con artist to win the Republican nomination? You have declared, "I can tell you I'm not a carbon copy of President Bush," but you offered only four more years of what seven of ten Americans now reject.

In 2006, when you returned from a trip to Iraq, you made all positive comments, checking off the administration's talking points for the war and ignoring the will of the American people. In early presidential primary debates, you adopted the administration's position in favor of torture and against the rule of law. Meticulously retrofitted and nattily dressed, "Matinee Mitt" portrayed a grim-faced tough guy battling "a global jihadist effort." You informed the electorate you would continue the Bush legacy of torture, and proudly proclaimed you wanted accused terrorist held at Guantanamo, "where they don't get the access to lawyers they get when they are on our soil." As the faithful roared their approval, you added, "We ought to double Guantanamo." If Joseph Smith and Brigham Young joined the delirium as they watched admiringly from Mormon Paradise, surely Thomas Jefferson and James Madison cringed in Mormon spirit prison.

Republican presidential candidates all naturally strive to share the Ronald Reagan mantle and perpetuate his legacy, and you're no exception. However, Reagan had convictions and controlled his consultants. You're controlled by consultants and ignore your convictions. Your campaign speeches repeated generic Republican positions that could be uttered by any conservative candidate and quite honestly, insult your intelligence, distract from your character and fail to display your competence. Even your old friend, Salt Lake City Mayor Rocky Anderson, scolded you because you "caved" on torture and the Iraq war. In June, 2007, interviewed on *Democracy Now* with host Amy Goodman, Anderson said seeing you flip-flop on these issues "was just absolutely incredible to me."

Facing angry Americans almost daily on the campaign trail, you finally admitted the post-invasion period was "mismanaged," and the administration failed to prepare for the insurgency or plan adequately for an Iraqi government handover. Then, you began positioning yourself as the candidate for political change. Mitt, it was awkward and disingenuous considering your years supporting Bush Administration policies. What a dance! First flip-flopping right, and then zigzagging toward the outside. What moves are next, an allemande left and a sashay toward the center? It requires a difficult display of footwork, but if anyone can wage a carefully choreographed campaign with flair, its slick dancing Mitt, the John Travolta of American politics.

During the 1970s and early 80s, I warned students in my Community College classroom that the far right posed the most danger to our political and economic freedoms. That was before Jerry Falwell endeared himself to Ronald Reagan, and the moral police began to exert so much political influence. The most libertarian Republicans aren't a major threat to the system. They're basically as impractical and innocuous as the left wing radicals who reside comfortably in their esoteric ivory towers. Libertarians think that about all we need to do is chip in a few bucks to build some roads and sewer lines. They don't understand capitalism needs visible hands to correct and complement the invisible hand of the marketplace. Of course, now, few want to be called liberal, particularly Democratic Presidential candidates. A pejorative today, but only a few decades ago the word liberal described someone who stood against big power and for individual achievement.

America's real societal danger comes from the reactionary religious right, which has the deadly force of a cultural Mac truck, and, given enough power, could knock America back into the dark ages—or nineteenth century Salt Lake City. This can't be allowed to happen. It's self-evident that open societies are more prosperous than totalitarian or theocratic, both socially and economically. In the past, you were a moderate Republican like your father, who stood by his political convictions and held his positions. Because of his moderate philosophies, your father must have struggled with other Republicans during his primary run for President, and it would be worse for him today. Moderates get run over by traffic from all directions, so you concluded you couldn't win the Republican nomination without a sudden conversion to conservatism. Still, I'm appalled that as a placebo conservative, you jumped in the driver's seat of the right wing's eighteen-wheeler and headed ninety miles an hour down the Presidential campaign trail. Remember, Mitt, moderates are responsible for saving civilizations from culturally dangerous rides with both reactionaries and radicals.

Besides the polls that reflect Mormon religious issues for you to overcome, a temporarily intimidated American media now has learned how to do its job again and often speaks sharply about the Iraq war. You have said you don't support media "censorship," but after you decided an ABC news report on the war went too far, you stated, the "media has responsibility to police itself." Perhaps, investigative reporters in the American Fourth Estate will make your presidential aspirations a referendum on both your political intentions and Mormonism's validity. Hopefully, rather than simply edit Church press releases, some reporters will look more closely at Mormon history, doctrines and publications. If the press doesn't police itself to your satisfaction, would you, under the guises of family values, national security or freedom of religion, use the Presidential bully pulpit to push for more American media intimidation and regulation?

Serious scrutiny of the LDS Church could be the kiss of death to your lifelong aspiration to be President because the Church's veil of secrecy can't withstand the light of day. Since the media is a tempting target for criticism by secretive organizations, will you be inclined to join those who seek to vilify the press? After wingnuts battered you in the conservative blogosphere for being too moderate, scrutiny spread into the mainstream media for the right reasons as you, like the Mormon Church, reinvented yourself. The Mormon image is manufactured by public relations executives, and your political image is created by campaign advisors. Closer press investigation will reveal the LDS Church is a ludicrous, even dangerous organization, and you, a product of multi-generational deception, were willing to do or say almost anything to win the Presidency on its behalf, including spending part of your personal fortune.

Mormon General Authorities want you to be President to hasten fulfillment of their mission statement, but don't like prying eyes. They spent decades, with considerable success, reinventing the Church to resemble Ozzie and Harriet.

Now, these men hope no one notices the surreptitious re-creation of Mormonism or its rapid financial growth. Presently, Church leaders refuse to reveal to members and the media that numerous truths discovered in recent decades are being ignored and damning documents suppressed. However, just because the Mormon Church changed its public image in the last two generations and presents perfect families like yours to America, the press won't allow the spin to continue unchallenged. The Mormon sitcom is as mythical as the Medusa and evidence of this is more prevalent than ever, thanks in large part to the Internet.

Mitt, Church leaders feign self-righteousness and claim their right to hide behind the First Amendment, but your Presidential bid makes it more difficult for the General Authorities to portray the Mormon Church as just another Christian denomination with a pristine image. Press-probing spells bad news for the LDS Church, your Presidential aspirations, and ultimately your legacy, unless you accept reality and react appropriately. If you step up to straighten this out, like you did the Salt Lake Olympics, a moderate and forgiving American public will respect you now and in the future. If honesty and integrity on your part become a political death wish to your campaign for higher public office, it's still the moral thing to do.

Where is the honesty and loyalty? That double-edged question is framing your presidential bid. Another important question was summed up by Alan Wolfe of Boston College who said, "The question is lingering: To what degree do ordinary Christians view Mormons as fellow Christians or as weird?" As more Americans look closely at the false reality behind the Mormon smiles and firm handshakes, they will find it weird, even scary, and vote accordingly. When thoughtful American voters comprehend the doctrines and goals of Mormonism, they won't want you imposing the Church's stated mission on our country, now or in the future. Your best option, and the righteous one, is to admit to the American people that Jesus of Nazareth is not portrayed in Mormon doctrine and worshipped in LDS chapels.

Americans must understand that complete Mormon political success would make our current neoconservative government look like a demon from the liberal left. An unbridled Mormon America would qualify for police state status. Stay tuned for this unfolding religious tale of Biblical proportions, non-Biblical doctrines and dramatically limited American civil liberties. Today, an increasingly larger number of Mormons are moving into governmental management positions at federal, state and local levels. Many have the same graduate degree that Church teachings motivated me to pursue. My graduate program at BYU, at what is now known as the George W. Romney Institute of Public Management, cranks out graduates faster than Brigham Young fathered children.

Historically, for reasons obvious to informed observers, the Mormon Church has supported a limited central government and states rights, but the infiltration of the American Commonwealth by Mormons continues to accelerate in the twenty-first century. Concern grows that a disproportionate numbers of federal, State and local Mormon officials are marching to the orders of the LDS Church. Mitt, do these government employees represent the American people, or are they serving a career Mormon mission to help fulfill prophecy? Do these men honor their Priesthood more than they respect the Constitution and Bill of Rights? Remember, several Mormon prophets and political leaders believed it would be necessary to destroy the Constitution in order to save it. Genuine concern should exist in America that the Church's religious agenda is more important to Mormon bureaucrats, and to you, than civil responsibilities to our nation. Author Charles L. Wood called it, *The Mormon Conspiracy.*

Mitt, do you believe the US Constitution is superseded by the Mormon hierarchical structure in Salt Lake City, and the *Book of Mormon* is more important than the Bible? American citizens have a right and responsibility to question your true intentions. It's a legitimate concern that, as President, you would pressure the State Department, for example, to leverage foreign aid, and use diplomatic means to advance the Church's worldwide missionary effort. Patronage powers could be used to stuff the federal government with even more devout Mormon bureaucrats, loyal above all else to LDS organizational goals. As President, you could further add to the Mormon deadwood stacked in our dysfunctional intelligence community that failed to provide the information we needed in recent years.

While Mormon members trooped into government service, you made systematic financial contributions to key fundamentalist religious organizations, which then suddenly endorsed you. At the same time, your campaign sought out specific individuals from these organizations and placed them on your payroll. These political prostitutes then became staff members or shills for you at political rallies. Members of the sanctimonious religious right are for sale, and you bought their support with organizational donations and large salaries. Hey, if you can't lick 'em, join or buy 'em, and then lick 'em.

Mitt, your recent political reinvention included changing positions on the one issue more frightening and perilous for America and the world than all others. To please visionless conservatives and business interest groups, you changed your environmental position and joined those who believe global warming isn't a moral question. Ignoring evidence, this crowd relegates global warming concerns to pop culture, and then haughtily dismisses them. Conservative skeptic and nay-sayer positions contradict the renowned cosmologist and mathematician Stephen Hawking who believes, "Global warming could kill millions. We should have a war on global warming rather than the war on terror."

Hawking is correct. In the next few decades, Bangkok is one of twenty-one cities worldwide, including New York and Los Angeles, vulnerable to rising seas related to climate change. According to U.S. and European experts, "More than one-tenth of the world's population, or 643 million people, live in low-lying areas at risk from climate change." Several threatened cities are key financial centers for Asia, Europe, the United States, and the Middle East. When global warming reaches critical mass, the maps of the world will be redrawn, and tens of millions of refuges will need unavailable aid.

Mitt, you once told a group of voters that you were terrified of global warm-ing. On another occasion, shortly after elected Massachusetts Governor in 2002, you held a press conference outside a coal-fired power plant to demand a clean-up plan within a year and vowed not to create jobs that kill people. Then, within three years, you pulled the plug on key elements of your environmental agenda. In December 2005, you withdrew Massachusetts from the Regional Greenhouse Gas Initiative, reversing course on the same day you announced you wouldn't seek reelection. Since then, you pushed for caps on fees charged to businesses that exceed targeted emissions standards. No doubt you reversed your environmental course to gain support from industry groups for your Presidential campaign. Granted, we're uncertain how severe climate change will be, but it must be addressed. The threat is stupefying, the opportunity tremendous, the waste incredible, and the time is now!

Nevertheless, you prefer to fight a global jihad on terrorism and rarely speak of environmental issues. Will you and your new political base saber rattle while glo-bal warming sucks the planet dry and redistributes moisture in devastating storms and droughts? Do you really understand who an American President must be after 2008? We can't expect international polluters to go green unless America leads by example. Countries like China already ask us why we aren't doing more. Great leadership is needed to create consensus among partisan political groups, and without it, progress on environmental issues will be stymied. Perhaps nations and businesses that are good planetary citizens will pay more for goods and ser-vices during the transition period—long term costs can't be quantified by present business models. However, to do nothing potentially means the death of civilization as we know it.

Earth's ecosystem is rapidly becoming imbalanced, temperatures are rising, and land-based ice slipping into the oceans will raise sea levels worldwide even more. Unprecedented water pools and crevasses are developing in the Antarctic and Greenland ice sheets. Coral reefs are bleached and dying, the icecaps are melting and polar bears are floating away to drown. The Artic icecaps are deteriorating more quickly than expected and will be gone in a half century. Even penguins eventually could be marching in mud. Pursue our present path of environmental denial, and the human race will be worried about more than just the polar bears and penguins—we will have placed ourselves on the endangered species list. Atmospheric scientists are startled at how quickly change is occurring in earth's large ice masses and as the glaciers recede, the world's drinking water is threatened. The disappearing ice has already made Alaska and Siberia vulnerable to waves that erode coastlines and some indigenous cultures have had to change hunting practices.

Mitt, the environmental issue is one of the biggest disqualifiers for your Presidential bid. Business and religious leaders who want you in the White House have shown little inclination to act, and your positions on the environment and global warming render you unsuitable to lead by example at home or abroad. Too far off target to resonate with moderate and liberal voters, you have positioned yourself only to serve the interest of industry. The Bush Administration's recent industry-friendly environmental proposals are too little, too late, mostly suited for photo ops, and the same people who posed with Bush would have your private telephone number on Pennsylvania Avenue, too. You flip-flopped on a problem far more important than contemporary bickering over social issues. You nonchalantly changed positions on something our generation must act on now, because surprising and disturbing events that can last for millennia could occur in decades.

Not a time for indifference, obfuscation and diversion, nevertheless, by your lack of concern, you reflect the position of those who believe global warming is just another kooky idea of the liberal left. You emphasized that Republicans should never abandon pro-growth conservative principals to embrace the environmental concerns of Al Gore. Mitt, politics aside, our children and grandchildren will face the consequences of skepticism, procrastination and moral inertia on global warming. Ecosystem warnings exist everywhere, like canaries dying in coal mines, yet Republican politicians—including Nevada's Governor—endorse more water guzzling, air polluting coal plants as the solution to our energy needs and do little to promote wind and solar energy.

Mitt, although you once seemed to understand, you now express little concern about the depth and breadth of the environmental crisis. Your policy positions on the environment are shamefully politically expedient and appear based on an end-days mentality. Conservative Christians are faithfully waiting to be ripped away from their cell phones and join the righteous Rapture into heaven. Consequently, the environment isn't particularly important because dark prophecies must be fulfilled before Jesus returns. In the specialized, Mormon version of the Second Coming, Joseph Smith will return with Jesus in tow. Together, they'll build the New Jerusalem in Missouri, with an Osmond Family concert to kick off construction. .

That scientists can trace back 650,000 years and show a direct correlation between carbon dioxide and the earth's temperature is dismissible by Christian fundamentalists and Mormons, who know the earth is really only 6,000 years old. It's early Sunday morning and time for the Millennium—although Jesus appears to be sleeping in. Whatever happens, Mitt, it won't be the Millennium where the lamb lies down with the lion and a Mormon Jesus presides over a perfected earth from a shining city on a hill in Jackson County, Missouri. Global warming is real, and we can't wait for divine intervention to solve our problems and save mankind. When melting ice sheets raise sea levels enough, Manhattan and Boston could compete to be the next Atlantis. I doubt you want to see those cities even partly disappear while you're building a larger conventional military to fight a global jihad against terrorists.

American Republicans and special interests in the highest political, business and media power positions ridicule irrefutable data, while greenhouse gas emissions raise temperatures and the earth's protective shell fills with more pollution. It's understandable, but unacceptable, that interest groups unconcerned about health care for millions of Americans also mock efforts to provide health care for Mother Earth. Geo-engineering advocates fear it's already too late to reverse the trend in time to forestall horrendous environmental consequences and propose deflecting sunlight with stratospheric sprays of sulfur, launching trillions of tiny orbiting mirrors and creating thousands of huge off-shore saltwater fountains. Such outlandish sun-shading measures would only treat the symptoms, but, with worldwide carbon dioxide emissions rising faster than the most pessimistic predictions, those actions—and more—may be necessary to save us until heavenly help arrives.

Citizens of the world seek environmental leadership from an American President prepared to act decisively, not one under oath to a nineteenth century religious cult. Earthly evidence of global warming is everywhere, and yet facts to support Mormonism are non-existent. Global warming is the reality and Mormonism the myth. Rather than blather about a Mormon celestial heaven for saved souls, mankind wants a multifaceted response to global environmental pressure on our earthly home. Mitt, the next President has a moral imperative to protect planet earth—not traditional marriage. Your personal priorities are confused and professionally, you represent constituencies unwilling to lead, follow or get out of the way on this vital issue. You're a leader of businessmen who pursue their self interests and religionists who believe Armageddon is imminent. The global warming crisis presents great economic opportunities and a chance to save our planet, but none of your key American constituent groups has shown much concern about the environmental side of the equation.

I know your Presidential policies won't be directly dictated by the Mormon Church. You wouldn't be merely part of the Mormon Living Prophet's daily puppet show, but your situation isn't comparable to that of John F. Kennedy. Besides your ancestral roots into Mormonism's first generation, you took solemn oaths to dedicate your time, talent and wealth to the Church of Jesus Christ of Latter Day Saints. The Mormon Prophet, or one of his Apostles, is positioned just a phone call or email away. Have you not made secret covenants to listen and obey? Unlike Thomas Jefferson, you can't claim exemption from religious debate, and unlike Jack Kennedy you can't simply dismiss the issue by telling American voter you aren't the Mormon candidate for Head of State. That you were running for Commander in Chief and not Theologian in Chief was only a cute campaign diversion from another important issue for Americans to consider. As President, your public decisions would be influenced by LDS Church Headquarters.

Dogged by the religious issue, and losing your lead in the Iowa polls, you finally made your "Faith in America" speech in December, 2007—as Kennedy did in 1960. The obvious observation is that you're not sleeping with any Hollywood babes or hanging out with mobsters. Kennedy was more likely to seek advice from Phyllis McGuire's made man than he was the Pope in Rome, and he said his public decisions wouldn't at all be influenced by the Catholic Church. In contrast, you're likely to consult regularly with the Mormon Prophet and Apostles on key national issues as part of your beliefs about soteriology—how the individual soul is saved, and eschatology—theories about the culmination of history.

Mitt, you even went as a far as to imply that you believe religious faith is necessary to be a successful President. So, your interwoven personal and religious beliefs will never be off limits for scrutiny because they could have a direct effect on his performance as United States President and leader of the western world.

Just for fun, Mitt, since you believe these peculiar, non-Christian doctrines concerning the state of the soul after death, and end-days activities, will Mormon leaders promise you the McGuire sisters for your eternal concubines? If they feel it necessary to retain your loyalty, the Council of Twelve may approve a bevy of current and former celebrity beauties as a future celestial bonus. Do you believe that's perhaps part of the God's eternal plan for you? Of course, these wicked party girls must repent and convert to Mormonism at some point—on earth or in the Mormon Spirit prison, and you must listen carefully to the latest LDS Prophet in the latter days. The Mormon fantasy for faithful male members is a state of exalted glory with great eternal sex for the guys who will become Gods. Mitt, do you really believe you can service an unlimited number of neglected beauty queens in eternity, even with an infinite Viagra prescription? How would you have time to travel, read a good book, go hunting, or help the other Gods manage the universe?

Carl Segan would say there are billions and billions of worlds to populate and if Joseph Smith and other Mormon Prophets are right, you will become a resurrected eternal erection with a giant sperm bank. I've been known to make a point too well, but the question remains: Where's your loyalty? Tell the American people if you believe all Mormon teachings and are in line to earn an infinite harem of women in an exclusive polygamist heaven. If you still believe these foundational Mormon doctrines and consider yourself destined for the Presidency as part of your progression along the celestial path, then I remind you: You're no John Kennedy. Kennedy wanted his women here and now.

Mitt, forget about somehow trying to be Kennedyesque—or Reaganesque. Stop the masquerade and make a truly majestic speech. It's time for an immortalizing effort founded on integrity and candor. Instead of calling "very unfair" those who say Mormonism is a cult, admit it is a cult, and truly clear the air. You once said giving your life for great things generates as much satisfaction in the effort as it does in the achievement. I couldn't agree more. So, discard your desire to prepare the world for the return of a phantom polygamist Jesus, and disregard your pending eternal stud-hood. Mitt, seek satisfaction in a noble calling to redirect our lost people living in an earthly state of ignorance and coveting a false future of blissful celestial blarney. Find courage to make a speech challenging Mormon leaders and confounding their apologists.

As a political scientist, I can't imagine a Mormon-controlled government that passes the American founders' freedom test. Rights the founding fathers believed to be self evident were, to early Mormon leaders, viewed as nuisances and obstacles, and twentieth century changes are only cosmetic. Mormon President and Prophet Wilford Woodruff said in April, 1898 that George Washington and other signers of the Declaration of Independence appeared to him in the St George Temple. He said spirits of the dead gathered around him and pleaded for assurances their Mormon temple ordinances would be completed. Woodruff stated, "I straightway went into the baptismal font and called upon brother McCallister to baptize me for the signers of the Declaration of Independence." Woodruff claimed a hundred men were there, including Columbus and John Wesley. If I didn't know better, I'd swear ol' Woody swilled some Mormon moonshine or twisted a joint of Mexican marijuana before he saw these apparitions.

It's difficult not to recoil and smirk when I imagine that the founding fathers, renaissance men, products of the Enlightenment and believers in reason and science, appeared before a Mormon Prophet to plead for their eternal lives in one of Joseph Smith's kingdoms of heaven. If this mind-boggling event had happened, those eighteenth century visionaries, many of whom were Freemasons, would have pleaded with Woodruff to protect the constitutional rights they worked so hard to safeguard for future Americans, including the Mormon people. The Constitutional framers were revolutionaries who detested kings, monarchies and theocracies. America's founders would have begged Woodruff to honor the basic tenants of tolerance, free speech, separation of powers and the separation of church and state, which they directly or indirectly wrote into the Constitution and Bill of Rights. Surely these men would have expressed distain for the LDS Church. Mormons hadn't supported Constitutional tenants in the eastern states, and Woodruff and previous prophets had disregarded freedom and liberty in the Utah Territory.

Mitt, you told columnist David Broder that you count on religious tolerance to defuse the Mormon issue in the Presidential campaign. Problematic, because what Mormons think of Christianity and gentiles is well documented and deeply embedded in our subculture. Brigham Young stated: "With regard to true theology, a more ignorant people never lived than the present so-called Christian world." Third Mormon President John Taylor said, "Christianity ... is a perfect pact of nonsense ... the devil could not invent a better engine to spread his work than the Christianity of the nineteenth century." Later, Taylor asked, "Where shall we look for the true order of authority of God? It cannot be found in any nation of Christendom."

Quotes condemning Christianity are abundant in Mormon history. Your ancestor, Apostle Orson Pratt, often as colorful to quote as Brigham Young, once announced to the world, "Both Catholic and Protestants are nothing less than the Whore of Babylon whom the Lord denounced by John the Revelator." On another occasion, he said, "The gates of Hell have prevailed and will continue to prevail over the Catholic mother of harlots and over all her Protestant daughters … the apostate Catholic Church, with all her popes and bishops, together with all her harlot daughters shall be hurled down to hell." Hope your "friend" Cardinal O'Malley, Catholic voters and the Protestant leaders don't see those remarks as you pursue the Presidency.

The Mormon story reminds me of the Cinderella fairy tale. Catholics are the wicked stepmother, Protestants the ugly stepsisters and Mormons none other than Cinderella, floating onto the ballroom floor in glass slippers to greet her eternal Prince. In the real world, the Roman Statesman, Cicero, philosophized there are gems of thought that are ageless and eternal. Generations ago, unwitting Mormons traded those gems away for a religious fairytale about fool's gold wrapped in a sheet. They chose to believe in magic peep stones Smith put in his hat to receive revelation and translate the *Book of Mormon*. Now, while Church leaders perpetuate the great hoax, you request tolerance from Christians. You expected to receive understanding and acceptance from Christian voters, but the Mormon religion is hostile to all denominations and remains disdainful of many of the individual liberties and freedoms we enjoy as Americans.

Speaking of your Presidential candidacy, you said, "We don't judge a candidate based on the theology of the religion they grew up in." That's only correct if he denounces it. American voters retain every right to judge whether you continue to believe in a strange, disproved cult and plan to carry its banner into the White House, either now or in the future. Another interesting quote you made concerning your Presidential bid and the Mormon religion is, "There will be a time when someone will go overboard, where someone will say something beyond the mark." You added, "And I hope I will be able to rise to the occasion in a way that is memorable." Mitt, I'm going beyond the mark by raising my voice and telling the truth about the Mormon Church. Is it asking too much for you or Church leaders to release members so they can learn to think for themselves? That would be right on the mark.

After fielding second rate political fighters from Republican gyms for almost four decades, Church leaders obviously hoped you wouldn't get knocked out in the Presidential trials. Utah Senator, Orrin Hatch, was never more than a punchy club fighter, but not you. You're their great white hope, with lightning quickness and a solid chin. You can float like a butterfly and sting like a bee. You bob and weave so deftly, political opponents put your picture on milk cartons in Massachusetts because you were gone so much no one could find you, let alone lay a glove on you. I kid you, Mitt. You're a man on a mission to be President, and that required constant traveling while Governor to solicit special interests groups. Nor have you forgotten the people of Massachusetts who elected you chief executive. You now ridicule the State on occasion to earn political points with conservative groups.

Speculation is that Church leaders might usher its members out of the Republican Party if they believe you were sucker-punched, hit with a low blow on the campaign trail, or, if you were not accepted by the Evangelicals you've worked so hard to please. An important question is what would constitute a sucker-punch? Does telling the truth about the LDS Church meet that criterion? Equally important, if the Church packs up its political marbles and pouts as it has in the past, where could this judgmental, intolerant, homophobic organization go? LDS Church leaders couldn't suddenly join the wicked Democratic Party, which supports issues they pontificate against as immoral and plainly evil. A third party movement is possible, but a successful American third party would more likely be a modern green party, not an old fashioned black and white gang with a regressive right-wing social agenda built into its base. However, since Mormons believe they will be alone in Heaven, it makes sense for them to form their own exclusive political party here on earth. That's a future decision for the LDS anointed ones and their Gods.

From the Church's infancy, Mormon leaders have waited in the wings to take control of America and supposedly save the Constitution, yet Utah is the reddest state behind the Bush Administration, whose national policies eroded it and international policies threatened it. Actually, it makes sense that Utah consistently gives President Bush the highest job-approval rating, because the sooner the American government collapses, the sooner the Mormon Church can assume its rightful leadership role. Did the majority of Mormon voters view this drugstore cowboy, George Bush, as the politician to lead them to Armageddon, so he deserved their support? Mitt, is the time almost here when the U.S. Constitution will hang by a thread? With America's international reputation shredded, our credibility in tatters, long-term budget projections exploded and the military ragged, are you saddled up and ready to ride to the rescue on the back of the White Horse Prophesy?

How can you believe, as we were taught, that the Constitution is divinely inspired, and cling to an organization that, if given the power, would set aside constitutional provisions at will? Remember, Mitt, the Mormon Church has a history of ignoring separation of church and state. James Madison explained the reasoning and justification for the concept when he said that it was the only way to avoid the ceaseless strives that had soaked the soil of Europe with blood for centuries. This Bush Administration has shown little respect for separation of church and state, and several other Constitutional and international legal concepts—yet LDS leaders obsequiously follow its short-sighted foreign and domestic policies. Kudos to Salt Lake City Mayor Rocky Anderson for attempting to wake up Utah Mormon sycophants so willingly loyal to whatever political authority figure Church leaders encourage them to accept. Once your friend, you cooled the relationship quickly when Mayor Anderson called for Bush's impeachment.

Key Mormon appointments to high level government positions solidified Church loyalty to the failed Bush Administration, and now Mormon Republicans count on you to become President of the United States and help them fulfill their multigenerational manifest destiny. Mitt, the Mormon cult can never fulfill its claim to members and, when given a chance in the last decade, Republicans failed to deliver on their promises to America. Since neither Mormons nor Republicans have real integrity or credibility today, where does that leave you and your lifelong beliefs and dreams? Instead of paying college students a commission to raise money for you, unethical under the standards of the Association of Professional Fundraisers, establish a team of biblical scholars to advise Church members on the real meaning of Biblical scriptures.

Mitt, show our people how *Old Testament* scriptures were frequently lifted from context by Church leaders to support Mormon heresy and how *New Testament* teachings don't jibe with the political agenda of the Republican Party's southern wing. Most new southern Republicans are political descendants of the old yellow dog Democrats, who bolted from the Republican Party after it ended slavery following the Civil War. Then, as segregationists, they returned to the Republican Party after the Democratic Party's 1960s Civil Rights movement frustrated and angered them. I call these white southerners Rin-Tin-Tin Republicans today because they remain lap-dog loyalists to the ugly wedge issues used by the new Republican Party to divide our society. The current favorite, of course, is gay rights, but Republican politicians use code words to play on racism still rampant in their ranks.

Mitt, on the surface, you have the administrative and personal skills to be a good President. You're talented, handsome and charismatic, but America needs a President who is more than posture and pose. Never in my lifetime has this country needed great leadership more than today. Though smart and methodical, your power-point stump speeches haven't showed courage and conviction, and your personal warmth and ability to connect with real people are as questionable as your core values. Americans want a sensible, personal human being for President, not a smarty-pants corporate wizard who almost never makes a gaffe as he presents one well-rehearsed graph after another. The nation isn't searching for a candidate presenting canned lines, glib responses and fast talk straight from an MBA act or a perfect man on his way the highest level of Mormon heaven. America isn't Staples, Dominos Pizza or the Celestial Kingdom.

Mitt, either you see it or you don't, and since you still don't see it, I can't quietly stand aside and watch you march into the American Presidency with your ankle chained to Joseph Smith. The White House must not be controlled by a man who believes in a phantom ancient culture, believes the fictitious *Book of Mormon* the most correct book on earth and who reveres Joseph Smith as a Christian prophet. Your political success would advance the Mormon cult kingdom, and that's unacceptable. Not on my watch! Like the little mouse waving a middle finger as the hawk swoops in, I have grabbed some cheese and joined those standing sentry atop the barricades defending freedom and enlightenment.

21

Collaring the Missionary Program

I can't define all the nuances of evil. Nevertheless, presenting and defending religious falsehoods—in the Mormon's case, a complex amalgamation of lies about eternity and the purpose of life—must rank with the great crimes against humanity. Mormonism is legally protected in America, even tax advantaged, but it's dangerous when those hiding behind the First Amendment have conspired to control the country and want to impose their mission statement on America and the world. Separation of Church and State can be maintained, and organized religion protected, without providing tax advantages to religious entities or permitting them to keep secret their finances. The U.S. Supreme Court has ruled that laws treating religious and non-religious groups equally don't violate the First Amendment, but Mormon attorneys argue for secrecy about Church finances and claim special tax privileges for Church businesses and missionaries.

A defiant LDS Church hasn't released financial information since 1959. It's their "secret of secrets," known only to an elite group in Salt Lake City and never shared with Church members or the media. The Mormon Church is one of the richest religions on earth, with billions on Wall Street and in real estate holdings roughly equivalent in size to the State of Delaware. In July, 2007, the Oregon Supreme Court rejected the Mormon Church's bid to shield detailed financial information about its net worth. An attorney defending the Church, Stephen F. English, said, "The Church respects the rule of law but has profound constitutional concerns based on its constitutional right to protect the free expression of its religion." The financial information wasn't released, and Mr. English took the Church's legal arguments before a circuit judge. The Oregon dispute involved a child molestation case against the Mormon Church, and the youth's attorney, Kelly Clark, argued "the same rules that apply to everybody else in society apply to the LDS Church."

Organizations like Mormonism and Scientology strengthen the case that all corporations should be taxed equally as part of their privilege to function. Two Mormon examples of tax dodging are exemptions on for-profit Church owned businesses and missionary support payments becoming tax deductible when parents first pay the Church. Mitt, tell the General Authorities to stop budgeting one billion dollars annually for their missionary program at taxpayer expense. Why should Americans subsidize Mormon corporate profits or their worldwide Missionary Program? Over the past decade, nonreligious corporate officers have been held more accountable by courts, the press and public for "cooking the books." Now, the Mormon General Authorities should give up their schemes to hide net worth and stop cooking their tax books.

In early 2006, I read comments a Harvard Business School professor, Clayton Christensen, made about the Church in reference to the Mormon missionary program in Massachusetts. Christensen proclaimed: "The truth has strong legs." This former Rhodes Scholar has a broad corporate and educational background, yet still believes Joseph Smith talked to Jesus and the *Book of Mormon* people were real. Amazing, even frightening, that he appears so bright and remains so lost. Fair to say this man, born and reared in Salt Lake City, was successfully programmed by the Church as a boy? For Christensen, Mormon leaders are the arbitrators of truth and his role in life crystal clear. He believes Massachusetts "is a perfect fertile ground" for the Mormon Church to spread its blarney to the Irish Catholics.

It reminded me of a story about the wide-eyed farm boy who returned home after a Disneyland vacation and told everyone he saw the real Goofy. Family and friends couldn't dissuade him, he knew the real Goofy when he saw him. Of course, faithful Mormons know that's impossible because the real Goofy died years ago, and the Church already did his Temple Work. What fun would a Mormon Celestial Kingdom be without a fully-loaded chain of Disneyland destinations, complete with all the original characters? Add some really cool Father Knows Best reruns, and the highest level of LDS heaven becomes glorious.

Just as the farm boy believed in the real Goofy, Elder Christensen continues to believe Joseph Smith was a prophet. Mitt, tell Christensen, along with all current missionaries—and the leaders who send them, that the Mormon version of truth is an imaginary character with a smiley mask, skinny legs, and no eyes. The creature dwells in a dark world, where group-think long ago ended legitimate discussion and independent inquiry. Unwittingly, Elder Christensen and the missionaries lied for the Lord when they bore witness to their version of truth for the media and Massachusetts gentiles. Indoctrinated and committed by their mission service, Clayton Christensen and those young missionaries are destined to be tunnel-visioned, card carrying members of the Mormon Myth Fraternity for life—unless you rescue them.

Church leaders should leave inactive members alone and stop sending missionaries where they aren't wanted. Today, three Church offices actively search for non-practicing Mormons across the US and Canada. Doesn't the Church think they find a Mormon chapel on their own if they want? When disillusioned Mormons desert and want to remain AWOL, missionaries are dispatched like sheep dogs to nip at their heels and herd them back into the compound. The LDS Church, one of the last bastions of missionary zeal, hunts down those who run from Mormonism and shamelessly invades the privacy of non-members. No other religion has an evangelical program this ambitious, and arguably, none are more wrong than Mormons. Young and uninformed, Mormon missionaries are more determined to push into peoples' homes to close the deal than the Fuller Brush man or encyclopedia salesmen.

In recent years, my friends and neighbors have been subjected to aggressive solicitations from fresh-faced Mormon youngsters certain their truth has strong legs. The missionary problem grew so troublesome, one Mormon neighbor asked me how to get both the Mormon home teachers and pesky missionaries to leave her inactive daughter in peace. Like many Mormon families, hers was conflicted about the Church's practices and doctrines. I informed her that members must write Church headquarters and formally request their names be removed from church records. I warned also that her daughter would be excommunicated. No one leaves the Church nicely.

Loyal Mormons frequently give private community gate codes to missionaries—every member a missionary—and once in, they work the neighborhoods door to door. Missionaries once told a neighbor her husband had made an appointment, so she almost let them in, only to discover later he hadn't. It was another lying for the Lord moment for chosen young men with an urgent calling. Dr. Joyce Brothers said membership in a religious group can give individuals such a strong sense of purpose, it overrides any kind of common sense reaction that normal people would have when someone politely says, "No thank you, I'm not interested." Saving souls is a tough business, and sometimes, extraordinary methods are required of special people given divine responsibilities.

As a general rule, the Church counts every member, including inactive members and non-baptized children less than eight years of age. Other churches remove people from the rolls if they stop attending, but not the Mormons. Some deceased members even languish on the membership rolls. LDS leaders inflate growth figures to claim bragging rights as the fastest growing church in the world. In 1973, Mark Cannon developed a geometric progression that predicted powerful Church growth through the remainder of the twentieth century—and he was right. LDS Church conversions exploded, and the Church grew from three million to twelve million members in thirty years. Mormonism no longer experiences these expansion numbers, and other religious groups are now growing faster.

Twenty first century data describe a Mormon Church with stalled growth rates in America and most foreign countries. The Church is currently in a churn phase, with nearly as many people defecting as converting. Thus, the Church grew by less than two percent in 2006 and was still under thirteen million members. Notre Dame Professor David Campbell pointed out what he called "the dirty little secret of Mormon growth." Though the Church's aggressive approach has created impressive results in the last few decades, "lots of baptisms don't necessarily translate into long-term membership." Mitt, electing you President would give Mormonism renewed legitimacy and could restart its growth pattern. Not an acceptable option.

The Mormon Church growth rate has stalled, but relentless efforts to prey on Christian denominations continue. I was pleased to hear a young man who attended my 2005 Community Lutheran Church workshop on Mormonism decided to stop dating a Mormon girl he considered marrying. He realized, once married, she would likely pester him to convert to Mormonism. Then, when the Lutheran youth group needed some religious armor to deflect assaults from aggressive Mormon students in the public high schools, I shared the defensive information they need, while emphasizing the importance of responding with kindness and understanding. I explained their young Mormon peers believe devoutly and feel their message vitally important. The child is father to the man, and Mormon pioneer family teenagers are products of intense intergenerational programming that created a false perspective and distorted the purpose for their lives. Members are assured their primary responsibility is to save humanity, so they program their children to spread the fabrications and build the kingdom.

My preschooler, who inherited the family musical talent, sings "Who let the Dogs out, who, who?" The Mormons have let their sheep dogs bark and run loose in neighborhoods around the world for generations. The problem is, this dog won't hunt! Mitt, put on that big dog face you showed me decades ago and tell the General Authorities this endless howling, barking and nipping at peoples' heels becomes more annoying each day. The yapping noise of fake Mormon news distracts from Christ's good news and discounts scientific knowledge. Reassuring to see the Church's growth has stalled, but now its time to put Mormonism in reverse—shrink it—or reform it into a Christian Church. Mitt, insist Mormon Inc. put its subsidized missionary program on a short leash or muzzle these mutts. It's grating, given twenty-first century realities, for religious mongrels to bark mindlessly, while the Mormon wagon train ambles on through the historical and scientific darkness.

22

Step up or Move on

Ultimately, the Mormon Church must make a major decision—hopefully sooner than later—to end the siege mentality and knee-jerk desire to circle wagons when faced with internal or external criticism. The wisest path for the LDS Church is to publicly disclaim its pagan aspects, disavow all false doctrines and become a Christian religion. The Church should officially denounce its non-Christian beliefs, discontinue all strange practices and apologize for past behavior. Then, our people can soften their presumptuous, judgmental attitudes and reign in the feelings of superiority toward non-Mormons. Mormons love to market themselves as the only real Christians, but they live an illusion and force out those who dare ask commonsense questions. Mitt, the LDS Church is a polluted form of the traditional Biblical Christian belief system and lacks genuine good news. It's immoral for Mormons to attack Christian Churches as historically corrupted and fallen, while simultaneously trying to assimilate into Christianity.

Admitting Joseph Smith, Brigham Young and those who succeeded them were false prophets need not be fatal to the Mormon subculture. On the contrary, accepting the truth will improve the Church in future generations. No longer required to defend the lie until they die, Church leaders and members could reallocate organizational resources into productive Christian services. Mitt, for a chance of success, change has to come from the top, and you must demand it. The LDS leaders will end their war on truth only when someone like you convinces them the war is lost. Tell the Prophet and Apostles to begin by relieving their paid apologists of duty. It's time for these pathetic paid soldiers to stop wildly firing weapons of mass distortion at Church members, the media and Christianity.

Instead of manipulating members and the press, Church leaders should permit vital information to flow freely, even though members initially will feel less self important, comfortable and secure. Granted, when leaders tell the truth and take appropriate steps to become Christians, the Church will lose some members. The

Fundamentalist Latter Day Saints groups will gain LDS members who prefer religious fiction to fact, but angels in Christian heaven will cheer when the Mormon Church stops its preposterous promenade and initiates programs to disseminate honest information to its members and the world community. It will be cathartic for angels, Mormons and humans.

The choice to become real Christians begins with our pioneer families and newer members learning the truth about Church history and doctrines. Then, Mormon leaders should make an international apology for the Church's practice of denouncing, condemning, raiding and lying to Christendom. For generations, Mormons badgered Christians to climb on their religious wagon train and follow false prophets down a long dusty trail. Now, a kindly-worded missive issued from the repentant Prophet and Apostles would be a welcome healing gesture to the Christian Churches. An apology to former Church members purged for daring to defy them and defend the truth would be welcomed, too. Mitt, heartbreaking stories abound in recent decades about individuals devastated and families emotionally fractured by Mormon leaders. I experienced the feelings of anguish, grief and loss suffered by others who left Mormonism in the late twentieth century.

If stronger and less egotistical, I would have abandoned my faith altogether over the past thirty years and joined the 93% of National Academy of Science members who reject the idea of God. In my last conversation with Grandpa Kelly, before a massive stroke left him unable to talk, he ignored my pleas to prepare to do his temple work with Grandma so he could make her and other family members happy. Grandpa cynically shook his head and told me when we die, we're dead. Never accepting that conclusion, I prayed to my personal God and hoped the pleadings didn't get spammed out of the billions of daily prayers he receives. It's scientifically contradictory, but I was too well programmed in childhood and remain too weak as an aging man to forgo all faith in a multi-universal God and his wondrous hearafter.

Counter culture icon, George Carlin, doesn't agree with me. He likes to keep faith simple and tangible, so he began worshipping the sun years ago. Carlin said the sun offers him everything he needs on a daily basis, and he can see it. If less spiritually needy, I might become a moon worshipper and pray to the man who lives there. We spent years watching for falling stars together and it doesn't hurt my eyes to gaze at him. Besides, he's a closer, more personal figure than the sun.

The LDS Church can prove it's really composed of Christian saints by displaying the courage—and humility, to renounce its false teachings about Jesus. Discarding harsh, confusing views about the nature of man—and absurd teaching about the universe and eternity—will cleanse the fabric of Mormonism and earn international respect. Many apostates, who miss catchy childhood hymns like *I'll be a sunbeam for Jesus*, might even return and bring their children and grandchildren to sing along in a Church that really believes in Jesus Christ. You can push stodgy Church leaders to reform so Mormonism can evolve into a real Christian church, like the Adventists and Reformed LDS Churches. In light of all the evidence condemning Mormon Prophets and their doctrines, it seems like the common sense decision to make. Then, I remember Mark Twain said common sense is not so common.

Mitt, because you want to lead the western world, saying the Mormon Church works for you and your family isn't good enough anymore. I realize the Church is good to you. It was good to me and others, so long as we didn't read the wrong books or ask rebellious questions. Cults, ponzi schemes and multi-level marketing pyramids always reward those who sign up early and defend the program. Now, the current Mormon Church, which, since 1838, had the temerity to call itself the Church of Jesus Christ of Latter Day Saints, is undergoing a slow, clandestine reform process, while continuing to hide or alter its history and foundational doctrines. This corporate deviousness traps Mormons in a lifetime of lies and delays the day of reckoning. Besides, if Mormon teachings were true, the Church would sell all Joseph Smith's doctrines proudly instead of being sneaky about it.

The historical relationship between science and religion is complex enough without attempting to build and maintain Christian faith on a magical foundation of fantasy less than two centuries old. In truth, Mormonism is a mesh of emotional ideas melded into a mangled mosaic of intellectual idiocies. Taking license with Shakespeare, confusion has made its religious masterpiece. Mitt, the Church of our forefathers ultimately will stop prospering if it insists on perpetuating proven delusions and make believe. LDS leaders should respect how difficult it is to have faith Christ died and was resurrected as described in the *New Testament* Gospels, without having missionaries and Sunday school teachers tell them to filter their faith in Christ through a nineteenth century prism of polytheism, polygamy, plagiarism and paganism. Only when it officially denounces the deviant teachings of Joseph Smith, Brigham Young, the Pratt brothers and others, can this ethnocentric organization become a Christian Church.

Mitt, tell Church leaders to admit the truth now. Though perhaps extreme and a bit melodramatic—even for the Mormon Church—a nice gesture would be symbolic excommunication for the dead ceremonies for Joseph Smith and Brigham Young. What a great first step before the LDS Church officially joins the Christian fold and converts all its pagan temples into something productive.

Smith and Young qualify for excommunication on a litany of charges, including adultery, falsely introducing polygamy as an eternal Christian practice, religiously institutionalizing the racism of their day, creating and promoting a fake new book given superior billing to the Bible, perverting the traditional Christian trinity, saying men can become Gods with physical bodies and claiming Jesus and Satan are our big brothers. Mitt, maybe you're the Devil's kid brother, but don't speak for me.

If Mormon leaders lack the courage to admit the deception and become a Christian church, they should lead members a separate way and become a new world religion. Mormons are admitted polytheists, while the other three worldly religions that sprang from Father Abraham's loins are monotheists. Mormons preach they are the true Christians, yet the LDS Church believe in doctrines more akin to *Old Testament* Judaism, the faith of Islam and forms of paganism. Mitt, maybe Mormons should show integrity, fully embrace all Joseph Smith's prophecies and stand proudly as a new religion. Church leaders admitting it's an organization of non-Christian beliefs would give them more credibility than muddling along behind their pumped up, polygamist, bureaucratic Jesus guy—and his dad who lives in the Kolob solar system.

LDS leaders are in an identity crisis and don't understand the Church can never build an honest future until it stops lying about its past and either denounces or fully accepts that past. Not knowing how to handle the rediscovered Joseph Smith and New Mormon History, Church leaders slink along in denial about whom and what they are and hope members and gentiles won't notice. What motivates the Mormons' determination to ignore the obvious and continue to preach religious tripe? Is it really as simple as corporate survival and following the dollar? If the Church can't find the courage to not covet the almighty dollar and publicly denounce its non-Christian teachings, it must bravely embrace its founding teachings and move on as a new world order. Mitt, insist the Church of our heritage either recant, apologize and join the Biblical Christian Churches, or announce it's not a Christian faith and stand along side the three major world religions. Whether the Mormon Church joins the Christians or moves on, I urge it to focus its financial services on living people and not continue squandering billions on the dead.

Then again, if there is no resurrected Jesus, one could argue without merit that it doesn't matter whether Mormons belong to cult. That was Thomas Ferguson's argument for letting Mormons continue faith in his Myth Fraternity, justified by his conclusion that Mormons' comforting beliefs are no better or worse than other groups. That argument assumes any form of ignorance is acceptable, even preferable, for millions of Mormons who fear contact with proper knowledge will create an epiphany, followed by spiritual panic and a paroxysm of tears. Without Jesus, all Christians and Mormons are living in a fantasy world, so it doesn't matter if my relatives want to pretend to save dead people and be prideful at the prospect of being thanked by them in a polygamist heaven. Still, if given an honest chance to chose, Mormon children, systematically programmed into the deception, would prefer to have mental and spiritual freedom.

Mitt, must another generation endure either a life in ignorance or face the emotional trauma of escaping over barbed wire walls? If Jesus is the resurrected Christ, then a new generation of children is being misled and because they believe in a false Christ, their eternal lives are at risk. Whether there's a resurrected Jesus, another universal deity, a God who lives outside the physics of our universe or no God at all, the Mormon people are misled. To continue misguiding them is immoral and needs to end. Whatever the case for Christian faith, it's difficult to imagine an omniscient, omnipresent entity—creator of the universe or universes—wants us to exist as spiritual cult-clingers hanging on desperately to a discordant, disproved belief system and rear another generation of equally delusional children. Not when this superior being placed us in interesting times, full of exciting historical and scientific discoveries that offer daily joy to ease our apprehensions about life after death.

Gambling isn't my game, which is smart for a resident of Las Vegas, but maybe I'm wrong about Mormonism. I'm definitely rolling the eternal dice. The odds are incredibly long, but possibly Joseph Smith was the greatest prophet of all time. When Patriarch J. Harold Brinley placed his hands on my head to bless me, there's a chance he received false inspiration that day. One of those evil spirits we were warned about as children may have whispered in Brinley's ear that I was valiant in my pre-earth life. Possibly Brinley was deceived when he claimed Jesus would magnify me if I raised my voice in defense of the truth. Or maybe, by behaving badly in this world, I've blow my one eternal chance to earn for all those eternal Mormon gospel and priesthood rewards. One thing is certain, working as the "Dow Jones guy" on local television for 10 years didn't qualify me for magnification—small screen.

It's a long shot, Mitt, but there's a remote chance the Mormon Church is the true Christian Church and the rest are corrupted imposters. In that case, you helped Jesus prepare the earth for inhabitance, while I perched my lazy behind on Heaven's fence to watch great intelligences in action. It's possible I spent the war in heaven sitting like a lump on a log with those no-account Negroes. Could it be you're one of the greatest organized intelligences to emerge from primordial life, and I was so weak and indecisive that I barely escaped the Curse of Cain? Maybe your destiny is to be President and expedite the Mormon Kingdom of Heaven on earth. If that's true, you'll be named to a spiritual Hall of Fame in a Mormon Millennial ceremony, and I'll eventually be shipped to hell in a hand-basket on Judgment Day.

If Joseph Smith's revelations and teachings are true, I could be judged by his Jesus to suffer a second death as a Son of Perdition and be disassembled as an organized intelligence for all eternity. I might be deemed so evil on that infamous Day of Judgment that I spontaneously burst into flames on the spot. However, I could get lucky and with an air of serendipity find myself assigned the Telestial Kingdom to live with angry eunuchs and bossy girls. It sounds like an awfully frigid place, but at least I won't be on fire. How miserable as I gnash my teeth and shiver where the Son of God doesn't shine. So sad forever because I'll know the Celestial life I could have had with Jesus had I been a righteous Mormon and obeyed our prophets on earth. If I get into the lowest level of Mormon heaven, I'll pray for pity visits from family and friends. Real Christian of everyone to take time from your busy schedules and come slumming—but no gloating, please!

Mitt, we bottom dwellers would be eternally grateful if you and the other Gods consider just one Disneyland for us drones. There will be billions of neutered guys and a few ornery women, who wouldn't "keep sweet," down there. It seems a reasonable request that we screw-ups in Heaven's basement have one measly franchise of our own. I only request a small amusement park, but real Disney characters could drop in once in a while. You know it will be endless misery without one place to have a little fun, especially knowing you Celestial studs still have your stones, almost all the girls, and a modern Disneyland chain, too. Standing forever in horrendously long lines to ride It's a Small World could be considered part of our eternal punishment.

On the other hand, if Joseph Smith was one of American history's greatest con men, which looks like a bet with the house rather than risking the farm, then escaping the emotional clutches of Mormonism is the greatest life achievement of those who found strength to leave the cult behind. Most worthy achievements come with a price tag, and unrepentant, excommunicated members paid the price. They had their cultural base ripped from under them, suffered emotional pain as their extended pioneer family standing diminished, often suffered severe career setbacks and lost lifelong Mormon friends. In retrospect, Mitt, the career part hasn't mattered to me for a long time. I realized years ago my early political career goals were misdirected by false teachings indoctrinated into me from child-hood. As far as family and friends are concerned, like most ex-Mormons, I will never give up on them as long as I live.

Conclusion
Set our People Free

It saddens, disappoints and still angers me to know that most of my relatives and Mormon friends will go to their graves believing Joseph Smith was a prophet. They're destined to die convinced he placed a magic stone in his hat to translate a gold-plated history of sophisticated early American peoples, and then restored the corrected Christian gospel under the auspices of Jesus Christ. I climbed the compound's barbed wire walls to get out, but I want my family and friends to find the compound door and walk out. I know how emotionally painful it will be for them initially. However, only then can future generations of my family, and yours, be free. Mitt, expedite a Mormon renaissance. Convince the LDS Church to end its war on intellect and encourage members to experience a modern day Great Awakening.

Even though intellectually free, I am still a small town boy in many respects. The kid who fell off the turnip truck looked a lot like me. Consequently, I yearn for a day when every Mormon, not just pioneer families, has the opportunity to experience the exhilaration of intellectual curiosity, realistic spirituality and the general richness of contemporary life. I envision an era when the Church's Priesthood leaders are hot bags of celestial gas pricked by sharp points of truth and forced to end their war on common sense and basic knowledge. A period when the Church's Native Americans, Pacific Islanders, Afro-Americans and women are free to find pleasure and pride in their ethnicities, cultures and genders. And of course, it will be a joyous occasion when apostates can interact openly and honestly with their Mormon families and friends without fear of judgment, recrimination or shunning.

Inclined to idealism and optimism, I have faith that truth will win this war—hopefully in my lifetime—which will be bad news for those bent on bending history to fit their desperate fantasies or financial goals. I'm pleased the American people used the 2006 mid-term elections to show the Republicans and Karl Rove they're not as stupid as they have been treated. Today, I pray that the Mormon people will rise from their spiritual slumber and prove they aren't as sheep-like as Church leaders think. Most pioneer family descendants, who still believe Mormonism devoutly and love it dearly, have the strength of character to accept the truth and ultimately will, even if it takes another generation or two.

Many LDS Church members are facing reality and leaving the Church now. Others just need someone like you to provide familial, financial and emotional cover. More members can be moved to rebel by the respected leadership and strong reassurances only you can provide. The day you declared for President, you said "Talk is easy, talk is cheap. It is only in the doing that hopes and dreams can come to life." Mitt, don't let the "speech of your life" be the canned contrivance you presented to Americans in December, 2007. Trying to put distance between youself and Mormonism is a turnoff to religious conservatives who disagree with Mormon theology, and stating that there should be some kind of religious litmus test for Presidential candidates is unfair and unconstitutional. Make a memorable speech to free Mormons from mysticism so they can develop hopes and dreams based on a more firm foundation. It's time to stop being a focus-group vetted political actor for gentiles and start giving an admiring Mormon audience some straight talk. Only when you become the Mormon peoples' humble best hope can you win genuine respect from the American public and the world.

Thomas Jefferson said however discomforting a free exchange of ideas may be, truth will emerge the victor. Win the intellectual fist fight for our pioneer families' hearts and minds with a solid combination of historical and scientific facts. "Truth," according to Sophocles, "is always the best argument," and the fists of truth must continually floor opponents if our western culture is to survive. I rest well at night knowing Jefferson and Sophocles weren't talking about the smiley-masked, skinny-legged, eyeless Mormon version of truth systematically reinforced by Mormon Church leaders and relentlessly preached by uninformed Mormon missionaries.

I want our Mormon baby boomers to accept the truth and begin an exodus out of the wilderness—with you leading the way. The arguments are simple and the facts clear. Either Joseph Smith spoke with Jesus and God the Father at age fourteen in a personal visitation, or he didn't. The *Book of Mormon* is either a thousand-year record of a family from Jerusalem, the forefathers of the people who built the Native American and Pacific Island cultures, or it isn't. After his resurrection, a polygamist Jesus Christ visited a great *Book of Mormon* civilization in the Americas, or he didn't. Heavenly visitors descended to ordain Joseph Smith and Oliver Cowdrey to eternal *Old Testament* Priesthoods, or they didn't.

Mormons have been given the sole authority and responsibility to save mankind, or they haven't.

Mitt, faithful Mormon Priesthood holders are going to become polygamist gods in eternity's Celestial Kingdom, or they aren't. The Mormon's sacred temple marriages and ongoing works for dead people are integral to the divine plans of Jesus Christ, or they aren't. You and I were chosen in the preexistence and foreordained before we were born to do the Mormon Gods' work on earth—and eventually become Gods ourselves—or we weren't. Either General Authority Paul H. Dunn's best friend died in his arms during World War II, or he didn't. President N. Eldon Tanner could read my mind forty years ago or he couldn't. Gordon Hinckley and numerous Mormon Church leaders were fooled by Mark Hofmann's Salamander letter and other forged documents, or they weren't. There can be neither compromise in the name of faith, nor denial to protect false hope. I know the answers to these questions and have accepted them.

This is my opportunity to bear testimony of the truth to you and all the Mormon people who choose to read it. I know Jesus Christ didn't found the Mormon Church, and I testify to you that Jesus and God the Father never visited Joseph Smith in a vision or authorize him to speak on their behalf. I know without doubt Joseph Smith was a charlatan and colorful product of his time, not a preordained prophet chosen as mankind's conduit to a communal heaven. I assure you, Joseph Smith wasn't a prophet sent bearing eternal ordinances by an omnipotent God or Gods. I swear on a stack of Bibles that the *Book of Mormon* is historical fiction conceived in the mind of Joseph Smith. I understand how discomforting this information is, and I sympathize with you and millions of others, but I know what I have said is true. I say it in the name of Jesus Christ, Amen.

The problem is too many members prefer false hope and emotional bondage to intellectual freedom, and neither my testimony nor yours will change their minds. Voltaire, a member of the same French Masonic Lodge as Benjamin Franklin, cynically declared, "It is hard to free fools from the chains they revere." Mormonism is a form of ancestor worship, and many pioneer descendants feel they betray their forefathers if they question the Church. Faithful members chose to remain blissfully ignorant in a difficult, complex world, while others are cultural Mormons who simply go-along. Many of the latter quietly become semiactive members of the Mormon Myth Fraternity to keep peace at home and work, but are so well programmed that they too, if pushed, will defend the Church like junk-yard dogs.

In his classic novel, *Escape from Freedom*, Erich Fromm wrote, "How willing man is to surrender his freedom to dictators of all kinds," and your ongoing performance on the national political stage gives legitimacy to dictatorial Mormon leaders. It's tragic because many of the most insecure, misinformed Mormons programmed to fear the truth and feel like victims can proclaim: "With so many people attacking us, and now Mitt Romney, it just proves we belong to the only true Church!" This beleaguered, irrational thinking became embedded in Mormon cultural genes during the first generation and will continue until someone of your stature speaks up and rebukes the religious dictators who benefit from members' emotional dependancy.

Einstein said, "The important thing is to never stop questioning." Unfortunately, to protect themselves from the unpredictability of our evolving world, self-absorbed Mormons prefer not to question the basis for their self-righteous social superiority and simultaneously hide in a persecution complex as if it were a bomb shelter. Nonetheless, I have faith the power of reason can change minds and create a foundation for a faith based in reality. Empowered Mormon pioneer descendents can truly honor their forefathers by using free agency to venture out into the sunlight, ask questions and follow the answers to intellectual and emotional freedom. Then, millions of deceived converts to the Church could also free themselves from the Great American Cult they unwittingly joined in recent decades.

Mitt, commit your fine mind, world-class education and advanced social skills to guide our people and their anachronistic Gods forward into the twenty-first century universe. Tell the chauvinistic, paternalistic, pioneer family Priesthood holders it's time for a reality check back on planet Earth. The moral move for Mormon leaders is to assure members they're no longer required to deify Joseph Smith and defy logic, history, physics, biology, archeology, anthropology and genetics. Instead of dutifully gulping down more public relations pabulum and sending their children, grandchildren and retired parents on missions to serve up spiritual baby food to the human race, Mormon baby boomers can be freed to sit at the adult table of life and enjoy its diverse intellectual menu.

Another quote from Einstein, one of my heroes, is: "The world we created is a product of our thinking. It cannot be changed without changing our thinking." Mitt, the Mormon universe into which we were programmed begs for new thinking today. I've changed my thinking and challenge you to transform yours. Once free, you can share the truth with millions of Mormons, open the compound door and place them on a path to freedom. Our people desperately need an open discussion based on intellectual, historical, and scientific honesty. I can't tell you exactly how to accomplish this great mission, but I offer my assistance to help figure it out and make it memorable.

The change process mandates the free exchange of ideas. Tell our pioneer families its okay to think objectively about their heritage for the first time in almost two centuries. Understanding how fundamental it is, Rene Descartes declared, "I think therefore I am." Mitt, please speak out and encourage the Mormons to think again. Do it for all the families divided and friendships broken by the Mormon Myth machine's cacophonous claims. Though it may be too late for many of our generational peers, it's sinful not to do it for the Mormon children. Demand the Church emotionally and spiritually release the well-meaning but uninformed missionary children in the field and the youngsters programmed in the Mormon Primary, Mutual, and Seminary programs. Do it for all those coming behind us, predestined for indoctrination into a pattern of fallacious thinking.

I have shared highlights of the New Mormon History with you—which is real LDS history uncovered and revealed in recent decades and also included scientific sources for an open minded review. You once said, "I want to surround myself with argumentative, bright people who aren't afraid to tell me their opinions." That's a respectable business and political management style, but how do you feel about a Cougar Club brother who ventured beyond opinion and told you the truth about the religion of our heritage? Time will tell.

Hope you've had as much fun trekking through time and space as I have. Now, the final earthly act has begun for us and, while it may not appear so, I wish God's speed for you, your children and posterity. Author Brian Greene wrote in *The Elegant Universe*: "Imagine that what we call the universe is actually only one tiny part of a vastly larger cosmological expanse, one of an enormous number of island universes scattered across a grand cosmological archipelago." Mitt, just imagine! I'm crossing my fingers that you will intellectually and religiously retrofit yourself and use your remaining time here to spark the Mormon peoples' imagination, encouraging new earthly and universal possibilities for our pioneer families and all LDS members. Since I'm keeping my fingers crossed, I must still believe in magic and miracles, too. May you live to be ninety and start Act III with a Big Bang!

Notes

Chapter Two

6. "I have to admit": Macomber, Shaun. Mighty Mitt Romney. *The American Spectator,* Cover Story. March, 2006.

6. "Hang by a thread": Sheffield, Carry. White Horse in the White House. *WSJ.Com,* November 3, 2006.

9. "Dare the world": Young, Brigham. *Journal of Discourses.* Volume 4: 77.

Chapter Three

15. "You can pick": Young, Brigham. *Journal of Discourses.* Volume 4: 77

Chapter Four

20. "would tread down his enemies": Marsh, Thomas. *History of the Church.* Volume 3, 167.

20. "War of extermination": Tanner, Sandra. *Salt Lake City Messenger.* May, 2006, 6.

22. "Hunt had long believed" Smith, Pauline Udall. *Captain Jefferson Hunt of the Mormon Battalion.* SLC, Utah: The Nicholas G. Morgan, Sr. Foundation, 1958, 164.

23. "More than all the riches": Pratt, Parley P. *Autobiography of Parley P. Pratt.* SLC, Utah: Deseret Book Store, Chapter 5.

24. "rake them down": Quinn, D. Michael. *The Mormon Hierarchy: Origins of Power.* Salt Lake City, Utah: Signature Books, 1994, 99–100.

26. "The great messiah, who was the founder": Von Wymetal, Wilhelm Ritter. *Joseph Smith's History Vault.* SLC, Utah: Tribune Printing & Publishing, 1886.

26. "God does not care": Von Wymetal, Ibid.

27. "The old materialism of Epicurus": Remy, Jules. *A Journey to the Great-Salt-Lake City*. New York: AMS Press, 1861.

Chapter Five

29. "One thing is clear": Smith, Wallace B. Exiles in Time. *Saints Herald*. 1992.

30. "I have a hard time with historians": Related by D. Michael Quinn. Pillars of my Faith. Talk at Sunstone Symposium, SLC, Utah, August 19, 1998.

30. "Some things that are true": Packer, Boyd K. The Mantle is Far, Far Greater than the Intellect. *BYU Studies 1981*, Volume 21, No. 3, 259.

30. "climate of academic freedom": Waterman, Bryan & Kogel, Brian. *The Lord's University: Freedom and Authority at BYU*. Salt Lake City, Utah: Signature Books, 1998.

32. "An idiosyncratic form of Christianity": Silk, Mark. Romney's Assimilationist Act raises more Mormon questions. *Salt Lake Tribune*. March 14, 2007.

36. "For many Mormons": Abanes, Richard. *Becoming Gods*. Eugene, Oregon: Harvest House Publishers, 2004.

Chapter Six

38. "The Church is about preaching": Allen, Mike. A Mormon as President. *Time*. November 26, 2006.

41. "Tyranny, like Hell": Payne, Thomas. *The American Crisis*. 1870. Amazon.

42. "There is a war going on": Packer, Boyd. Speech to the Annual Church Education Symposium, 1981.

44. "If faith will not bear": Smith, George A. *Journal of Discourses*. Volume 14, 1878, 21.

Chapter Seven

49. "The cultural mindset of the Church": 60 Minutes. *CBS*. April 7, 1996.

50. "You have to appreciate what its like": Clark, Kim. *Religious News Service Website*. August 31, 2005.

51. "You chose your party's agenda": Morrison, Jane Ann's column. *Las Vegas Review Journal.* August 19, 2006.

51. "Is soft-spoken and polite": Giroux, Greg. *New York Times.* January 29, 2007.

Chapter Eight

53. "scientology plus 125 years": Weisberg, Jacob. Romney's Religion. *Slate.* December 20, 2006.

54. "It does not matter": Oaks, Dallen. Reading Church History. Ninth Annual CES Symposium at BYU. August 16, 1985.

56. "Perfect people would be awfully tiresome": Prince, Gregory A. & Wright, Wm Robert. *David O. McKay and the rise of Modern Mormonism.* SLC, Utah: University Of Utah, 2005.

56. "peculiar evil": Mill, John Stuart. *On liberty.* Indianapolis, Maryland: Bobbs-Merrill Co, 1956.

60. "Faith is one of the forces": Carnegie, Dale. *How to Stop Worrying and Start Living.* New York: Simon and Schuster, 1951.

63. "A great miracle": Hinckley, Gordon B. LDS Semi-Annual Conference. SLC, Utah: October, 2007.

Chapter Nine

67. "Individuals and thinking members": Hinckley, Gordon B. Larry King Live. *CNN.* September 8, 1998.

69. "So self-created was he": Bloom, Harold. *The American Religion.* Chu Hartley Publishers LlC, 2nd edition, 2006.

71. "If this court record is authentic": Nibley, Hugh. *The Myth Makers* SLC, Utah: Bookcraft, 3rd edition, 1979.

73. "If the First Vision did not occur": Hinckley, Gordon B. *Teachings of Gordon B Hinckley.* SLC, Utah: Deseret Book Company, 1997.

75. "It is thought by some": Smith, Joseph Fielding. *Essentials of Church History.* SLC, Utah: Deseret Book Company; 24th edition, 1971.

75. "There was a general spirit": Pratt, Parley P. *Autobiography*, Ibid.

76. "Two or three were wounded": Complex Authorship. *History of the Church.* SLC, Utah: Deseret Book Company, Volume 7, 103.

Chapter Ten

78. "He was either a Prophet of God": Smith, Joseph Fielding. *Doctrines of Salvation.* SLC, Utah: Bookcraft Publishers, Volume 1, 1954.

78. "Some revelations are of God": Newell, Linda King & Avery, Valeen Tippetts. *Mormon Enigma: Emma Hale Smith.* USA: Doubleday, 2nd edition, 1994.

79. "Revelations have been revised": Tanner, Jerald and Sandra. *Changing the revelations: The case against Mormonism.* SLC, Utah: Utah lighthouse Ministry, 1967.

Chapter eleven

84. "Must be either true of false": Pratt, Orson. *Divine Authority of the Book of Mormon.* Liverpool, England, 1851.

84. "Seems to be merely prosy detail": Twain, Mark. *Roughing It.* Hartford, Conn: American Publishing Co., 1886

85. "We do not have to prove": *Book of Mormon Student Manual.* SLC, Utah: Church Education System, 1989.

86. "All of one breed and brand": Roberts, B. H. *Studies of the Book of Mormon.* SLC, Utah: Signature Books, 2nd edition, 1992.

86. "Myth Fraternity": Larson, Stan. *Quest for the Gold Plates.* USA: Freethinking Press, 1996.

90. "nasty, filthy affair": Cowdrey, Oliver. Letter to brother, Warren, 1838. Wikipedia.

92. "white, and exceedingly fair and beautiful": Nephi 12:23. *Book of Mormon.* SLC, Utah: LDS Church.

92. "A dark, a filthy, and loathsome people": Mormon 5:15. Ibid.

Chapter Twelve

96. "We consider it a divine institution": Young, Brigham. Interview with Horace Greeley. *New York Tribune*. August 20, 1859.

97. "But let them apostatize": Young, Brigham. *Journal of Discourses*. Volume 5, 332.

97. "The Negro in the preexistence": Peterson, Mark E. Race Problems—as they affect the Church. Address at BYU, 1954.

98. "There is no definitive account": Roberts, B. H. *Comprehensive History of the Church*. SLC, Utah: LDS Church, 1930.

98, "More detailed and miraculous": Palmer, Grant H. *An Insider's View of Mormon Origins*. SLC, Utah: Signature Books, 2002.

Chapter Thirteen

103. "to have their blood spilt": Young, Brigham. *Journal of Discourses*, Volume 4, 219.

104. "The whole government is gone": Campbell, Eugene E. *Establishing Zion*. SLC, Utah: Signature Books, 1988, chapter 17.

105. "We are the smartest people": Young, Brigham. Judgment according to Work. Discourse in the Salt Lake Tabernacle, January, 1858.

Chapter Fourteen

108. "What is eternal life": Smith, Joseph Fielding. *Doctrines of Salvation*. SLC, Utah: Bookcraft Publishing, Volume 2, 9.

109. "Insomuch as this Church of Jesus Christ": Taylor, John. *Three Nights of Public Discussion*. Liverpool, England, 1850.

110. "If plural marriage is not true": Pratt, Orson. *Journal of Discourses*, Volume 21, 296.

110. "married his fifth wife in 1897": Dobner, Jennifer & Johnson, Glen. *Deseret Morning News*. February, 25, 2007.

111. "The only men who become Gods": Young, Brigham. *Journal of Discourses*, Volume 11, 269.

111. "A belief in the doctrine of plurality of wives": Grant, Jedediah M. *Journal of Discourses*, Volume 1, 345.

111. "This law of monogamy": Pratt, Orson. *Journal of Discourses*, Volume 13, 195.

113. "Obviously, the holy practice": McConke, Bruce R. *Mormon Doctrine*. SLC, Utah: Bookcraft Publishing, 1958 edition, 522.

113. "will perhaps be saved in the Celestial Kingdom": Brigham Young. *Deseret News*. SLC, Utah, September, 17, 1873.

114. "Be silent or I will ruin your character": Von Wymetal, Ibid.

114. "I have noticed that a man": Kimball, Heber C. *Journal of Discourses*, Volume 5, 22.

114. "The brother missionaries": Hirshon, Stanley P. *The Lion of the Lord: A Biography of Brigham Young*. New York: Random House, 1969. p129.

115. "All sense of morality": Young, Ann-Eliza. *Wife, No. 19*. Conn: 1875, 70–71.

117. "traditional Christian standard of marriage": Newell, Linda King & Avery, Valeen Tippetts, Ibid.

121. "I believe there are few significant developments": Tanner, Jerald and Sandra. *Changing World of Mormonism*. SLC, Utah: Utah Lighthouse Ministry, 1981, 546.

121. "The greatest responsibility in this world": Smith, Joseph Fielding. *Teachings of the Prophet Joseph Smith*. SLC, Utah: Deseret Books, 1838, 356.

121. "The greatest commandment given us": Smith, Joseph Fielding. Ibid, Volume 2, 149.

123. "ordinances instituted in the heavens": *Ensign Magazine.* SLC, Utah: LDS Church. August, 2001, 22.

124. "unchanged and unaltered": Smith, Joseph F. Fashion and the Violation of Covenant and Duty. *Improvement Era.* August 9, 1906.

Chapter Sixteen

132. "He could not get the Saints to live it": May, Dean L. *Utah History Encyclopedia.* SLC, Utah: University of Utah Press. 1994.

Chapter Seventeen

139. "A three-day old human embryo": Harris, Sam. *Letter to a Christian Nation.* New York: Alfred A. Knopf, 2006.

146. "About a thousand years": Harris, Sam, Ibid.

146. "Our country now appears": Harris, Sam, Ibid.

Chapter Eighteen

148. "It was appalling": Cillizza, Chris & Mosk, Matthew. Swift Boat Figure joins Romney. *Washington Post.* March 17, 2007.

Chapter Twenty

162. "This is not a democracy": Quinn, D. Michael. *Elder Statesman: Biography of J. Rueben Clark.* SLCD, Utah: Signature Books, 2002.

167. "The question is lingering": Paulson, Michael. *The Boston Globe.* March 24, 2006.

169. "Global warming could kill millions": Nuclear Scientists move Doomsday Clock toward midnight. *USA Today, London, AP.* January 17, 2007.

169. "More than one-tenth of the world's population": *Associated Press, Las Vegas Review Journal.* Oct 22, 2007.

173. "I went straightway into the baptismal font": Woodruff, Wilford. *Journal of Discourses,* Volume 19, 229.

174. "With regard to true theology": Young, Brigham. *Journal of Discourses*, Volume 8, 199.

174. "Christianity ... is a perfect pack of nonsense": Taylor, John. *Journal of Discourses*, Volume 6, 167.

174. "Where shall we look": Taylor, John. *Journal of Discourses*, Volume 10, 167.

174. "Both the Catholics and Protestants": Pratt Orson. *The Seer.* Washington D.C. 1853, 155.

174. "The gates of hell have prevailed": Pratt, Orson. *Pamplets,* Liverpool, England. 1851, 112.

Chapter Twenty-one

179. "The Church respects the rule of law": Green, Ashbel S. *The Oregonian Newspaper.* July 12, 2007.

180. "The truth has strong legs": Lindsay, Jay. LDS Church seeing growth in Massachusetts. *Associated Press.* January 28, 2006.

182. "the dirty little secret": Lindsay, Jay. Ibid.

Conclusion

192. "Talk is easy": Sidoti, Liz. Mitt Romney makes 2008 run official. *Associated Press.* February 14, 2007.

195. "Imagine what we call the universe": Green, Brian. *The Elegant Universe.* New York: Vintage Book, 1999, 366.

Selective Bibliography and Recommended Reading

Books

Abanes, Richard. *Becoming Gods: A closer look at 21st-Century Mormonism*. Oregon: Harvest House Publishers, 2004.

Abanes, Richard. *One Nation under Gods: A history of the Mormon Church*. New York: Four Wall Eight Windows, 2003.

Bushman, Richard Lyman. *Joseph Smith, Rough Stone Rolling*. New York, 2005.

Denton. Sally. *American Massacre*. New York: Vintage Books, 2003.

Green, Brian. *The Elegant Universe*. New York: Vintage Books, 2000.

Harris, Sam. *Letter to a Christian Nation*. New York: Alfred A. Knopf, 2006.

Hassan, Steven. *Combating Cult Mind Control*. Rochester, Vermont: Park Street Press, 1998.

Hitchens, Christopher. *God is not great: How Religion Poisons Everything*. New York: Hachette Book Group USA, 2007.

Krakauer, Jon. *Under the Banner of Heaven*. New York: Doubleday, 2003.

Newell, Linda King and Avery, Valeen Tippetts. *Mormon Enigma: Emma Hale Smith*. Chicago, Illinois: University of Illinois Press, Second Edition, 1994.

Palmer, Grant H. *An Insider's View of Mormon Origins*. Salt Lake City: Signature Books, 2002.

Sagan, Carl and Shklovskii, I. S. *Intelligent Life in the Universe*. San Francisco: Holden-Day Inc., 1966.

Smith, Joseph, Jr. *Book of Mormon.* Salt Lake City: LDS Church, 1969.

Smith, Joseph, Jr. *Doctrine and Covenants.* Salt Lake City: LDS Church. 1969.

Smith, Joseph, Jr. *Pearl of Great Price.* Salt Lake City: LDS Church, 1969.

Southerton, Simon G. *Losing a Lost Tribe, Native Americans, DNA and the Mormon Church.* Salt Lake City: Signature Books, 2004.

Tanner, Jerald and Sandra. *Mormonism, Shadow or Reality.* Salt Lake City, Utah: Utah Lighthouse Ministry, Fifth Addition, 1987.

Wood, Charles L. *The Mormon Conspiracy.* California: Black Forest Press, 2004.

Magazines and Periodicals

Time, New York, New York.

Smithsonian, Washington D C.

National Geographic, Tampa, Florida.

The Economist, London, England.

Newspapers

Boston Globe, Boston, Massachusetts.

Des Moines Register, Des Moines, Iowa.

Las Vegas Review Journal, Las Vegas, Nevada.

Las Vegas Sun, Las Vegas, Nevada.

New York Times, New York, New York.

Salt Lake Tribune, Salt Lake City, Utah.

Washington Post, Washington D. C.

Selected Glossary of LDS Terms

Aaronic Priesthood: The lower of two priesthood divisions in the LDS Church. It was supposedly restored to earth in 1829, when John the Baptist returned from heaven to ordain Joseph Smith and Oliver Cowdrey. Boys twelve years old and up are ordained, in ascending order, to titles of deacon, teacher and priest.

Apostles: Sometimes a reference to the original twelve Apostles. More often a reference to the twelve current Mormon Apostles, who hold the Melchizedek Priesthood and serve directly under the Mormon First Presidency.

Apostasy: Refers to a period in time when people or individuals rebel against the prophets of God. More specifically, for Mormons it references what is called the "Great Apostasy," a period beginning after the original apostles were killed and ending with the "Dispensation of the fullness of times," when Joseph Smith restored the complete gospel.

Apostate: An individual who rebels against the prophets of God. In the Mormon Church, this specifically means anyone who no longer accepts their prophets and is excommunicated.

Book of Mormon: One of the standard works of the LDS Church. This book was translated by Joseph Smith from ancient metal plates and published in 1829. It deals mainly with the religious history of a group of Israelites who came to America circa 600 B.C., and ends circa 400 A.D.

Blood Atonement: A Mormon doctrine introduced by Joseph Smith that states some human acts are so sinful, repentance is not enough. The person must be killed and blood allowed to flow on the ground so that he can be saved.

Brigham Young: The second Mormon Prophet and pioneer leader well-known for leading the Saints west.

BYU: Brigham Young University, the Mormons Church-operated University, located in Provo, Utah.

Celestial Kingdom: The highest of the three Mormon kingdoms of heaven, which also has three subdivisions. There, people will live with the Heavenly Father and Jesus and progress eternally. Some men will become Gods with plural wives and worlds to create and rule.

Celestial Marriage: Being married in the temple for time and eternity, which is essential to exaltation. It is also called eternal marriage or temple marriage.

Beside being encouraged for all worthy living Mormons, it is performed vicariously for the dead by temple workers using genealogy records as part of God's plan of salvation for all mankind.

Council of Fifty: An LDS organization established by Joseph Smith in 1844 to symbolize and represent a future theocratic Kingdom of God on the earth. Smith and Brigham Young hoped to create this kingdom in preparation for the Millennium. Little is known about it.

Curse of Cain: A confusing concept used by Mormons until 1978 to deny priesthoods to African-Americans and people of color around the world. The Pearl of Great Price says the people of Canaan were a despised people who became black, and that the descendants of Ham could not have the right to the priesthood.

Danites: A secret society of about 400 Mormon men organized in 1838 with Joseph Smith's endorsement. Sworn to defend the prophet, "right or wrong," they took their name from the *Book of Daniel* in the *Old Testament* and were also know as the Sons of Dan. Members of the group fought in the Missouri Mormon war against the State militia.

Disciplinary Council: A group of Mormon Melchizedek Priesthood holders with authority to disfellowship or excommunicate members.

Dispensation: A period of time in which truth from heaven is given to people on earth through prophets. Joseph Smith purportedly opened the Dispensation of the Fullness of Times.

Doctrine and Covenants: One of the four Mormon Standard Works containing revelations given to Joseph Smith and a few other latter-day Prophets of the Church.

End days: The last days of earth as we know it before biblical prophesy is fulfilled, and Jesus comes to rule over the earth in the Millennium.

Endowment: The initiatory temple ceremony rite that consists of being washed, receiving a new name, receiving sacred garments, viewing the LDS version of creation and the fall and learning various handshakes that are essential for exaltation. Endowments are also performed vicariously for the dead.

Eternal Progression: The concept that a person can progress through three estates of existence (primordial, mortal and post-mortal) and ultimately obtain godhood.

First Presidency: The Mormon Prophet and his two councilors.

First vision: The term used to describe Joseph Smith's account of the heavenly encounter he supposedly experience in 1820 at age fourteen. Mormons believe it proves him a prophet. Although altered over the years, Smith claimed he was visited by God the Father and Jesus Christ who told him all the Christian churches were wrong, and he was to restore the perfect gospel to earth.

Foreordination: Callings given by the Heavenly Father to his spirit children, who then come to earth at a preplanned time and place with specific assignments in mortal life.

General Authority: Refers to the LDS leaders who have the highest authority, including the First Presidency, the Council of the Twelve, The First and Second Councils of Seventy and the Presiding Bishopric.

Gentiles: Anyone who is not a Latter Day Saint, including Jews.

God: Mormons believe their Father in Heaven was once a man who subsequently obtained godhood. He is a glorified and perfected man with a body of flesh and blood. Human men can become a god like him.

Godhood: The goal of Mormon men is to attain godhood in the Celestial Kingdom, have their own spirit children and create new worlds for them to populate.

Gods: Mormons believe innumerable men have already eternally progressed to become Gods, and many more will progress to godhood in the future.

Golden Plates: The plates on which the Book of Mormon supposedly was written. The Angel Moroni led Joseph Smith to the place in the Hill Cumorah where they were allegedly buried for over 1500 years.

Gordon B. Hinckley: Current Prophet and President of the LDS Church. Mormons believe he has the authority to lead the Church as did Joseph Smith, Brigham Young and others.

Hill Comorah: Location in upstate New York where Joseph Smith claims the Angel Moroni lead him to find the gold plates used to write the Book of Mormon.

Home Teachers: Members assigned by the Ward Bishop to visit members monthly. They were formerly called Ward Teachers.

Jack Mormon: A slang expression for an inactive Mormon.

Lamanites: Most commonly used by Mormons today as a term for American Indians. According to the Book of Mormon, this branch of Lehi's descendants became unfaithful and was cursed with a dark skin. They eventually killed all the Nephites, who also became wicked. Mormons believe Lamanites are the ancestors of the American Indians.

Lying for the Lord: Refers to the practice of lying to protect the image inside and outside the Mormon religion. From Joseph Smith's denial of having more than one wife to Gordon B. Hinckley's dishonest comments on Sixty Minutes about polygamy, Mormons history is replete with examples of Mormon lying.

For loyal Mormons, the welfare of the Church is more important than the principle of honesty.

Kingdom of God: The Church of Jesus Christ of Latter Day Saints on earth; also the Celestial Kingdom.

Melchizedek Priesthood: The greater of two Church priesthoods supposedly restored in 1829 to Joseph Smith and Oliver Cowdrey when Peter, James and John returned from heaven.

Mesoamerica: The cultural areas within which a number of pre-Columbian societies flourished before the Spanish colonization of the Americas. The areas included some of the most complex and advanced cultures in the Americas, including the Olmec, Teotihuacan, Mayan and Aztec.

Miracle of the Seagulls: According to Mormon lore, legions of seagulls appeared in June, 1848 to partially save the pioneers' first food crop. The seagulls ate mass quantities of crickets, drank some water, regurgitated and continued to eat more crickets. Though called Mormon crickets, they are not true crickets but belong to the katydid family.

Mormon Battalion: President James K. Polk instructed Secretary of War, William L. March, to enlist a battalion of 500 Mormon men to assist in the Mexican-American War. The force, which included 32 women as laundresses, traveled 2000 miles from Council Bluffs, Iowa to San Diego, California in 1846–47, the longest march in military history.

Mormon Gods: The Church teaches the Trinity is composed of three separate beings, and there are multiple polygamist gods throughout the universe. God was once a man, and men can become gods.

Mormon Militia: A term used to reference Mormon men both before and after the Church's move west. Joseph Smith formed a militia in Nauvoo, Illinois known as the Nauvoo Legion. The Utah Mormon militia was involved in the Utah War with the Federal government in the 1850s and participated in the 1857 Mountain Meadow Massacre.

Mormon: The name of a mighty Nephite warrior in the Book of Mormon from whom the common name for the LDS Church is derived.

Mormon Missionaries: Young Mormon men at age nineteen and young women of twenty-one can serve as full time missionaries in locations around the world for eighteen to twenty-four months. Their assignment is to teach people about the restored gospel. Those who go overseas receive foreign language training.

Mormon Trail: The American heartland trail used by Mormons, trappers, Indians and others. It stretched 1300 miles from Nauvoo, Illinois to Salt Lake City and was used by 70,000 Mormon pioneers between 1846 and 1869.

Moroni: The son of Mormon who supposedly appeared to Joseph Smith as an angel and led him to the gold plates. His statue adorns the top spire of Mormon Temples.

Nephites: According the Book of Mormon, they were the descendants of Nephi, son of a Jew named Lehi. Lehi and his family were supposedly guided by God from Judah to America in a wooden submarine circa 600 years B.C. Much of the Book of Mormon is a description of endless wars between Lehi's descendants, the Nephites and the Lamananites.

Ordinances: Sacred rites and ceremonies necessary for Eternal Progression.

Ozzie and Harriet: This was a 1950s family oriented television sitcom about the Nelson family, which included sons, David and Ricky.

Patriarch: One of the offices of the Melchizedek Priesthood whose primary responsibility is to give patriarchal blessings.

Patriarchal Blessing: Each member of the Church is entitled to receive a one-time blessing from a Patriarch.

Pearl of Great Price: One of four LDS Standard Works, it contains a selection of Joseph Smith's revelations and translations not found in the Doctrine and Covenants, including the Book of Moses and the Book of Abraham.

Plural Marriage: A term Mormons prefer over polygamy. Joseph Smith initiated this practice by revelation in 1844, but it was practiced years before by select Mormon leaders. Despite being officially discontinued in 1890, it continued into the twentieth century and according to the 132nd section of the Doctrine and Covenants, is considered the eternal order of the highest level of the Celestial Kingdom.

Polygamy: See plural marriage.

Prophet: The term initially used by Mormons to identify the founder, Joseph Smith. Today, Mormons believe they are led by living prophets, and the word refers to the president of the LDS Church.

Relief Society: The main LDS Church woman's organization. It meets every Sunday while the men meet in their various priesthood quorums. Its functions include Sunday instruction, monthly homemaking instruction and aiding in the welfare program.

Restored Gospel: Mormons claim the complete gospel of Jesus Christ was lost or distorted over the centuries and Joseph Smith was called to restore it in it fullness. The complete gospel is the full plan of salvation, which embraces all that is necessary to be saved and exalted.

Returned Missionaries: Designation given young Mormon men and women who have completed a two year mission for the Church and returned home.

St. George Temple: The temple built in St. George, Utah in the late nineteenth century.

Sacrament Meeting: Part of the Sunday Worship service. The meeting features talks by members of the ward and distribution of the sacrament.

Saints: The term Mormons use to describe themselves. Since Joseph Smith believed he lived in the last days, he named his creation the Church of Jesus Christ of Latter Day Saints.

Salamander letter: A notorious forged document created by Mark Hofmann in the early 1980s. It referred to a salamander and drew upon legends about certain animals having supernatural powers and tied it to Joseph Smith's magic activities. Several Mormon leaders were initially fooled or unable to discern its authenticity, until others suggested it was a forgery.

Spirit Prison: The place where all non-LDS people go immediately following death. Mormon Missionaries go there from Mormon Paradise and preach the gospel. Those who respond positively progress toward the Celestial Kingdom, aided by the performance of temple ordinances done for them by Mormon temple workers still living on earth.

Stake President: A man who presides over a group of wards.

Standards Committee: A group of men who hold hearings for BYU students accused of breaking rules set by the Church-operated school. They have the power to expel students.

Standard Works: The volumes of scripture officially accepted by the LDS Church: The *Book of Mormon, Doctrine and Covenants, King James Bible* and *Pearl of Great Price.*

Telestial Kingdom: It is the lowest kingdom of heaven and never visited by God the Father or Jesus. The final destination of carnal and wicked people, it will be visited only by the Holy Ghost. Still, it is compared in glory to the stars and said to surpass mortal understanding.

Terrestrial Kingdom: The middle kingdom of heaven where people will be visited by Jesus but not God the Father. This will be the final destination of honorable people and non-valiant (Jack) Mormons.

Temples: Places where worthy Mormons go to perform sacred rituals for both the living and the dead, including endowments, baptisms and eternal Marriages.

Temple Garments: There are two kinds of temple garments. One special type of garments only is worn in the temple, and the other sacred undergarments are worn at all times by worthy members who feel they give them supernatural protection.

Temple Marriage: See celestial marriage.

Temple Recommend: A certificate issued to Mormons, usually by their Bishops, verifying their worthiness to enter the temples.

Temple Work: An expression to describe ordinances performed in temples by the living for themselves and for the dead.

Testimony Meeting: Once a month, ward members use Sacrament meetings to bear their testimonies. Members can stand up to testify they know Joseph Smith was a prophet who restored the gospel, the Book of Mormon is the word of God, and the Mormon Church is the only true church. They believe they receive this testimony through feelings not facts and are encouraged to build their testimonies by bearing it often.

United Order: One of several nineteenth century Church programs established to manage and administer the Law of Consecration. Members would deed all their property to the United Order and receive an inheritance or stewardship. First initiated by Joseph Smith in February, 1831 as "an everlasting order," it was similar to other utopian societies formed in the U.S. and Europe during the Second Great Awakening.

Veil: Most commonly used as a term of death. Dying is passing through the veil. Veils are part of the temple ceremony used to symbolize the passing from one state of eternal existence to another.

Ward: The smallest ecclesiastical unit of the LDS Church, equivalent to the local congregation. A developed ward usually has about 500 people and is also called a branch.

White Horse Prophesy: An LDS belief stated and restated for generations by Church leaders that the U.S. Constitution will hang by a thread, and the Mormon priesthood holders will save it.

Word of Wisdom: A revelation concerning health practices given to Joseph Smith in 1833 and recorded in Section 89 of the Doctrine and Covenants. Mormons reference it to abstain from tobacco, alcohol, coffee, etc.

Zion: A commonly used LDS term that has various meanings. It can refer to The Church of Jesus Christ of Latter Day Saints, Utah or Independence, Missouri where the Mormons believe Jesus will set up his kingdom headquarters when he returns, or wherever the righteous live.

Index

978-0-595-51178-5
0-595-51178-3

www.ingramcontent.com/pod-product-compliance
Lightning Source LLC
Chambersburg PA
CBHW051232050326
40689CB00007B/894